THIS CHAIR ROCKS

A MANIFESTO AGAINST AGEISM

Also by Ashton Applewhite

Cutting Loose: Why Women Who End Their Marriages Do So Well

THIS CHAIR ROCKS

A MANIFESTO
AGAINST AGEISM

ASHTON APPLEWHITE

CELADON
BOOKS

NEW YORK

www.celadonbooks.com

Excerpt from "Here" from *Begin Again: Collected Poems* by Grace Paley. Copyright ©
2000 by Grace Paley. Reprinted by permission of Farrar, Straus, and Giroux.

Library of Congress Control Number: 2018961339

ISBN 978-1-250-31148-1 (hardcover)
ISBN 978-1-250-29724-2 (ebook)

Our books may be purchased in bulk for promotional, educational, or business
use. Please contact your local bookseller or the Macmillan Corporate and
Premium Sales Department at 1-800-221-7945, extension 5442, or by email at
MacmillanSpecialMarkets@macmillan.com.

Originally self-published by Networked Books, Inc.

First Celadon Edition: March 2019

10 9 8 7 6 5 4 3 2 1

To the memory of Robert Neil Butler
—mentor, activist, physician, humanist—
who kicked the whole thing off

CONTENTS

We contain all the ages we have ever been.

—*Anne Lamott*

THIS CHAIR ROCKS

A MANIFESTO
AGAINST AGEISM

INTRODUCTION

I've never lied about my age—I have no problem saying "I'm sixty-six" loud and clear—but I sure know a lot of people who do. People who've lied on résumés and on airplanes and on dates. There was the opera singer who fudged upward at the beginning of her career so she could get cast as Norma, but was holding at thirty-nine. And the woman who loved passing off her granddaughters as her kids, and who was regularly connected to her bank's fraud department because she couldn't remember what birth date she was using.

I would never have been able to keep my stories straight either—one reason I told the truth. Another was because the typical response wasn't so terrible: "You look great for your age!" I inherited my mother's no-gray-hair genes, I've always had plenty of energy and no plans to slow down, and I certainly never felt like any of the labels out there—"senior," "cougar," "woman of a certain age"—applied to me. But if I was so cool with it, why didn't "You look great for your age" feel like a compliment? The fact was that the hazy prospect of growing old filled me with something between free-floating anxiety and stomach-churning dread. I didn't want to think about it until I had to, and when it crossed my mind, I flipped the channel. Why not, as long as I could "pass" for younger, right?

That wasn't a very solid strategy. Birthday cards circulated regularly around the charmless cubicles of the office at the American Museum of Natural History, where I worked with a guy named Ray for fifteen years. Ray and I didn't have much in common. He handled the accounts; I wrote. He lived in the suburbs; I didn't own a car. He was conservative; I'm progressive. With his fringe of snow-white hair, if he had gained weight and worn red, he would've made

1

a perfect Santa Claus. He was proud of being cantankerous and was always muttering about his aches and pains, and he couldn't wait to retire to Florida. So when I learned that Ray and I were exactly the same age, I panicked. I thought, "What if everyone finds out? They'll think *I'm* old too."

That wasn't just condescending and mean-spirited of me; it was idiotic. My museum coworkers, Ray included, were an intelligent bunch. They didn't have any trouble telling the two of us apart, and difficulties were unlikely to crop up. Why, then, was I so flipped out about landing with Ray on the same side of some hypothetical old/young divide? Why did I imagine that this would erase our individuality, and diminish me so frighteningly? Was I driven by fear of losing my looks? Of growing frail? Of my own mortality? Wouldn't I be better off making my peace with the passage of time than waging a battle no one could ever win?

I wish I could report that I found the answers in one blinding epiphany. Instead, it's been a gradual awakening over the past twelve years. There have been many glum days at the keyboard, and some sleepless nights dictating brilliant insights into my phone, most of which were a lot less brilliant in the morning light. I had the good fortune to be mentored by Dr. Robert Butler, coiner of the term "ageism," before his death in 2010. I attended seminars for journalists who cover the "age beat," inhaled countless books and articles, and started thinking out loud in blog form. I delved into a world of advertisements and movies, policies and bylaws, and products and promotions that had shaped my unconscious beliefs with one overarching message: old = no good. Or, as the Twitterverse might put it: It sucks to be old.

A chance dinner conversation in 2007 with my partner's mother, Ruth Stein, got me started on this journey. In their eighties at the time, she and her husband, Bill, were booksellers, and that night she said, "I think you should write about something people ask us all the time: 'So when are you going to retire?'" The idea was upbeat and sound bite–friendly. I started learning about longevity, interviewing people over eighty who work, and blogging about it.

I headed to Santa Fe, where I had family to stay with. My first interview was with eighty-eight-year-old folk artist Marcia Muth on the porch of her little adobe house, shaded by a tree festooned with shiny compact disks and surrounded by her hubcap collection. Muth had been raised in Fort Wayne, Indiana, by her grandparents, to whom she was "a disappointment, because I liked classical music, I liked Shakespeare, I loved poetry. To them, work was having a store." She went on to become a law librarian, poet, publisher, and, in her fifties, a successful folk art painter and teacher. A newspaper clipping on the wall quoted Muth's advice to her Elderhostel students: "You are never too old, and it's never too late."

Embarrassed by her lack of formal training, Muth painted in secret for ten years. When a local artist dropped by and caught her scurrying to hide her brushes, he offered her some advice: "Don't take any lessons. Just keep going." She did, and it became a way of life that she was grateful to have found in her middle years. Chronic bronchitis had ended her teaching career a few years earlier and tethered her to an oxygen tank, but "it doesn't interfere with the painting, that's the important thing," she said. "Your life does change as you get older," she told me. "You get into what's important and what's not." She and her partner went out less and moved more slowly, but her work continued to improve as she got better at listening to herself. "Don't fear old age," she advised. "Your years can be just as wonderful as you get rid of some of the anxiety people suffer from. And I find my eighties have been even more fun than my seventies were."

The possibility that life could become *more fun* in your eighties had never crossed my mind. Nor that growing a little shorter of breath each year would fail to terrify. Nor that an ever more circumscribed life could be an ever greater source of personal growth and specific pleasures. Nor that such joyful clarity would be rooted in awareness—not denial—that time was short and therefore to be

3

savored. After this first jolt of fresh old air, I kept going. From pediatricians to park rangers, Americans of advanced years and all stripes told me about their work behind steering wheels and desks and band saws and television cameras and how they'd gotten there.

It came as no surprise that they were as different from one another as could be, not to mention from the stereotype of the doddering ancient. But something *did* surprise me: the discrepancy between what I'd simply assumed it was like to be eighty or ninety and what I was encountering firsthand. The more I read and the more experts I talked to, the clearer it became that these older workers were typical of a large and fast-growing cohort of older Americans. Why the disconnect between what I had imagined about old age and the reality that was coming into view? Had I bought into some kind of party line? What were some of my assumptions about what the future held?

My darkest nightmare was the possibility of ending my days drooling under a bad botanical print in some ghastly institutional hallway. If asked what percentage of Americans over sixty-five lived in nursing homes, I'd have ventured, "Maybe thirty?" I'd never have arrived at the actual number: 2.5 percent, down from 5 percent over the last decade! Even for people eighty-five and up, the number is only 9 percent.[1]

Only 2.5 percent of Americans over sixty-five live in nursing homes.

What about being sick, and helpless? It turns out that over three-quarters of the "oldest old"—ages eighty-five and up—can go about their everyday activities without any personal assistance.[2] Probably not shoveling their driveways or doing Costco runs, but dressing, cooking, and wiping their own butts. People get chronic illnesses, but they learn to live with them. The vast majority of older Americans live interdependently until they come down with whatever kills them.

What about the specter of dementia? Everyone seemed to know a horror story. My memory's never been any good, so maybe I won't notice if I develop Alzheimer's disease. It's a terrifying prospect. But even as the population ages, dementia rates are dropping.[3] The real epidemic is *anxiety* about memory loss. Remember the two and a half percent of people over sixty-five living in nursing homes? Ninety percent of the remainder can think just fine.[4] Here too, the vast majority of older Americans will land in the rest of the pie chart, slowed somewhat but fully capable of finding their slippers sooner or later and making their way in the world.

How about my assumption that old people no longer have sex? It's true that sexual activity tends to decrease with age. It's equally true that retirement homes are hotbeds of lust and romance, as evidenced by skyrocketing sexually transmitted disease rates in people over fifty. Sex and arousal do change, but often for the better, especially for women.

I also figured that old people were depressed. After all, they were *old*, and they were going to die soon. Their droopy faces were all the evidence I needed. It turns out that older people enjoy *better* mental health than the young or middle-aged.[5] Who knew? Here's the kicker: People are happiest at the beginnings and the ends of their lives.[6] If you don't want to take my word for it, Google "U-curve of happiness." Even as age strips us of things we cherished—physical strength, beloved friends, toned flesh—we grow more content.

The more I learned, the better I felt about the years ahead—no small accomplishment in itself. I had to acknowledge that the goalposts were shifting, but also that I remained very much in the game. I've always loved bicycling in the city, but now I wear a helmet and stay in the slow lane. I still barrel along the sidewalk, but recently had to slow down in order to keep pace with a seventy-four-year-old friend whose knees were killing her. Arthritis. She marveled that time and cartilage had waylaid her in this way, and I realized that I, too, will marvel when it happens to me. Like her, I'll figure out how to deal with it. I'll buy a cane just like she did, and keep on going. Just not as fast.

Specific concerns replaced nameless dread. I was onto something. Clearly, hitting ninety was going to be different—and way better—than the inexorable slide toward depression, diapers, and puffy white shoes I'd once envisioned, although I'm still worried about the shoes.

Things started looking so much rosier that I graduated to what I came to call I'm Not Ray–Stage Two: trumpet the fact that Ray and I are the same age, because see how much younger *I* look! Sliding happily to the other end of the spectrum, I spent several years chasing the idea that enough spinach, Sudoku, and positive thinking could "put old on hold." This approach goes by all kinds of peppy names, like successful aging and productive aging, and it moves a lot of product aimed at keeping us "ageless." It sounds comforting and it feels empowering.

But a question tugged at my sleeve. Was I actually coming to terms with what it meant to grow older? Or had I merely swapped my don't-want-to-think-about-it foxhole for a hamster wheel to keep uncomfortable reckonings at bay—and Ray at a distance? Replaced dread with denial, in effect?

Hitting sixty felt just *fine*. I *knew* the years were bestowing more than they took away. I knew it from my own experience, and my research continued to confirm that I was no exception and that the years ahead had even more to offer. But I had yet to internalize that knowledge, to integrate it into my beliefs and attitudes, to embed it into my sense of self and my place in the world, to make it my own. I had to acknowledge and start letting go of the prejudices about aging that had been drummed into me since childhood by the media and popular culture. *Wrinkles are ugly. Old people are incompetent. It's sad to be old.* Absorbing these fallacies had been effortless. Banishing them is unsettling, and infinitely harder. Present tense because I'm still at it, as I'm reminded on a regular basis.

What was the hardest prejudice to let go of? A prejudice against myself—my own future, older self—as inferior to my younger self. That's the linchpin of age denial. Whatever form it takes, from a cutesy "Just say I'm over (fill in the number)" to faces frozen by needle and knife, denial creates an artificial, destructive, and unsustainable divide between who we are and who we will become. Concealing or disavowing our age gives the number power over us that it doesn't deserve. Accepting our age, on the other hand, paves the way to acknowledging it with ease, even pride.

I am not saying that aging is easy. We're all worried about some aspect of getting old, whether it's running out of money or getting sick or ending up alone, and those fears are legitimate and real. But it never dawns on most of us that the experience of reaching old age—or middle age, or even just aging past youth—can be better or worse depending on the culture in which it takes place. And American culture is grotesquely youth-centric. Depictions of older people tend to be extreme. At one end of the spectrum, a silver-maned dude, beloved of marketers, surfs a turquoise wave. At the other end, beloved of the aging-industrial complex, a tiny woman withers in a hospital bed. These people exist, but they are hardly typical. The vast majority of us will end up in the middle, muscles and memory slowed, but out in the world and—with some help—able to enjoy our lives to the end.

I had to make my way to I'm Not Ray–Stage Three: I'm not Ray. Ray recently retired to Florida, where I bet he's going to be happy as a clam; it's the old age he wants. I'm making my way toward the old age I want, and it won't look like his. I'm not planning to retire anytime soon, nor am I going to take up pole dancing or marathon running. I feel just fine about it. All aging is "successful"—not just the sporty version. Otherwise you're dead.

> **All aging is "successful"—not just the sporty version. Otherwise you're dead.**

A bunch of pieces fell into place with that realization, but a fundamental, underlying question remained: Why had my vision of late life been so out of sync with the lived reality? Why had I bought into an unexamined narrative for all these years instead of taking comfort and guidance in the evidence around me? These facts were easy to come by, so why didn't more people know them? What Kool-Aid had we drunk? What was it in the culture that had me and so many others so freaked out about the prospect of living to eighty or ninety? The answer, which grew into an itch that I had to scratch and ultimately a book that I had to write, is ageism—the relegation of older people to second-class citizenship, along with the disrespecting of youth. Here's the formal definition: discrimination and stereotyping on the basis of a person's age. We're ageist when we feel or behave differently toward a person or a group on the basis of how old we think they are. "Ageism" isn't a household word yet, nor a sexy one, but neither was "sexism" until the women's movement turned it into a howl for equal rights.

As with all "isms," stereotyping lies at the heart of ageism: the assumption that all members of a group are the same. It's why people think everyone in a retirement home is the same age— old—even though residents can range from fifty-year-olds to centenarians. (Can you imagine thinking the same way about a group of twenty- to seventy-year-olds?) And the longer we live, as more experiences inform our uniqueness, the more *different* from one another we become. Think about it: Which group is likely to have more in common, a bunch of seventeen-year-olds or a bunch of seventy-seven-year-olds? As doctors put it, "If you've seen one eighty-year-old, you've seen *one* eighty-year-old."

All "isms"—ageism, racism, sexism—are socially constructed ideas. That means we make them up, and they change over time. Like all discrimination, ageism legitimizes and sustains inequalities between groups, in this case, between the young and the no-longer-young. Different kinds of discrimination—including racism, sexism, ageism, ableism, and homophobia—interact, creating layers of oppression in the lives of individuals and groups. The oppression is reflected in and reinforced by society through the economic, legal, medical, commercial, and other systems that each of us navigates in daily life. Unless we challenge stigma, we reproduce it.

Like racism and sexism, ageism is not about how we look. It's about what people in power want our appearance to mean. Ageism occurs when a group, whether politicians or marketers or employment agencies, uses that power to oppress or exploit or silence or simply ignore people who are much younger or significantly older. We experience ageism any time someone assumes we're "too old" for something—a task, a relationship, a haircut—instead of finding out who we are and what we're capable of. Or if someone assumes that we're "too young": ageism cuts both ways, and young people experience a lot of it. That's what's going on when people grumble about lazy Millennials or complain that "kids are like that."

Now I see ageism everywhere. When old pals cringe at public mention of how long they've known each other instead of savoring their shared history. When men and women feel compelled to lie about their age on online dating sites. When people bridle at being kindly offered a seat on the bus. On billboards and television, in hospitals and hotels, over dinner and on the subway. ("At age eighty, who doesn't need a facelift?" a poster announcing a subway station renovation asks brightly.) In the incessant barrage of messages from every quarter that consigns the no-longer-young to the margins of society. In our mindless absorption of those messages and numb collusion in our own disenfranchisement.

I've learned that most of what I thought I knew about the aging process was wrong. That staying in the dark serves powerful commercial and political interests that don't serve mine. And that seeing clearly is healthier and happier. Yet, despite the twentieth century's unprecedented longevity boom, age bias is only beginning to bleep onto the cultural radar—it's the last socially sanctioned prejudice. We know that diversity means including people of different races, genders, abilities, and sexual orientation; why is age typically omitted? Racist and sexist comments no longer get a pass, but who even blinks when older people are described as worthless? Or incompetent, or "out of it," or boring, or even repulsive?

Age is a criterion of diversity.

Suppose we could see these hurtful stereotypes for what they are—not to mention the external policies and procedures that put the "ism" after "age." Suppose we could step off the treadmill of age denial and begin to see how ageism segregates and diminishes our prospects. Catch our breath, then start challenging the discriminatory structures and erroneous beliefs that attempt to shape our aging. Until then, ageism will pit us against each other; it will rob society of an immense accrual of knowledge and experience; and it will poison our futures by framing longer, healthier lives as problems instead of the remarkable achievements and opportunities they represent.

A good place to start is by jettisoning some language. "The elderly"? Yuck, partly because I've never heard anyone use the word to describe themselves. Also because "elderly" comes paired with "the," which implies membership in some homogenous group. "Seniors"? Ugh. "Elders" works in some cultures but feels alien to me, and I don't like the way it implies that people deserve respect simply by virtue of their age; children, too, deserve respect. Since the only unobjectionable term used to describe older people is "older people," I've shortened the term to "olders" and use it, along with "youngers," as a noun. It's clear and value-neutral, and it emphasizes that age is a continuum. There is no old/young divide. We're always older than some people and younger than others. Since no one on the planet is getting any younger, let's stop using "aging" as a pejorative—"aging Boomers," for example, as though it were yet another bit of self-indulgence on the part of that pesky generation, or "aging entertainers," as though their fans were cryogenically preserved.

It always drove me nuts when some clown called me "young lady" and expected me to feel complimented, but I didn't know why until I started thinking deeply about it. Made to our face, comments like these are disguised as praise. We tend to ignore them because the reference to being no-longer-young is embarrassing. And it's embarrassing to be called out as older until we quit being embarrassed about it. Well, I'm not anymore. When someone says, "You look great for your age," I no longer mutter an awkward thanks. I say brightly, "You look great for your age too!" When it dawned on me that one of the reasons older women are invisible is because so many dye their hair to cover their gray, I bleached mine white to see what it was like. When my back hurts, instead of automatically blaming it on my osteo-you-name-it, I stop to think whether shoveling or weeding could be to blame. I started a Q&A blog called *Yo, Is This Ageist?* where people can ask me whether something they've seen or heard or done is offensive or not. And I wrote this book.

Although we age in different ways and at different rates, everyone wakes up a day older. Aging is difficult, but few of us opt out, and the passage of time confers very real benefits upon us. By blinding us to those benefits and heightening our fears, ageism makes growing older in America far harder than it has to be. That's why I've embarked on a crusade to overturn American culture's dumb and destructive obsession with youth, and challenge the way people at both ends of the age spectrum are devalued and disrespected.

When someone says, "You look great for your age," I no longer mutter an awkward thanks. I say brightly, "You look great for your age too!"

As I've gone on this journey from the personal to the political, it's become clear that ageism is woven deeply into our capitalist system, and that upending it will involve social and political upheaval. Ageism, unlike aging, is not inevitable. In the twentieth century, the civil rights and women's movements woke mainstream America up to entrenched systems of racism and sexism. More recently, disability rights and gay rights and trans rights activists have brought ableism and homophobia and transphobia to the streets and the courts of law. It is high time to add ageism to the roster, to include age in our criteria for diversity, and to mobilize against discrimination on the basis of age. It's as unacceptable as discrimination on the basis of any aspect of ourselves other than our characters.

If marriage equality is here to stay, why not age equality? If gay pride has gone mainstream, and millions of Americans now proudly identify as disabled, why not age pride? The only reason that idea sounds outlandish is because this is the first time you've encountered it. It won't be the last. Longevity is here to stay. Everyone is aging. Ending ageism benefits us all.

Why add another "ism" to the list when so many, racism in particular, call out for action? Here's the thing: We don't have to choose. When we make the world a better place to grow old in, we make it a better place in which to be from somewhere else, to have a disability or be queer or non-white or non-rich. Just as different forms of oppression reinforce and compound each other—that's intersectionality, a term coined by feminist and civil rights activist Kimberlé Crenshaw—so do different forms of activism, because they chip away at the fear and ignorance that all prejudice relies upon. Ageism is the perfect target for compound advocacy because everyone experiences it. And when we show up *at all ages* for whatever cause tugs at our sleeve—save the whales, the clinic, the democracy—we not only make that effort more effective, we dismantle ageism in the process.

This book is a call to wake up to the ageism in and around us, embrace a more nuanced and accurate view of growing older, cheer up, and push back. What ideas about aging have each of us internalized without even realizing it? Where have those ideas come from, and what purpose do they serve? How do they play out across our lives, from office to bedroom, in muscle and memory, and what changes inside us once we perceive these destructive forces at work? What might an age-friendly world—friendly to *all* ages, that is—look like? What can we do, individually and collectively, to provoke the necessary shift in consciousness, and catalyze a radical age movement to make it happen?

Let's find out.

CHAPTER ONE

WHERE AGEISM COMES FROM AND WHAT IT DOES

When geriatrician Robert Butler coined the term "ageism" in 1969—not long after "sexism" made its debut—he defined it as a combination of prejudicial attitudes toward older people, old age, and aging itself; discriminatory practices against olders; and institutional practices and policies that perpetuate stereotypes about them. The term was quickly adopted by the media and added to the *Oxford English Dictionary*. Almost half a century later, it's barely made inroads into public consciousness, not to mention provoked outcry.

Negative messages about aging cast a shadow across the entire life of every American, stunting our prospects, economy, and civic life. This is oppression: being controlled or treated unjustly. However, most Americans have yet to put their concerns about aging in a social or political context. When I ask people if they know what ageism is, most reflect for a moment, compare the word to other "isms," and realize what it must mean. The concept rings true, and they nod. But it's still a new idea to most. And unless social oppression is called out, we don't see it as oppression. Perpetuating it doesn't require conscious prejudice or deliberate discrimination. This lesser life is "just the way it is," and the way it probably always will be.

IT WASN'T ALWAYS LIKE THIS

In most prehistoric and agrarian societies, the few people who lived to old age were esteemed as teachers and custodians of culture. Religion gave older men power. History was a living thing passed down across generations. This oral tradition took a serious hit with the invention of the printing press, when books became alternative repositories of knowledge. As long as old age remained relatively rare, though, olders retained social standing as possessors of valuable skills and information. The young United States was a gerontocracy, which served the older men who held the reins; younger citizens had to age into positions of authority.

The nineteenth and twentieth centuries ushered in a reversal. Modernity brought massive transitions that reduced the visibility of older members of society, diminished their opportunities, and eroded their authority. Rapid social change made learning about the past seem less relevant. Aging turned from a natural process into a social problem to be "solved" by programs like Social Security and "retirement villages." The nursing home, a "shotgun marriage of the poorhouse and the hospital" in geriatrician Bill Thomas's memorable phrase, came into being and created a growth industry. The historians Thomas R. Cole and David Hackett Fischer have documented how, at the start of the nineteenth century, the idea of aging as part of the human condition, with its inevitable limits, increasingly gave way to a conception of old age as a biomedical problem to which there might be a scientific solution. What was lost was a sense of the life span, with each stage having value and meaning.

Propelled by postwar leisure and prosperity, the explosion of consumer culture, and research into a stage of life newly dubbed "adolescence," youth culture emerged as a distinct twentieth-century phenomenon. As this "cult of youth" grew, gerontophobia—fear of aging and dislike, even hatred, of old people—gained traction. Those of us who grew up in the 1960s and '70s were warned not to trust anyone over thirty, perhaps the first overt exhortation to take sides across a generational divide. The decades beyond thirty appeared ever less enviable. "Will you still need me, will you still feed me, when I'm sixty-four?" crooned the Beatles.

GROWING OLD HAS BECOME SHAMEFUL

The status of older Americans is rooted not only in historic and economic circumstances but also in deeply human fears about the inherent vulnerabilities of old age: the loss of mobility, visibility, and autonomy. Not all of these transitions befall us all, and only two unwelcome ones are inevitable: We'll lose people we've known all our lives, and some part of our bodies will fall apart. These changes are natural. But we live in a culture that has yet to develop the language and tools to help us deal with them. That's partly because these changes make us feel vulnerable, partly because longer lives are such a new phenomenon, and partly because of ageism, both internalized and in the culture at large. As a result, all too often these transitions are characterized by shame and loss of self-esteem.

Internalized, these fears and anxieties pave the way for a host of unhealthy behaviors that include denial, overcompensation, and worse: actual contempt, which legitimizes stigma and discrimination. Two characteristics of marginalized populations are self-loathing and passivity—what my daughter tactfully dubbed the "yuck/pity factor" that the prospect of growing old invokes in so many.

As a friend who bought a house from a wheelchair user observed, "Damn, it's nice to have wide doorways, and a toilet positioned this way—they should just do it for everyone." That's the premise of universal design—that products designed for older people and people with disabilities work great for everyone else too. Age-friendly products improve the built environment and make it more accessible, but stigma keeps them off the market. Realtors advise removing ramps and grip bars before putting a house on the market, as though no buyer could see accessibility as a bonus or aging into it as a necessity. Alas, thanks to internalized ageism, they've got a point.

Stigma trumps even the bottom line. There's a fast-growing "silver market," especially for products that promote "age-independence technology," yet advertisers continue to pay a premium to target eighteen-to-thirty-five-year-olds. Despite the significant purchasing power of older buyers, retailers are uneasy about stocking products for them and companies are leery of investing. Unless they're selling health aids, brands don't want to be associated with the no-longer-young set either. Just as telling is the resistance of older consumers themselves to buying products that might telegraph poor eyesight or balance.

Instead we blame ourselves for a vast range of circumstances not of our making and over which we have no control. Difficulties turn us into "problem people." When labels are hard to read or handrails missing or containers hard to open, we fault ourselves for not being more limber or dexterous or better prepared. Watching an older person struggling to heave herself out of a low chair, we assume her leg muscles are weak or her balance is shot, instead of considering the inadequacies of seating so deep or low to the ground. If we see a teenager perched on a kindergartener's chair, we don't bemoan the fact that his legs got so huge. Kiddie chairs aren't designed for teenagers any more than armchairs are designed for ninety-year-olds.

As we age, we blame ourselves for a vast range of circumstances not of our making and over which we have no control.

The issue is not competence, or incompetence, but it's hard to keep sight of that in an ageist world. These obstacles are less of a problem than the underlying policies and prejudices that reduce access and independence. We blame our own aging, instead of the ageism that renders these natural transitions shameful and these barriers acceptable. Discrimination—not aging—is the barrier to full participation in the world around us.

AGEISM MAKES US DREAD OUR FUTURES

It doesn't make much sense to discriminate against a group that we aspire to join. Or to rail about olders sucking up "entitlements"—which they *earned*—when both the need and the antagonism will come our way in turn. Ageism is a prejudice against our own future selves, as Todd Nelson and many other age scholars have observed, and has the dubious distinction of being the only "ism" related to a universal condition. It takes root in denial of the fact that we're going to get old. That we *are* aging. Its hallmark is the irrational insistence that older people are Other, not Us—not even future us—and we go to great lengths to distance ourselves from that future state. "My mom is ninety, but she's not *old*," someone insisted to me not long ago, as though it were contagious. We exaggerate difference and overlook what we have in common, as with older people who spurn senior centers "full of old people in wheelchairs" lest they be tarnished by association.

In childhood we're maddened when grown-ups don't treat us with respect—that's ageism too—but unable to imagine that our speech will someday quaver, skin crease, gait falter. Over time it gets harder to sustain that illusion, and a punitive psychological bind tightens its grip. Unless we come to terms with the transition, we hate what we are becoming. Historian David Hackett Fischer is blisteringly clear about the implications of this damaging divide, "destructive most of all to those who adopt it—for in the end it is always directed inward upon the mind it occupies."[1] That's the nature of prejudice: always ignorant, usually hostile. It begins as a distaste for others, and in the case of age (as opposed to race or sex), it turns into distaste for oneself.

This self-hatred takes many forms. It's manifest in the widespread effort to "pass" for younger, the way people of color have passed for white and gay people for straight; behavior spurred both by the desire to protect ourselves from discrimination and by internalized disgust. It underlies disparaging comments like, "I know that this isn't true of anyone else in the room, but I'm not getting any younger" and "You don't have to say *when* I graduated," both of which I've heard verbatim from people on the front lines of aging policy. You'd think they'd be a little more self-aware, but many are invested in deficit models of aging. They're experts in the important task of caring for the frailest and neediest—that's how they get funded and promoted—and they have yet to reconcile that view of old age with what lies ahead for themselves. At the other end of the spectrum, many experts are proponents of the successful aging model, which holds that healthy behaviors and "can-do" strategies can hold aging at bay. That's still denial, a high-end version that tends to overlook the very important role of socioeconomic class and potential disability in shaping how "successfully" we age.

We're so busy feeling young that we stay blind to the ageism in and around us and never learn to defend ourselves against it. Older people tend to identify with younger ones as strongly as youngers themselves do. Other groups that experience prejudice, like gays or people with autism, develop buffers that can reinforce group identity, and even pride, at belonging to what sociologists call an outgroup. Olders are apparently the only group whose attitudes about old age are as disparaging as those held by the in-group, the young.[2] Talk about not wanting to belong to any club that would have you as a member! Which would be funnier, and a lot less ironic, if it weren't the club that everyone is counting on getting into.

AGEISM LEGITIMIZES ABUSE, AND ACTUALLY SHORTENS LIVES

Why are stereotypes so insidious? Because when they apply to others, there's no need to defend ourselves against them. They're easily, often unconsciously, absorbed into our ways of thinking. Stereotyping obstructs empathy, cutting people off from the experience of others—even if, as is the case with ageism, those "others" are our own future selves. "Ageism allows the younger generations to see older people as different than themselves; thus they subtly cease to identify with their elders as human beings," Robert Butler wrote in *Why Survive? Being Old in America*, which won him a Pulitzer Prize.[3] When we see people as other than us—other color, other nationality, other religion—their welfare seems less of a human right. That's why at least five out of six cases of elder abuse go unreported.[4]

Elder abuse can take many forms: neglect or abandonment; physical abuse (including the inappropriate use of drugs or confinement); emotional abuse such as intimidation or humiliation; sexual abuse; healthcare fraud; and financial exploitation. Because of age-ism, elder abuse is less familiar to emergency room staff and law enforcement officers than other forms of domestic violence, and the public is less equipped to recognize it. "If nobody knows that I'm be-ing abused, or I never *hear* about elder abuse and I think I'm the only one it's happening to, I'm embarrassed and ashamed so I just keep my mouth shut," explains Mary Anne Corasaniti, ex-director of New York State's Onondaga County elder abuse program. It's why some people rationalize exploiting olders with the repugnant excuse that the person is too old to notice.

Condescension alone actually shortens lives. What profession-als call "elderspeak"—the belittling "sweeties" and "dearies" that people use to address older people—does more than rankle. It rein-forces stereotypes of incapacity and incompetence, which leads to poorer health, including shorter life spans. People with positive per-ceptions of aging actually live longer—a whopping seven and a half years longer, on average—in part because they're motivated to take better care of themselves.[5] Dementia confers no immunity. Nursing home residents with severe Alzheimer's have been shown to react aggressively to infantilizing language. Overaccommodation also harms—behavior like using simpler words and sentences or speak-ing louder and more slowly than we would to a younger person, in-stead of first ascertaining that the person is in fact confused or hard of hearing. Targets of this demeaning behavior appear to "instantly age," speaking, moving, and thinking less capably.[6]

Internalized stereotypes also interfere with the value that people place on their own lives. Take the sad story of Bob Bergeron, a therapist in New York whose suicide at forty-seven took his friends by surprise. Described as "relentlessly cheery," Bergeron had friends and family, financial security, and no history of depression. Extraor-dinarily beautiful as a young man, he was writing a self-help guide called *The Right Side of Forty: The Complete Guide to Happiness for Gay Men at Midlife and Beyond.* In Bergeron's suicide note, next to an arrow pointing to the title page of his manuscript, he wrote, "It's a lie based on bad information." He was new to the struggles of the writing life and alone on New Year's Eve; not a good combination. Belonging to a subculture that fetishizes youthful beauty and conventional sexual prowess did him no favors either. Bergeron's greater tragedy, though, was to inhabit a world so bereft of alternative narratives that dread overtook him. That's why we need more rich, complex stories that shrug off the mantle of decline and show there's no "right" or "wrong" side to forty—or any other age.

In another study, people were exposed to negative or positive stereotypes of old age, then asked to request or reject life-prolonging medical treatment in a hypothetical situation. As expected, the negatively primed subjects were more likely to opt out.[7] We see these values in the cultural controversy around assisted suicide, where the indignation index drops sharply when the population in question consists of the very old or severely disabled.

American culture barrages the old and disabled with the message that their lives are not worthwhile, nor worth paying for.

Conversations need to factor into a cultural climate that barrages the old and disabled with the message that their lives are not worthwhile, nor worth paying for.

Euthanizing older people has a history in fiction that goes back at least as far as the Victorian-era novelist Anthony Trollope. Published in 1882, his novel *The Fixed Period* proposed mandatory euthanasia at age sixty-eight, ostensibly to relieve suffering. In satirist Christopher Buckley's novel *Boomsday*, Millennials rise up. The movement's prophetic leader urges folks to stop paying taxes that subsidize retirement, and create financial incentives for Boomers to commit suicide. The description of a seminar hosted by New York University in June 2013 called "Love and Let Die: An All-Day Consideration of Ballooning Longevity, the Quality of Life, and the Coming Generational Smash-up" posited that "We may well be approaching a situation in which we as a society will have to choose between living in a world where an eighty-five-year-old is routinely granted five hip operations, or one in which we can still afford, say, primary school."

If someone botched my first four hip operations, I'd like a crack at a fifth, thank you very much. It's not as though funding for primary school comes out of the same bucket as funding for joint replacements (and universal healthcare and decent public education would render the example meaningless). It's not a question of resources but of how they're distributed. People at both ends of the age spectrum are least likely to be economically productive in a capitalist system, and therefore the most likely to be discriminated against. For all the "family values" rhetoric coming out of Capitol Hill, programs for kids are underfunded because kids don't vote and because the kids whose parents have political influence need those programs less. As with other "isms," ageism pits the disenfranchised against each other in order to maintain the power of the ruling class.

"Kids vs. canes" is a false dichotomy that gerontologists have debunked countless times, but it makes great headlines. As it is, older people are lacking from the landscape, and pro-aging voices are rare. If ageism continues to go unchallenged, a dystopian future where they are missing entirely begins to seem conceivable. Given the remarkable set of achievements that longevity represents, that would be an ironic and tragic outcome.

LONGER LIVES ARE A BASIC INDICATOR OF HUMAN PROGRESS

Growing old isn't new. What's new is how many of us now routinely do so. The first leap in life span occurred some thirty thousand years ago, during the Paleolithic era, when people started living past the age of thirty. That's when modern humans began flourishing, making art, using symbols, and thriving, despite the bitter cold of the last Ice Age. Why? Because thirty is old enough to be a grandparent, which conveys evolutionary advantages. Older people are repositories of knowledge, skilled in avoiding danger and storing food and knowing who's related to whom, and at passing along these complex skills.

The next big shift occurred some 150 years ago, propelled by the extraordinary scientific and technological advances that began with the Industrial Revolution. As more children survived to adulthood, women began having fewer of them. (Somewhat counterintuitively, the main determinant of population aging is dropping fertility rates, not rising life expectancy.) The proportion of older people increased, and the life span in the developed world has since doubled. In the twentieth century, in the U.S. alone, the American life span increased by a staggering thirty years. This largely reflects the fact that more Americans are surviving to adulthood, but we're living longer, too, gaining on average ten biological years since our grandparents' era. In effect, thanks largely to clean water and antibiotics, we've redistributed death from the young to the old.

"It is, frankly, insane to look at an ageing population and not rejoice," writes *Guardian* columnist Zoe Williams about the U.S. Census Bureau's 2008 report on the unprecedented aging of the world population. "Why do we even have a concept of public health, of cooperation, of sharing knowledge, if not to extend life, wherever we find it?"[8] A blue-chip roster of speakers at the 2012 Age Boom seminar for journalists in New York referred to the longevity revolution as "the most important phenomenon of our time in the world, more than the bomb, the Pill, or the Internet," as "an extraordinary opportunity to solve almost all of our problems," and as "potentially the biggest achievement in the history of the species." Describing "a new stage of human history," Linda Fried, Dean of Columbia University's Mailman School of Public Health, referred to "the only natural resource that's actually increasing: the social capital of millions more healthy, well-educated adults." A growing body of knowledge from very different schools of thought—including the Rand Corporation, University of Chicago, Queen's University Belfast, and Harvard and Yale Universities—now acknowledges that health, along with the longevity it brings, are important economic drivers that generate wealth by affecting healthcare costs, labor-force participation rates (given the appropriate incentives), worker productivity, and the financing of pension systems.[9]

YET THERE'S MORE HAND-WRINGING
THAN BACK-PATTING GOING ON

A little less worried about the tug of time on your own prospects? It's no time to relax! Journalist Paul Kleyman's witty coinage—"global wrinkling"—evokes both the scale of this massive demographic shift and the free-floating anxiety that accompanies it. Global wrinkling is typically portrayed as a social problem, even a disaster in the making. Anxious times feed what Fried called "a deficit accounting of what it means to be an aging society." When times are tough, we look for scapegoats. We project our personal worries about getting older onto the demographic phenomenon of population aging. And indeed, unless we prepare wisely for this demographic shift, we could turn feat into fiasco.

In October 2010, demographer Philip Longman warned of a "'gray tsunami' sweeping the planet."[10] The phrase summons a frankly terrifying vision of a giant wave of old people looming on the horizon, poised to drain the public coffers, swamp the healthcare system, and suck the wealth of future generations out to sea. Journalists jumped on it, and "gray tsunami" has since become widely adopted shorthand for the socioeconomic threat posed by an aging population.

"Is the progressive aging of society really equivalent to the instantaneous devastation of cities?" asks University of Toronto Assistant Professor Andrea Charise. As she notes, this language divides society into two opposing groups, the "needy old" and everyone else, and "traffics in the politics of panic"[11] so successfully that all other narratives are effectively pushed aside. It's not the first politically charged use of this kind of language. In the late nineteenth century, the influx of Asian immigrants was referred to as the "yellow peril." A "rising tide" has been used to describe a whole host of diseases deemed threatening to society, from tuberculosis and syphilis in the nineteenth century to HIV/AIDS in the twentieth century and Alzheimer's disease in the twenty-first.

Talk of plague and poverty justifies prejudice against older people, legitimizes their abandonment, and fans the flames of intergenerational conflict. It also obscures the fact that what we're facing is no tsunami. It's a demographic wave that scientists have been tracking for decades, and it's washing over a floodplain, not crashing without warning on a defenseless shore. Since the wave has been on the horizon since the 1950s, why is society so ill-prepared? Why not conceive of it as a "silver reservoir," as social gerontologist Jeannette Leardi proposes? The "tsunami" could fill that reservoir.

Part of our ambivalence about aging is just human. Nobody wants to die young, but concerns about scaling up the financial and physical support that long lives require are widespread and legitimate. Things are changing so fast that we're carving out entirely new biological and social turf. Roles for this new cohort of older people have yet to evolve. The institutions around us were created when lives were shorter. For example, the notion that education is for the young, employment for people in middle age, and leisure for the old is clearly obsolete, but we have yet to revise these structures in substantial ways, or invent new ones. Science has leapfrogged culture, and society hasn't had time to catch up. Humans are notoriously slow to reframe perception and behavior.

Sociologists call this "structural lag." It happens when elements of a social system change at different rates and get out of sync. Small wonder that so many of our attitudes toward old age are irrational or downright contradictory. Americans over fifty control approximately 70 percent of the country's disposable income, yet we are ignored by marketers. How can age be a burden, as the headlines insist, and also the gift that a thousand cloying affirmations rightly declare it to be?

GLOBALIZATION IS FUELING
THE DEVALUATION OF OLDER PEOPLE

Operating in the global economy means competing intensely for any kind of economic edge. The difference between success and failure hinges on slim and fast-moving margins. As the quest for wealth and power has gone global, the people who inhabit that globe are rapidly growing older. Those trends are colliding.

According to the "gray tsunami" narrative, an aging population makes it impossible to compete in the global economy. A young labor force, on the other hand, attracts global businesses and investors. Call it "global age arbitrage,"[12] a term coined by business reporter Ted C. Fishman, author of *The Shock of Gray*, a preview of the global effects of the longevity boom. (Arbitrage means buying an asset cheaply and promptly selling it elsewhere at a profit.)

Global competition for "economic youth" is driving political and institutional ambivalence about the longevity boom, and the interests of the very young and very old—the most exploitable labor force, and therefore least valuable—are linked. Writing about how the government defines poverty, journalism professor Thomas B. Edsall observed that "both the beginning and the end of life are becoming increasingly subject to market decisions, cost-benefit analyses, and bottom-line considerations that had not been so glaringly explicit in the past."[13] Olders are perceived as a drag on the economy because of the way the economy is structured, and the structure has yet to be revised in order to take advantage of the vast new untapped resource we represent.

The language is cold-blooded, the trajectory is evident, and the culprit is clear. As Fishman put it, "The high costs of keeping our aging population healthy and out of poverty has caused the United States and other rich democracies to lose their economic and political footing."[14] In other words, according to this school of thought, Western imperialism is in decline not because of the accumulation of toxic debt that threatened the global banking system, or the effects of climate change, or the stagnation of real wages, or high youth unemployment rates, or crumbling public infrastructures, or a workforce left behind by automation and the information economy, or because the middle class is under siege and wealth is being concentrated in ever fewer hands. The problem is too many old people!

This is hogwash. In *The Imaginary Time Bomb*, British economist Phil Mullan exposes the reactionary analyses of people like Fishman and makes a persuasive case that the modern world's growing preoccupation with aging has little or nothing to do with demography. Instead, it is used to justify further reductions in the role of government in the economy and the curbing of the welfare state. "Often what is presented as a population problem is better understood as a moral or ideological problem which assumes a demographic form," writes sociologist Frank Furedi in the preface.[15] This justification for austerity "lies in the socially constructed notion that federal spending on the elderly and the poor is the cause of the problems of the US economy," writes Mullan.[16] Blaming aging for the problems that afflict the U.S. economy—the way Fishman, Longman, and so many alarmist demographers do—obscures their origins in global capitalism.

THESE ARE SOME OF THE MYTHS USED TO ADVANCE THIS ANTI-OLDERS AGENDA:

- **Society will be swamped by all these old people!**

Consider the oft-repeated statistic that as of 2015 there were more Americans over sixty than under fifteen. Yes, there are a ton more old people in the boat, but there are also a lot fewer kids. Will we be drowned in a glut of olders, or starved by a dearth of youngers? Another way to look at it is that by 2020 there'll be one older adult for every child—far better for the children's welfare than the inverse, when birth rates and infant mortality were high.

It's helpful to keep in mind that the projections that have people so worked up are largely the result of a specific historical phenomenon: the cohort effect of the postwar generation growing old—the proverbial bulge in the python. Tellingly, relatively few U.S. population graphs extend past midcentury, by which time the proportion of people over sixty-five will be in decline. Even countries that are rapidly aging can produce "youth bulges," Longman points out, describing them as looming disasters "with all the attendant social consequences, from more violence to economic dislocation."[17] Can't win for losing.

• **An older population will bog everyone else down in caring for the sick and the frail.**

The longevity boom does indeed call for massive investment into the biology of aging and related medical issues. New and often expensive medical treatments make it possible to prevent or treat many more conditions than fifty years ago. The caregiver crisis is real and growing more acute. But the assumption that older people are inevitable money pits for health dollars is incorrect. Medical expenses are highest in the period just before we die, but that's true whether we die at eighteen or eighty, and evidence suggests that how long we're sick affects spending more than how old we are.[18] The postwar generation is the healthiest one in history. One study of twenty-two wealthy countries (including the U.S.) actually found population aging *negatively* correlated with health expenditures.[19] Rather it was people with debilitating illnesses or injuries—regardless of age—who used the most resources. According to the World Health Organization, aging has far less influence on healthcare expenditures than several other factors. For example, between 1940 and 1990, when the U.S. population aged most rapidly, aging appears to have contributed only around 2 percent to the increase in health expenditures. Technology-related changes were responsible for between 38 and 65 percent of that growth.[20]

People aren't just living longer; they're healthier and are disabled for fewer years of their lives than older people of decades ago. According to the U.S. Department of Health and Human Services, the share of U.S. healthcare spending going toward nursing and retirement homes has declined since 2000 and been flat since 2006.[21] The ten-year MacArthur Foundation Study of Aging in America concluded that once people reach sixty-five, their added years don't have a major impact on Medicare costs, although this may change as the number of people living with Alzheimer's disease increases.[22] People over eighty actually cost less to care for at the end of life than people in their sixties and seventies, possibly because aggressive interventions become less common. Chronic conditions pile up, but they don't keep most older Americans from functioning in the world, helping their neighbors, and enjoying their lives.

- **Olders are a drag on the economy.**

Absolutely not. People fifty and up fuel the significant, fast-growing, and often overlooked "longevity economy." According to AARP, spending by the fifty-plus population amounted to $5.6 trillion in 2015. Factor in the effects of this direct spending as it circulates through the economy and the contribution to GDP amounted to $7.6 trillion. Overall, this spending supported more than 89.4 million jobs in 2015—61 percent of all U.S. jobs.[23] By 2032 the fifty-plus age-group is projected to drive more than half of U.S. economic activity, as their spending fuels industries that include apparel, healthcare, education, leisure, and entertainment.[24] The trend is global. As Joseph Coughlin, director of the MIT AgeLab, writes in *The Longevity Economy*, "It's no exaggeration to say that the world's most advanced economies will soon revolve around the needs, wants, and whims of grandparents."[25]

The U.S. also has more older workers than ever before. By staying employed longer, generating tax revenue, and continuing to earn and to spend, olders are fueling economic growth far longer than previous generations did. As they age and transition out of the workforce, people will need more help with tasks like home maintenance, driving, and downsizing, all of which generate jobs. Older people also drive investment in a multitude of new products and ser-

vices, especially technologically innovative ones. And while "entrepreneur" might conjure up an image of a kid in that proverbial
garage, twice as many successful American entrepreneurs are over
age fifty as in their early twenties.[26] Labor statistics capture only part
of the economic contribution of older Americans, whose unpaid
volunteer work in 2015 was valued at $75 billion. As Baby Boomers
transition out of the workforce, this figure will rise.[27]

• **One generation benefits at the expense of another.**

For starters, the common—and intuitively attractive—perception
that distinct "generations" share and represent a set of experiences
and characteristics has no scientific basis. The variation *within*
members of a given group—people born between 1980 and 2000,
for example—is greater than the variation *between* generations (as is
also the case with people of a given race or ethnicity). Most studies
that claim to demonstrate generational differences show something
else instead, as with the ageist trope that Millennials in the workplace are spoiled and dissatisfied. The same was true of GenXers
and Baby Boomers at that age; as we get older we tend to move into
jobs that suit us better. It's an age effect, not a generational effect.[28]

The tension between generations is indeed worth studying,
but mostly as a red herring and a symptom of how aging has been
reframed as a problem. The postwar generation in the U.S. had the
good fortune to come of age in an era of unheralded peace and
prosperity. It's understandable for younger people to resent that
good fortune, and to feel as though the Boomers have pulled up
the drawbridge after themselves. But pitting groups against each
other—old against young or, in this case, vice versa—is a time-
honored tactic used by the wealthy and powerful to divide those
who might otherwise unite against them in pursuit of a fairer
world for all. It's like setting groups of low-wage workers against
each other, or the interests of stay-at-home moms against women in
the paid workforce. The underlying issue is a living wage for all, and
redress requires collective action. When issues are instead framed

as zero-sum—more for "them" means less for "us"—it's harder to see that the public good is at stake and the issue affects everyone.

Because conflict sells papers, the media perpetuate the myth that intergenerational competition is inevitable, and people readily buy into it. Barricades are easier to build than bridges. But they're a lot less useful, and at a minimum this kind of thinking is short-sighted, as when older people complain about school taxes. Don't they want the guy delivering their oxygen tank to be able to read the instructions? Having an educated workforce is better for everyone: individuals, families, communities, and society as a whole.

Pitting the generations against each other also obscures the key fact that income inequality does not discriminate by age. The wealthiest 1 percent consists of people of all ages, just like the ninety-nine. As leading economists have been arguing for years, growing wealth disparity *within* different age cohorts (not between them) underlies the shrinking prospects of ordinary Americans. Much of the intergenerational angst centers on the loaded term "old-age dependency ratio," which compares the number of people over sixty-five to those aged fifteen to sixty-four, typically framed as the ratio of "dependents" to those of "working age." With the number of people over sixty-five growing and the number in the workforce shrinking, the reasoning is that outnumbered youngers—often referred to as Gen Xers, Millennials, and Generation Z—will be left to shoulder enormous burdens. In fact, the proportion of older workers has been falling pretty steadily for over one hundred years. As Mullan observed about the United Kingdom, "The number of working people 'supporting' each pensioner has fallen from fourteen to one in 1900 to four to one in 1990, and hardly anybody noticed."[29]

In recent years, many scholars have criticized this dependency ratio because of its crudeness as a measure and because of its blatant anti-olders ideology.[30] It's based on the assumption that people become economic deadweight as soon as they hit sixty-five, when the reality is far more nuanced. Older Americans draw heavily on their own resources in retirement, and many never become wholly dependent on government support. Many people require benefits well before age sixty-five, and a growing proportion remain employed long after it.

Fortunately the World Bank has developed a long-overdue alternative formula, called the adult dependency ratio, which takes these trends into account. Instead of comparing the ratio of older to younger workers, it compares the ratio of inactive adults to adults who remain economically productive. This ratio stays more or less constant until it eventually declines, and depicts a far more reassuring economic forecast.[31]

Economic dependence is hardly a one-way proposition. More resources have *always* flowed from older generations to younger ones than the reverse. Older people provide as much or more care than they receive, and people over seventy-five spend more time looking after someone, usually a partner, than young people do.[32] In 2012 the Pew Research Center reported that one out of every ten children in the U.S. lived with a grandparent, most often in the grandparent's house under the grandparent's care.[33] Many programs that benefit olders benefit youngers, too, like Social Security and Medicare payments that keep olders self-sufficient while their kids are busy raising *their* kids. In an era of stagnant wages and rising tuitions, more and more olders are helping grandchildren pay for college.

Families are multigenerational, after all. When fundamental problems with the housing and job markets go unaddressed, everyone suffers: the jobless "boomerang generation" of Millennials living with their parents; their parents—the "sandwich" generation—who are doing the lion's share of wage-earning and caregiving for both younger and older family members; and, in a longer-lived world, even a "club sandwich" generation of adults who look after grandchildren, help their own offspring, and tend to their own nonagenarian relatives. Although much of this assistance goes unpaid, it has economic value, and it allows others to do paid work. That's why the MacArthur Foundation paper *Facts & Fictions about an Aging America* concluded

31

that there's no evidence of "significant intergenerational conflict over old-age entitlements. In fact, quite the opposite appears to be true."[34]

Another false dichotomy is that older workers take jobs away from younger ones. When jobs are scarce, this is true in the narrowest sense, but people seldom compete for the same jobs across generations. A different 2012 Pew Research Center study of employment rates over the last forty years found that rates for younger and older workers are actually *positively* correlated.[35] In other words, as more olders stayed on the job, the employment rate and number of hours worked also improved for younger people. A 2015 study in the UK also found that higher employment rates among older workers benefited youngers, as older workers had more money to spend, thus creating more jobs.[36] The challenge is to create enough jobs to prevent resentment and envy from affecting relations between generations—to create a world, in the words of historian David Hackett Fischer, "in which the deep eternal differences between age and youth are recognized and respected without being organized into a system of social inequality."[37]

• Social Security bankrupted! Medicare exhausted!

A large population over the age of sixty-five will strain federal programs, and the government's future financial obligations, currently underfunded, are indeed significant. Social Security, which is notably well-managed at low cost, can be fixed with relatively small adjustments, such as raising the cutoff point for taxing earnings. (Because high-end earnings have grown faster than average, today only about 83.5 percent of earnings are taxed, as compared to 90 percent in 1983.)[38] Nor is the longevity boom to blame for the mess American healthcare is in. The failure lies in the way the system is organized. Designed as an acute care program, Medicare needs to be overhauled to deliver care management to people with disabilities and chronic illness—an aging America, in other words.

Compare the U.S. to Canada, whose citizens have free universal healthcare. In 2012 the Canadian Institute for Health Information (CIHI) reviewed thirty-five years of healthcare costs with a focus on the effect of an aging population. Contrary to the conventional belief that an aging population will overrun hospitals and drain healthcare budgets, the CIHI reported that elderly related care actually added *less than 1 percent* to public-sector health spending each year, despite the fact that olders are proportionately higher users of hospital and physician services, home care, and prescription drugs.[39] In other words, spending on seniors is not growing faster than spending on the population at large. A lifetime of governmental assistance has reduced the vulnerability of older Canadians to illness and disability in old age.

Their American counterparts, on the other hand, still evince the lifelong effects of a system that leaves the poor in the lurch, whether old or young—the people who need healthcare the most, so that they don't get sick and stay sick. Note: *lifelong*. The cumulative effects of poverty, stress, and harsh work environments manifest over time in illnesses that are often attributed to aging but actually reflect persistent disadvantage. As they mount, the personal and financial consequences reflect the growing cost of gross social inequality.

- **We can't afford longevity.**

We can if we want to. A blue-chip panel of experts convened in 2015 by the Leadership Council of Aging Organizations concurred that we can provide for the healthcare and retirement income security needs of older Americans by using existing resources more efficiently.[40] It's the right move economically as well as ethically. Over the last century, national GDPs around the world, along with life spans, have rapidly increased.[41] Health and longevity generate wealth.

Spending money on older people is often portrayed as a cost. It is an investment, not just for ethical reasons and not only because everyone will benefit down the line. Better health systems would cost less and keep people healthier, enabling them to work longer and contribute more to the economy. A sustainable long-term care system would allow the women who currently perform the bulk of this unpaid labor to stay in the workforce, enable people with significant disabilities to continue to live the way they would like to, and encourage risk-sharing and bonding across communities. Supporting engagement for olders in the arts and education improves cognition, bolsters social ties, and benefits the quality of life of everyone involved.

Spending money on older people is often portrayed as a cost. It is an investment.

Older people do indeed receive a disproportionate amount of government and welfare spending: more healthcare, more personal social services, and of course, by definition, all retirement benefits. Is this really outrageous, or even surprising? Isn't this what the system was designed for—to provide for those who can't provide for themselves anymore? Between one-fifth and two-thirds of today's older Americans haven't saved enough for retirement.[42] As author Susan Jacoby observed in *Never Say Die,* "a decent life for the old old cannot, in most cases, be financed by individuals."[43] Providing them with a modicum of financial security into their eighties and nineties will require significant government support.

A big GDP is less important than political will and long-term planning. Resources are not inherently scarce; the United States spends almost as much on its military as all the other nations of the world combined.[44] This "scarcity" is the result of policy decisions in a society whose oldest—and youngest—citizens are demeaned and disregarded.

Life spans are our most basic measure of well-being. For the best crack at reaching ninety, become a wealthy Asian-American man. Yet more advisable, decamp to Anguilla, Austria, Australia, or any of the forty-two other countries that ranked above the United States in global life expectancy in 2017.[45] (Monaco tops the list with a life expectancy of 89.40; the U.S. is in forty-third place at 80; Chad has the lowest at a shocking 50.60.)

Shamefully, in a historic reversal, the life expectancy of the poorest Americans is falling. Studies describe a society in which socioeconomic status is destiny. In 2016, economists at the Brookings Institution found that for men born in 1920, there was a six-year difference in life expectancy between the top 10 percent of earners and the bottom 10 percent. For men born in 1950, that difference had more than doubled to fourteen years. For women, the gap grew to thirteen years from 4.7 years.[46] In regions with higher income and education levels, life spans rose. Thus, even as the gap in life expectancy narrows between men and women and between blacks and whites, it widens between the haves and the have-nots.

THE PERFECT STORM: WHEN AGE, CLASS, AND ENVIRONMENTAL CATASTROPHE COLLIDE

In late life, almost everyone finds out what it's like to be excluded from mainstream discourse and possibility. As writer Walter Mosley put it, "When you become old, you become black . . . anybody that's poor, who gets really old, anybody who suffers some kind of traumatic physical ailment, they realize what it is to be pushed aside by a society that's moving ahead only with what they believe is good—the experience that black people have had in America forever. If you're old, you're not good; if you're paraplegic, you're not good; if you're black, you're not good."[47]

These lines are never more clearly drawn than during natural disasters, when poor people, people of color, and older people die in disproportionate numbers. Chicago's 1995 heat wave claimed 729 lives. Most of the victims were olders living in the heart of the city, isolated by urban decay, afraid to open doors and windows and unable to afford air-conditioning. Blacks were more likely to die than whites, who were more likely to die than Latinos, who tend to live in densely populated neighborhoods and face less isolation.

Of the nearly one thousand people who died when Hurricane Katrina hit the Gulf Coast in August 2005, almost half were seventy-five or older, and more than half of those were black. New

Orleans is both a poor city and a segregated one. Hardest hit were the immobile and impoverished. The deaths of many more older residents can be attributed to the stress of being evacuated and losing their homes.

Almost half of those who died when Superstorm Sandy blew into the mid-Atlantic coast in October 2012 were over sixty-five. As with Katrina, most died on the day of the storm, and most drowned alone. Some were homebound; others chose to stay put. Those in institutions also suffered. Evacuating more than forty nursing homes and adult homes in low-lying areas for Tropical Storm Irene a year earlier had cost millions of dollars. As Sandy approached, officials recommended against evacuation. The hurricane severely flooded at least twenty-nine facilities in Queens and Brooklyn. Over four thousand nursing home residents and fifteen hundred adult home residents sat in the cold and dark for at least three days before being transported through debris-filled floodwaters to crowded, ill-equipped shelters and homes as far away as Albany. Many low-income olders were trapped for days without power in housing projects as well, left behind in every sense by an ageist world.

WHAT DOES IT MEAN TO BE AN AGING SOCIETY?

At one end of the spectrum is "shortgevity," a term coined by Dr. Robert Butler to describe countries where people don't live long and healthily enough to be productive. The United States is not among them—far from it—but both temperament and circumstance stand between many Americans and old age, not to mention a good old age. Not everyone ages well, because of who they are (depressed, reckless, extremely self-involved) or what they are (poor, frail, isolated, African American, Native American, female), and many don't live long enough to grow old.

For those of us with access to healthcare and education, however, for the first time in human history four living generations will become commonplace. We're going to have more time to figure out what we want to do with our lives, more time to accomplish it and share what we know, and more time to wind down with those we love.

To take advantage of this "longevity dividend," we need to quit the reflexive hand-wringing, challenge the ageist assumptions that underlie it, and think realistically and imaginatively about the kinds of intergenerational contracts an equitable future will require—a task all ages would do well to engage in together. Stripping older people of their ability to contribute places a true burden on young adults, who are supposed to mate, breed, establish careers, and start saving for retirement by age thirty-five or so—another example of how ageism affects *everyone*. The mutually advantageous alternative is to see age as an asset. Exploit the "experience dividend" that this new cohort embodies. Acknowledge that olders are not mere burdens but contribute to society, and that their value as human beings is independent of conventional economic productivity. As Marina Gorbis, executive director of the Institute for the Future, puts it, "Productivity is for machines."

That cultural shift is within our grasp. Allocating resources according to whiteness or maleness now seems unthinkable, but it went unquestioned until not long ago (and in many arenas still does). Slavery was fundamental to the American economy until the abolitionist movement turned it into a crisis. Brutal segregation was a reality for black South Africans until the anti-apartheid movement rose up against it. Not until the women's movement emerged did women challenge their second-class status. All these struggles are ongoing, and none are easy. It took nearly a century for American women to win the right to vote, a struggle tainted by racism on the part of white suffragettes, and the ugly legacy of slavery continues to blight the lives of African Americans. It'll take time to develop a culture that acknowledges and reflects on the emerging meanings of longevity, but the conversation is beginning. Let's flip it, as Laura Carstensen, director of the Stanford Center on Longevity, suggests, "from one about growing old to one about living long."

CHAPTER TWO

OUR AGES, OURSELVES: IDENTITY

When I started this project, "How old do you feel?" didn't seem like a loaded question. The widespread tendency to knock a few years off your age seemed optimistic at best and harmless at worst. At fifty-five I *felt* fully engaged, at the height of my intellectual powers, reluctant to trade my bikini for a one-piece with a little skirt, or otherwise trim my sails. In other words, I felt "young." By the same token, feeling "old" was invariably a complaint, meaning feeling ill or unattractive, maybe a little blue or slow off the mark.

What I had yet to pin down was the way language reinforces the idea that feeling good = feeling "young" and feeling bad = feeling "old." Why the quotation marks? Because none of these states of mind are intrinsically linked to what age we happen to be. If we break an ankle, we feel debilitated. Get a promotion, we're filled with confidence. Lose someone we love, depressed. Make a new friend, energized. These feelings, just like these events, can crop up at any point in our lives. Our obsession with youth blinds us to that fact.

"Young" and "old" are useful words with specific meanings. The first means "having lived for a short time," the second "having lived for a long time" or "no longer young" (although I prefer "old*er*" for the second meaning). The words don't mean attractive/ugly or trendy/out of touch or foolish/wise; they're not a binary. Steeped in age denial, we don't notice that such equations are flawed. The question is not how old we feel, but how we feel about "old"—or about just not being young anymore.

Old age is so stigmatized that we go to great lengths to distance ourselves from it. *How to Age*, an excellent primer by medical sociologist Anne Karpf, tells of a sixty-one-year-old woman who observed that when she enters a room and sees nothing but gray heads, she honestly forgets, for one awful moment, that she's one of them. (I'm Not Ray–Stage One!) "This is like people who say, 'I don't feel old,'" Karpf comments, "as though there were some special feeling that age brings, instead of just being themselves but older."[1] We don't wake up one morning hijacked by Oldness. As the years pass we remain ourselves, just older. Of course we can't know what the future holds, but when aging past youth seems dreadful, clinging to youth seems the only option. The more time goes by, the more damage that strategy does to our sense of self and our place in the world.

> *The more time goes by, the more damage clinging to youth does to our sense of self and our place in the world.*

THE EMERGENCE OF YOUTH CREEP

Until the second half of the nineteenth century, explains Patricia Cohen in *In Our Prime: The Invention of Middle Age*, "Age was not an essential ingredient of one's identity."[2] Milestones like marriage, offspring, and illness sufficed for a population divided into ten-year cohorts, and life was a lot shorter. Players of the original game of *Life*, created by Milton Bradley in 1860, could ascend from "infancy" to a square in the far corner marked "50—Happy Old Age."

By 1900, as life spans increased and narrower categories became statistically useful, the census began asking for exact dates of birth, and "How old are you?" became a prime identifier for Americans of all ages. The widespread tendency to knock a few years off your age probably cropped up not long afterward, as the social meaning of the number shifted. Clearly part of the creep is based on measurable social change. Young people used to finish school, get married, and have kids in their early twenties; now it often take decades to pass those adult milestones. In 1978, *Webster's Dictionary* defined middle age as "between forty and sixty." Merriam-Webster Online now pegs it as "the period of life from about forty-five to about sixty-four."

Only a few of the sixty-year-old respondents to a 1963 study of 1,700 older Americans classified themselves as old, and barely half of the eighty-year-olds, a small percentage of whom persisted in describing themselves as young.[3] A Pew Research Center study conducted forty-six years later not only confirmed that "you're never too old to feel young," but showed that "the older people get, the younger they feel—relatively speaking."[4] The "thirty-nine syndrome"—refusing to admit that you're over forty, a masculine weakness, not a feminine one, by the way—peaks at around fifty but never entirely disappears. Comedian Jack Benny famously celebrated his thirty-ninth birthday forty-one times.

IT'S NOT JUST A NUMBER

How tempting it is to emulate Benny, to lie or fudge or just omit that pesky number, at least for as long as we can get away with it. Having come of age during the youth-glorifying sixties, couldn't my generation claim a little extra indulgence? Certainly most of us can identify with financier Bernard Baruch, who lived to ninety-five and declared old age to be "always fifteen years older than I am." It's true that most thirty-year-olds can't imagine being eighty, but their parents don't make it any easier when they pretend they can't either. Age is indeed "only a number," as long as that number reflects how many times we've circled the sun.

Like many of the octogenarians I interviewed, retired psychotherapist Bill Krakauer registered "a little bit of a shock" every time he looked in the mirror, saying "I feel like a young guy." I know the feeling, but it's less unnerving now that I know it's close to universal. When he launched a new career as an actor, Krakauer told his agent, "I'll be eighty in a few months." She drew in her breath and hissed, "Don't tell anybody. Don't tell *anybody*!" She didn't want people assuming he was too old for a part and he didn't want people treating him with kid gloves, so they happily colluded.

My mother painted over her bathroom mirror, not a tactic I'd recommend. Writer and television commentator Andy Rooney took a more oblique approach. Spotting his reflection in store windows, he'd wonder, "Who is that stooped old man over there?" So he stopped looking in windows. Rooney was a staple on *Sixty Minutes* for thirty years, stepping down—from television, not from writing— at ninety-two. Denial works, at least until the bill comes due.

Line up a random bunch of seventy-year-olds and it'll be hard to believe they share a birth year. Since we age at very different rates, it makes a certain sense to reject identifying with our chronological age. That's one reason so many octogenarians maintain, truthfully, that they still feel fifty, forty, or even thirty inside. The other reason is internalized ageism, which is why the disavowal of chronological age is so problematic. It gives the number more power than it deserves, contributes to ageist assumptions about what age signifies and ageist stereotypes about what age looks like, and distances us from our cohorts.

INTERNALIZED STEREOTYPES BECOME SELF-FULFILLING PROPHECIES

Nobody's born ageist, but it starts young. Research suggests that children develop negative stereotypes about old age in early childhood, around the same time that attitudes about race and gender begin to form.[5] As a kid I knew I was never going to turn into one of those grown-ups who incomprehensibly preferred sitting to racing around, and that my bruised shins and scabby knees would exile me permanently from the land of stockings and heels. I was a conspicuously late bloomer, I have yet to get the hang of heels, and my thoughts didn't turn to aging until I was in my fifties. We age slowly, which is one reason we don't pay much attention to its grim portrayal. Negative stereotypes abound, and when we're young we don't see any reason to examine them critically—which is hard work, another disincentive.

Unexamined, these beliefs and opinions become fixed, forming what psychologists call "premature cognitive commitments"— mind-sets that we're unlikely to reconsider even when it would work to our own benefit and even when it affects actual behavior. For example, social scientists primed a group of college students with negative age stereotypes by having them unscramble sentences that included words like forgetful, Florida, and bingo. Afterward, the students were observed walking to the elevator *measurably more slowly* than a control group.[6] Steps slowed simply because a subliminal script said it was time to totter.

My nights on the dance floor now end in a hot bath with ice packs on both knees. (Looks ridiculous, feels great.) I'd been assuming that this was just the price of admission at my age. I'd lost sight of the fact that my back was feeling fine, or that the jumping around might have taken a toll on my younger companions as well. In other words, that tasks or circumstance—a concrete floor, hours bent over a desk, cooking for forty—might be as much or more to blame. When I mentioned this to Keith VonEmmeler, a then-twenty-six-year-old aerialist, his brow furrowed. "I was sore after a couple of hours of training the other night, and said to myself, 'Damn, I'm too young to be this sore.' But when I think about it, that's what I get for not stretching or training for over a week."

Unless we confront these expectations of impairment and insignificance, they build up over the decades, making older adults themselves the worst ageists of all. We rule out activities or outfits or relationships preemptively because they might not be "age-appropriate," especially any with a tinge of sexuality—a double taboo. Over time, as age-related stereotypes grow more relevant, people tend to act as though they were accurate, creating self-fulfilling prophecies.[7] We blame every ache on age and every memory lapse on incipient dementia, losing sight of the fact that the other knee doesn't hurt and that kids, too, forget stuff all the time.

Yale psychologist and age scholar Becca Levy calls this kind of behavior "stereotype embodiment theory." In a series of experiments, she flashed a series of words positively or negatively associated with aging on a screen, too briefly for the subjects to become aware of them. The experiments demonstrated that older people exposed to the positive messages about late life showed better recall and more confidence in their abilities than those exposed to negative ones. The decline has nothing to do with physiology. It's psychological. Borne out by research on memory loss in general,[8] the effect of cultural expectations on recall and performance is powerful. It's the same reason fifteen-year-old girls excel on science tests in countries where they don't face strong gender bias.

Call it "stereotype threat," a term coined by social psychologist Claude Steele to describe apprehension about being seen through the lens of a negative stereotype or the fear of behaving in a way that inadvertently confirms the stereotype. Call it subconscious self-handicapping. Whatever name it goes by, the phenomenon undercuts performance and well-being until the underlying assumptions are exposed and invalidated.

WHETHER PATHETIC OR HEROIC, STEREOTYPES OPPRESS

We're all familiar with depictions of old women as lovable grannies or evil witches, and old men reduced to silent graybeards or hapless fools. All are caricatures. Whether they set too high a standard or too low, stereotypes are a way to avoid dealing with people as individuals, and to keep them at a distance.

When we internalize stereotypes of olders as useless and debilitated, it's understandable that we experience aging as trauma—the betrayal of the body and the dissolution of our place in the world along with it. This is a fundamental challenge to a healthy sense of self, although the apprehension is typically accepted at face value. Take former *New York Times* blogger Judith Warner's plaint about being elbowed off stage as another generation moves into the spotlight and hogs all the fun. "I now see the passage of time more as a kind of bell curve," she wrote. "Years of ascension, soaring anticipation, followed by a plateau—which is not so bad, really—and then, no way to sugarcoat this: a rather precipitous decline." Only forty-four years old, Warner bid so long forever to "excitement, discovery, intensity."[9] Feigning transgression, she added, "You are not supposed to think this, much less say it!" Has Warner never met someone over fifty who's embraced a cause, fallen in love, seized the day? Of course she has, but ageist stereotypes push those positive examples to the back of the line and lead us to question our own abilities.

When I interviewed park ranger Betty Soskin, she was working as an outreach specialist and interpreter at Rosie the Riveter National Historical Park in Richmond, CA. Her long history in the area made her an invaluable asset, not least because, as she put it, "I'm at an age where I know how all the stories turned out." Soskin described "hitting the age wall" twice during a training session at the Grand Canyon. One task involved blending in with tourists to observe concessionaires in national parks. "A saleswoman asked me, 'Are you here with Elderhostel?' and all of a sudden I became an old lady," Soskin recounted. "I was doing my job as a student, but I suddenly felt like someone who had wandered away from her tour group and was lost. And I suddenly began to walk more slowly. A physical and psychological change came over me as a result of that simple question."

On the way home, she and a companion ate fried rattlesnake at the Cowboy Club, then pulled up in their convertible at the vortex, a famous rock formation in Sedona believed to channel energy flow, and started up the gravelly sandstone incline. Soskin was scrambling along in her blue jeans until she happened to overhear "this conversation among a group of elders about how one of them had gotten paralyzed with fear and gotten stuck and 'oh, how awful!' And I stopped in my tracks. Because all of a sudden I identified not with my friend who was headed up the incline and who was twenty years younger than I, but with the elders standing nearby." We're all vulnerable to being shaped to some degree by the expectations of others. It requires our acquiescence, as Soskin was acutely aware. "I gave them that power," she noted, "because I could go on up that incline with no problem."

Exceptionally active, Soskin could scramble her way out of that mind-set, but America's "can-do" ethic can be almost as problematic as the ageist script of learned helplessness. People with disabilities have a term for uplifting pictures of disabled people doing things the rest of us might not expect them to be doing, like skiing or kissing: "inspiration porn." Also a name for the protagonists: "supercrips." Enter the "supergeezer." At eighty, Japanese climber Yuichiro Miura made it to the top of Mount Everest. At eighty-five, fashion designer Gloria Vanderbilt published a steamily explicit erotic novel. Former President George H. W. Bush celebrated his ninetieth birthday by jumping out of a plane.

That smattering of octogenarian CEOs, nonagenarian performers, and centenarian diploma-earners are standard-bearers, all. The media loves 'em. But placing them on pedestals distracts from the social and economic factors that shrink the worlds of most older and disabled people. It also reflects a culture that venerates actors, musicians, and athletes in ways that reinforce ageist, racist, and sexist stereotypes.

Celebrity culture is ground zero. "Pop: come for the sexism, stay for the ageism," wrote music critic Sasha Frere-Jones about Britney Spears, noting that the thirty-two-year-old former child star "has long faced the specter of becoming old in pop years."[10] (Are pop years like dog years?) Athletes fare little better. Reluctant to acknowledge a hero's physical decline, fans collude in the pretense that stars who slow, like Yankee shortstop Derek Jeter, who retired at forty with uncommon grace, are simply in prolonged slumps. Denial turns a natural progression into a personal failure.

The notion that the postwar generation will rock and roll its way through old age is another ageist myth. Many olders just want to be able to pay their bills and spend time doing things they like with people they love. Others, myself among them, have bigger plans than ever. There's no norm, no average way of aging, as would be abundantly clear if age denial—aka "agelessness"—weren't fundamental to the supergeezer and celebrity scripts. The struggles of daily life can take just as much courage, and life writ small be just as full of meaning. We could use more examples in the media, many more, of olders living ordinary lives, neither drooling nor dazzling. Of course that's not what sells papers or garners click-throughs, so it will be up to us to hold up the vast and varied middle ground as equally valid examples of how to age.

AGE CONFERS CONTENTMENT

Which group is happier, a bunch of thirty-five-year-olds or a bunch of eighty-five-year-olds? The thirty-five-year-olds, right? That's what both groups answer. But ask each to assess its own well-being and the older people come out ahead—in study after study, from Australia to Zimbabwe. Data from a University of Warwick study on two million people from eighty nations show an extraordinarily consistent pattern: whether rich or poor, single or married, childfree or fertile, people were most miserable in middle age and happiest in childhood and at the ends of their lives.[11]

People in their eighties and nineties readily admit that life is difficult and growing more so, but they also keep the things that make it worthwhile firmly in view. The source of this conscious contentment appears to be internal, deeply human, and inherent to growing old. Aging itself confers very effective coping mechanisms upon most of us. Perhaps the shift is based in brain chemistry, or maybe we just get better at appreciating what we have. Whatever its basis, as we hit the homestretch, most of us make peace with our pasts and enjoy the present as never before.

WE EACH AGE DIFFERENTLY:
MENTALLY, PHYSICALLY, AND SOCIALLY

Human variability makes chronological age an increasingly unreliable benchmark of pretty much anything about a person: what she "should" look like, or be listening to, or feel about thongs or the Internet of Things. Categories make life simpler, and generalizations are inevitable, but sorting by capacity and inclination makes more sense. There are even more ways of getting from sixty to ninety than there are of getting from thirty to sixty. That's why "You look great for your age!" offends: It relies on internalized ageism to work as a compliment, and it implies that people "your age" look a certain way. Aging does indeed have hallmarks, tactfully identified by Pew Center researchers as forgetfulness, bladder control problems, decreased sexual activity, being retired, and having grandchildren and gray hair.

Chronological age is an increasingly unreliable benchmark of pretty much anything about a person.

Some are inevitable if we live long enough. But which ones, when, and how we deal with them, vary enormously.

THERE'S NO SUCH THING AS "AGE-APPROPRIATE"

Aging is, obviously, a process. The older we grow, the more complexly layered identity becomes, the fatter the file in which our knowledge and memories are stored, in which, in turn, our sense of self resides. In Lynne Segal's philosophical take in her book *Out of Time: The Pleasures and the Perils of Aging*, what really matters are the narratives we create, "the stories we tell ourselves of how to 'be our age as we age.'"[12] The central task, in other words, is to figure out what's us-appropriate at any point, not necessarily what biology predicts or an ageist culture ordains. There's no such thing as age-appropriate.

Acutely aware of how much has changed, we also feel the same. That's why so many people maintain, "I'm still a kid inside." The feeling is genuine, but it reflects the way an ageist culture divides us into young and no-longer-young. We experience this as conflict: a "true" and more pleasing self, obscured by sags and wrinkles, struggling to remain visible and relevant. This way of thinking is a trap.

Age is real, but it is not a fixed characteristic like eye color or skin color or, typically, sex. Age is an observation used to place ourselves relative to others. Ask an eight-year-old where the children are, and she will invariably scan the room for younger kids. Age is both fixed and fluid, as is the way we experience it. At the time of this writing, I'm sixty-six. How I *feel* about it at a given moment depends on whether my knees hurt, who else is on the bus, and infinite other variables. Different mental and physical states coexist. "We are, at every moment, younger and older," writes Wendy Lustbader in her book *Life Gets Better: The Unexpected Pleasures of Growing Older.*[13] Referring to "the radical ambiguities of old age," Segal calls this disorientation "temporal vertigo." As we age, she writes, "we also retain, in one manifestation or another, traces of all the selves we have been . . . rendering us psychically, in one sense, all ages and no age."

Swedish sociologist Lars Tornstam, who's been studying the aging process for three decades, sees many older people who continue to mature socially and psychologically, a process that he calls gerotranscendence. He describes the first "sign of gerotranscendence" as "a feeling of being a child, a young person, an adult, middle age and old—all at once!"[14] What abundance! There's much that I don't remember but much that I do, from skinned knees and learning to type and kiss and conjugate and calm a baby and how to walk on ice just last winter. (Center of gravity on the front leg, like a penguin.) Unless we fall into the tiny minority hijacked by severe, late-stage dementia, all those selves will remain available to us until the end.

Like everything else about old age, people undoubtedly experience these transitions in countless unique ways, some inhabiting an increasingly distilled sense of self and others exploring a multiplicity of identities. Toward the end of the television series *The Big C*—spoiler alert!—after Laura Linney's character has moved to a hospice, she hangs young-and-healthy photographs of all the residents around their necks one night to remind the dining room staff of the places in the world the dying once occupied. The dance between all the selves we've inhabited across the years never stops.

"The great thing about getting older," according to writer Madeleine L'Engle, "is that you don't lose all the other ages you've been."

This is not "agelessness." Offering neutral ground, an end run around all these messy ambiguities, "agelessness" sounds so seductive, doesn't it? On a tube of eye cream, "agelessness" promises to erase the trace of time. In pop culture it describes people who "stay young" into their fifties and sixties. In gerontology, it suggests that a youthful spirit can remain unaltered within an aging body. None of these scenarios is possible, and they're all ageist. As sociologist Molly Andrews has argued, "the current tendency toward 'agelessness' is itself a form of ageism, depriving the old of one of their most hard-earned resources: their age."[15]

Rather this is "agefulness": an accretion of all the things we've done and been, not catalogued or curated but stored random access within our bones and brains, that makes us who we are. Hag, spinster, crone? Old fogey, old fart, old goat? Little old lady, dirty old man, sweet old thing? Geezer, biddy, codger, coot? Those stereotypes are ours to reject or subvert on the way to more compelling and accurate aspirational identities. At the moment I'm leaning toward hag, something a driver actually called me last year when I banged on the trunk of his car after he bombed through the pedestrian crosswalk. Hag, outside of Shakespeare—*really*? Maybe it was my funny fake-fur cat hat that undid him.

"I wish I were young again." People say this all the time. When pressed, however, few would actually move their game pieces back to the beginning of the board, or anywhere close, unless they could transport their present-day consciousness back in time as well. Adolescence again? No, thanks. I'd love my eighteen-year-old cartilage back, but I dance more now because I'm less self-conscious and prioritize better. Whatever our trajectories, however we've navigated loving and letting go, whether of children or houses or dreams, we are the sum of those experiences and what we learned from them. They make us us. That is agefulness, rich and deep and invaluable.

PUSH BACK!

REJECT THE BOGUS OLD/YOUNG BINARY

When the 2011 Fall Fashion issue of *New York* magazine landed in my mailbox, it had a chic young woman on its cover. Yawn. "When it came time to cast the cover, we decided . . . to embrace a more expansive view of beauty," an editor's note explained. "We came up with four cover subjects: an eighty-one-year-old woman; a nineteen-year-old man who can pass quite convincingly as a woman; a mother and daughter . . . ; and an old-fashioned yet newfangled muse." Turned out that my copy featured the nineteen-year-old, and I stopped yawning. It was Serbo-Croatian teenager Andrej Pejić, who modeled both women's and men's clothing and hit the big time when French *Vogue* dressed him in a skirt. Saying, "I've left my gender open to artistic interpretation"[16] at the time, the model has since transitioned to womanhood.

Those in the genderqueer vanguard like Pejić bravely reject biological and cultural constraints. In response, the culture is shifting. Gender used to be viewed as a rigid binary, male or female, but we now understand that it's far more fluid. If *gender* can be conceived of this way, why on earth not age, which is inherently, obviously, a continuum? Especially in view of the fact that in late life, as hormones change, gender roles begin to merge. Many women become more assertive and men more emotionally attuned. Age is relative: We're always younger than some and older than others. Even nonagenarians are quick to point out that Mrs. So-and-So down the hall is older than they are. If we can shake off the far more rigid shackles of gender, why not embrace a more fluid, friendly, and, frankly, far more rational view of age?

Any compartmentalization is problematic. Take "middle age," to which so many cling like flotation cushions, although who knows where the middle lies anymore? According to Patricia Cohen, middle age was invented around the turn of the twentieth century, when the bulk of the population began living decades past their child-rearing years. Capitalism, vanity, and fear of mortality all swiftly combined to pathologize this grim development and commercialize the remedies. Sound familiar? The point, of course, is that the same applies to the way late life is typically viewed.

This punishing old/young binary—old/no-longer-young, actually—consigns two-thirds of us to second-class status, a meekly self-enforced exile to the wrong side of the velvet rope. The exile starts ever younger. Describing a *New York* magazine feature on internet celebrity, the New York University Local blog wrote, "It makes us feel some toxic combination of alienation, self-righteousness, nostalgia, and a smattering of annoyance. Do we feel OLD?? . . . Is the only salvation the silent grave?"[17] The bloggers were *college students*—still on the "right" side of that rope, but already oppressed by ageist norms. The birthday card rack sets the bar at twenty-nine. I hate to admit it, but one reason I got married at 29.9 was because I didn't want to be single at thirty. The marriage turned out very differently than I thought it would, as did turning forty, fifty, and sixty, and I bet the birthdays ahead will pack their share of surprises.

CLAIM YOUR AGE— AND QUESTION ITS SIGNIFICANCE

Few people frankly acknowledge that they're fine with their age; they're more likely to offer it up with a resigned shrug or a self-deprecating anecdote. Well-meaning readers regularly offer a tip to a journalist colleague who covers the "age beat" and dubbed herself the Aging Reporter: Surely she'd made this regrettable association by mistake? Surely she'd fare better with a cheerier title?

Coming out generally means identifying an attribute that would otherwise be hidden, and offers membership to a welcoming community. Identifying yourself as old, on the other hand, observes critic Elaine Showalter, "is to admit something everyone can see, and is thus somehow more shaming, carrying more of a stigma. We're supposed to deny being old; it is seen as an insulting, or at least unwelcome, self-description, unless jocular and well-padded with euphemisms."[10] Even well-padded, it deprecates. Euphemisms demean, like the sportscaster who crowed, "Diana Nyad is sixty-four years young!" when the marathon swimmer succeeded at her fifth attempt to swim from Cuba to Florida. Better to remember Nyad's own words, spoken through parched and swollen lips: "You're never too old to chase your dream."

The alternative is age acceptance: acknowledging the accomplishment of having come this far—however far that happens to be—and making peace with it. From acceptance to declaration is no great leap. It's not "age outing" if we out ourselves, and when we slip the cultural noose we rob the number of that power over us. Lots of people, for example, recall claiming their first senior discount—or, horrors, being offered one!—with real dismay. If there's no shame, the discount becomes just that: a price break free of ambivalence, not to mention mortification.

What's the best answer to "How old are you?" Tell the truth, then ask why it matters. Ask what shifted in the questioner's mind once they had a number. Ask why they think they needed to know. The information feels foundational, but it isn't. We ask partly out of sheer habit, carried over from childhood, when a month was an eternity and each year marked developmental changes and new freedoms. "The kids drive me crazy asking how old I am," said eighty-year-old Detroit schoolteacher Penny Kyle. "I don't mind telling my age, but I know on the job it can cause you a problem, so I always say I'm a hundred and four." Ha!

What's the best answer to "How old are you?" Tell the truth. Then ask what difference the number makes.

We also ask how old people are because age functions as a convenient shorthand, a way to contextualize accomplishments and calibrate expectations. It's lazy, though, and utterly unreliable, and arguably impertinent. A woman who attended one of my talks answers the question by retorting, "How much do you weigh?"

Scientist Silvia Curado refuses to give her age, not because she wants people to take her for younger but because she refuses to be pigeonholed in a way that she finds "reductive and usually faulty." Her consciousness makes it a political act. Social worker Natalia Granger has another radical suggestion: Follow the example of gender-nonconforming people, who reject roles and stereotypes based on the sex they were assigned at birth. When asked for your age, identify as age-nonconforming.

Author and environmental activist Colin Beavan announced on Facebook that he was "coming out as age queer. I am not comfortable with the roles and stereotypes associated with the age of the body I was born into," he wrote. "My body's age is not my age. From now on, I will be identifying as thirty-seven." I love the culture hack but want to modify it, because identifying as thirty-seven (still "young") is a form of denial. Colin is in his fifties. I'm eleven years older than he is. I'm good with that, and he's getting there; after a back-and-forth, he decided to stop identifying with a specific age. I want to be age queer by rejecting not my age but the fixed meanings that people assign to it—the roles and stereotypes that Colin, too, declines to abide by. I claim my age at the same time that I challenge its primacy and its value as a signifier.

REJECT AGE AS A FIRST-ORDER IDENTIFIER (THINK OF IT AS A THOUGHT EXPERIMENT)

The habit of wanting to know a person's age is hard to break. It's the first question that springs to mind when a friend says they're dating someone new, although I no longer ask it. Take the journalistic convention of including ages in newspaper stories. Two stories in the same week, one about a forty-two-year-old nursing student running for homecoming queen and another about a ninety-one-year-old mayor swindling River Falls, Alabama, out of $201,000, got me thinking about it. Dolores Barclay, a veteran Associated Press reporter, fielded my question.

"It is just another essential fact to include about the subjects we cover. It's part of the 'who' in reporting," Barclay responded.[19] "Age is often relevant to certain stories as well. For example, if we write about a 'senior citizen' or 'older person' who takes her first sky dive, does the story have more impact if the subject is seventy or if she's ninety-nine? Or if we're profiling the accomplishments of a musician who has had an illustrious and amazing career, don't we want to know how old he is? What if he's only twenty-four, but reading the story we might think he's sixty?"

Okay, what if? The week before I'd happened to attend the dazzling U.S. debut of South Korean classical guitarist Kyuhee Park at Carnegie Hall. She could have been thirteen or twenty-three years old, and I was itching to know. It turned out that she was twenty-seven, which made the experience no less rapturous. It did make me wish that I'd spent less time being distracted by the itch. The media focus relentlessly on the age of celebrities, especially women like Madonna who decline to "age gracefully." "I find whenever someone writes anything about me, my age is right after my name," Madonna said. "It's almost like they're saying, 'Here she is, but remember she's this age, so she's not that relevant anymore.' Or 'Let's punish her by reminding her and everyone else.' When you put someone's age down, you're limiting them."[20]

Or protecting them, which is little better. The first attitude desexualizes, and the second incapacitates. Why shouldn't River Falls Mayor Mary Ella Hixon, whose ten-year sentence was commuted to five on probation, do some time for stealing $201,000 from her town? Although his client was clearly *compos mentis*, an attorney for the defense maintained that she "was being taken advantage of." "Had it not been a ninety-one-year-old woman, I would have stood on my head to make sure she went to prison," the Covington County district attorney told the Associated Press. Apparently citizens in the know had been reluctant to blow the whistle, he said, "for fear of being ostracized or because it was a proverbial 'little old lady.'"[21] The only non-ageist position in the story is the acknowledgment that

Hixon was powerful enough to silence her critics. A forty-two-year-old homecoming queen, on the other hand? Now *that's* news!

Obviously the subject's age belongs in obituaries and profiles of child prodigies, but its reflexive inclusion in other kinds of stories is nothing but a bad habit. Race is no longer an obligatory part of the "who" of a story unless it's a story about race relations—just the opposite, in fact, for the same reason. Because it's sexist to foreground a woman's marital status, Ms. has supplanted Miss or Mrs. as an identifier. Why should age be different? There are plenty of ways to clue readers in the rare event that it's actually relevant to the story. A little confusion could rattle a lot of assumptions about what people are capable of at a given stage of life, or what they have in common across age divides, which would be all to the good.

Another thought experiment: Suppose date of birth was omitted from medical records? Inconceivable, right? OK, maybe buried on page 3. But wouldn't it be great if physicians had to assess and prescribe based on each person's physical and mental condition, free of bias about which symptoms were likely to crop up at a given stage of life, and which were "worth treating"? It's why geriatrician Mark Lachs named his book *Treat Me, Not My Age.*

TAKE A PAGE FROM THE DISABILITY RIGHTS PLAYBOOK: THINK PERSON FIRST

To avoid reducing people to labels or medical diagnoses, disability etiquette prescribes "people first" language: talking about people with mental illness (instead of mentally ill); people who have autism or epilepsy (not autistic or epileptic); wheelchair users (instead of wheelchair-bound or confined to); and so on. The disability is a characteristic of the person; it does not define them.

When I initially heard "person first" language, it seemed cumbersome and slightly silly. The term "ableism" has been in use for at least thirty years to describe discrimination against people with disabilities, but it seemed an annoying invention by the Politically

Correct Thought Police. A friend who works in the field brought me around by saying tartly, "You wouldn't refer to 'my cancerous mother,' now would you?" It's worth keeping in mind that cancer was deeply stigmatized until quite recently and treated like a shameful family secret. Mores change, thank heavens.

So here's yet another thought experiment: How about learning from the disability rights movement and attempting to conceive of ourselves and those around us as "people with age" instead of as X- or Y-year-olds? Age becomes just another attribute, like being a good speller or Filipino or a Cubs fan. People could "have years" just as people with dementia "have trouble thinking" and others a knack for putting people at ease or a tin ear. Age needn't set apart, nor be set apart from other identifiers. Person first, as Bill Krakauer discovered when he started taking acting classes. "So here are these bunch of kids and they see an old guy, right? After a while it quiets down. It takes a few weeks, but everybody forgets. I stop looking at them like young people, and they stop looking at me like an old guy and we're all just people."

TAKE HEART: THERE'S NO "RIGHT" PATH

"Aren't we all supposed to aspire toward 'Active Aging?'" asks ethicist H. R. Moody in his *Human Values in Aging* newsletter.[22] Perhaps not, he suggests. Perhaps doing less frees us up to accomplish more of what matters most to us. Perhaps the trick lies in figuring out what matters most—a tall order in view of the fact that most Americans' self-worth is intimately bound up in self-reliance and conventional economic productivity. Americans value *doing* over *being*, and I'm no exception. Reminded that I'm rounding the third turn on the track, my impulse is to get cracking on that bucket list. "No wonder cultures where being is devalued and doing over-valued regard old age with such contempt and dread!" Anne Karpf observes in her book *How to Age*.[23] The whole point about aging "well," she says, is to become more liberated from social expectations and prioritize what feels right for us: tidal breezes for Ray, midtown fumes for me.

It can be hard to resist the "successful" or "productive" model of aging, since it provides an optimistic counterpoint to the standard narrative of decline. Gerontologists like the terminology because it's upbeat. Conservatives like it because it legitimizes reducing government support by placing the burden of how we age on the individual. The positive language is seductive, as is its premise, because we really, really want to think we can keep doing the things we love forever. We often can—versions of them, that is. Motivation is important, as is keeping mentally and physically active, making a living, helping others, having goals, all those good things. But the goalposts shift. We'd do well to keep in mind that many of those activities are predominantly available to the lucky and reasonably well-off, and to decouple self-worth from long-standing measures of earning power or physical prowess. Much is not under our control, and many supports require policy-level implementation.

Sanitized or romanticized exemplars of "successful aging"— those silver-maned couples waltzing on the foredeck of a cruise ship—set an unreasonable standard and suggest that less "successful" agers are responsible for their circumstances. Why does NPR's Ina Jaffe dislike the term "successful aging" so heartily? "It means there's one more opportunity for me to fail."[24] As age scholar Margaret Cruikshank has observed, the model overlooks the very important role class plays in determining who gets to age in the first place, not to mention how "successfully." "No amount of individual effort or sturdy self-reliance can gain for working-class people or people of color the advantages enjoyed by the white middle class, especially by men," she writes in her book *Learning to Be Old*.[25] Everyone can make sensible choices, but barriers like heavy caregiving responsibilities, inadequate healthcare, and neighborhoods with few resources make it more difficult. Blaming the poor for "bad choices"—and poverty itself on weakness—makes aging another arena in which we succeed or fail based on terms that are far from neutral.

Many choices are unlikely to be ours, and have little to do with willpower or personal virtue or whether our software skills are up to date. Both the losses and the pleasures are likely to take us by surprise. "The mistake we make in middle age is thinking that good aging means continuing to be the way we were at fifty. Maybe it's not," says Tornstam.[26] Instead he sees many olders who continue to mature socially and psychologically, in ways that may surprise or dismay. Hallmarks of this process include less fear of death and disease, deeper relationships with fewer people, coupled with an increased desire for solitude, and diminished commitment to old habits, routines, and principles. The assumption that older people become "set in their ways" is an ageist cliché. Lives can indeed become constrained by disability or living on a fixed income or conforming to an institutional schedule. But the ultimate creatures of habit are children, and odds are that people who find comfort in routine were always like that.

If I had a nickel for every story I've been sent about olders doing the limbo or DJing or skipping rope, I'd be rich. I don't post them because they get plenty of press without my help, and because it reinforces the notion that the older people who deserve admiration are those who can look and behave like younger ones. These overachievers are outliers. They're terrific and they're inspirational, but it's also okay to sit on the porch. If a mom's wanderlust fades or an uncle quits his bowling league, we're likely to wring our hands and blame illness or depression. In fact such transitions may reflect greater self-esteem, more spontaneity, or a need for time to reflect on larger questions—what Tornstam describes in his theory of gerotranscendence as "a shift in meta perspective, from a materialistic and rational view of the world to a more cosmic and transcendent one, normally accompanied by an increase in life satisfaction." More basis for the growing body of evidence that emotional well-being increases with age.

BECOME AN OLD PERSON IN TRAINING

How then to bridge the personal and the political? To integrate the real and the aspirational? In 2008 I heard geriatrician Joanne Lynn describe herself as an old person in training, and I've been one ever since. I know I'm not young. I don't see myself as old. I know a lot of people feel the same way. They're in the grips of a cruel paradox: They aspire to grow old yet dread the prospect. They spend a lot of energy sustaining the illusion that the old are somehow *not us*. Becoming an Old Person in Training bridges the us/them divide, and loosens the grip of that exhausting illusion.

Becoming an Old Person in Training acknowledges the inevitability of oldness while relegating it to the future, albeit at an ever-smaller remove. It swaps purpose and intent for dread and denial. It connects us empathically with our future selves. As Simone de Beauvoir put it, rather more grandly: "If we do not know who we are going to be, we cannot know who we are: Let us recognize ourselves in this old man or in that old woman. It must be done if we are to take upon ourselves the entirety of our human state." In a world increasingly segregated by race and class as well as by age, reaching over those divisions to acknowledge the one path we all will travel is a radical act.

Becoming an Old Person in Training means ditching preconceptions, looking at and listening carefully to the olders around us, and re-envisioning our place among them. It means looking *at* older people instead of past them, remembering they were once our age, seeing resilience alongside infirmity, allowing for sensuality, enlarging our notion of beauty, and acknowledging that an apartment or a room or even just a bed can be home to an internal world as rich as ours and very possibly richer. It means thoughtful peeks through the periscope of an open mind at the terrain we will some day inhabit.

Thinking way ahead doesn't come naturally: As a species, humans evolved to choose present gratification over future well-being. That's why becoming an Old Person in Training takes imagination. In her book *A Long Bright Future*, Stanford psychologist Laura Carstensen describes the importance of generating realistic, humane visions of our future selves—what we'll want to be doing and be capable of—and embarking on the tasks and changes and sacrifices that will get us there. "If we can't picture ourselves teaching, laughing, loving, and contributing to society when we're ninety and 100, then good luck is about the only thing that will get us there," she writes.[27]

As an Old Person in Training, I see the ninety-year-old me as withered and teetery, but also curious and content. Envisioning her won't make it happen, but I sure can't get there without the aspiration. It means working against the human tendency to underestimate how much we'll change in the future. Rich, complex stories about the past tend to yield vague, prosaic projections of a future in which things stay pretty much the same. Maybe that's because the unknown breeds unease; maybe it's because predicting the future is more difficult than reminiscing; maybe it's because the task holds less appeal in a youth-centric society. Work through that and it becomes easier to imagine ourselves doing different things with new friends in places we have yet to visit—or staying home, if that's our pleasure.

The sooner growing older is stripped of reflexive dread, the better equipped we are to benefit from the countless ways in which it can enrich us.

The consensus from people over eighty, who should know, is that young people worry way too much about getting old, so the earlier we make this imaginative leap, the better. The sooner this lifelong process is stripped of reflexive dread, the better equipped we are to benefit from the countless ways in which it can enrich us. Some people are born with this awareness, and so have longer to develop the capacities that will serve them well later on. Anne Karpf describes them as the ability to keep making new friends, to value internal resources, and to be able to let go. She also notes that the values most admired in the industrialized world—high personal and economic productivity—do little to help us age. We would do both ourselves and the planet a favor, she observes, if we reject those values for more humanitarian and communitarian ones.

AIM FOR "AGEFULNESS"

Becoming an Old Person in Training also makes it easier to think critically about what age means in this society, and the forces at work behind depictions of older people as useless and pathetic. Shame can damage self-esteem and quality of life as much as externally imposed stereotyping. Becoming an Old Person in Training is a political act, because it derails this shame and self-loathing. It undoes the "otherness" that powers ageism (and racism, and nationalism). It makes room for empathy, and action. It robs the caricatures of crone or geezer of their power and frees us to become our full—our ageful—selves.

I may be jumping onto podiums instead of out of airplanes—I have a long way to go on the "being over doing" front—but I'm not running away from aging. That sets me apart from the aspirational supergeezers, as well as from an awful lot of other "aging experts" who are invested either in a deficit model of aging (helping the frail and needy age) or its misleading opposite (successful aging!). I hope to set an example of radical aging: acknowledging my mortality; embracing aging as a natural process; wrestling with the countless paradoxes this involves (for a while my working title for this project was *Both Are True*); and rustling up companions along the way. We're all old people in training, whether we know it yet or not, and our numbers will swell as we reject demeaning stereotypes and claim our aging selves.

CHAPTER THREE

FORGET MEMORY: THE OLDER BRAIN

The possibility of becoming less mobile has never kept me up at night. I'd grab a walker, or get strapping lads to carry me about. But lose my marbles? *That* prospect used to terrify me. Didn't every "it's right on the tip of my tongue" spaz-out signal more precious neurons decamping for good? If I lived long enough, wouldn't the tendrils of dementia, or serious memory loss, inevitably unfurl in their place? Nope, not even close. It's still my worst fear, but I no longer think it's inevitable, or even likely.

- Serious mental decline is not a normal or inevitable part of aging. According to the MacArthur Foundation Study of Successful Aging, "Declines rarely affect all kinds of cognitive performance; second, most of the losses come late in life; and third, many older people are not significantly affected by even minor losses of mental ability."[1]
- Most forgetfulness is not Alzheimer's, or dementia, or even necessarily a sign of cognitive impairment.[2]
- About 20 percent of people in their nineties seem to escape cognitive decline entirely, and continue to perform as well as middle-aged people.[3]

Even as the population ages, dementia rates are falling—significantly. The total number of cases is rising along with the number of olders in the population, but the likelihood of any given person getting dementia has gotten lower and lower. And people are being diagnosed at older and older ages.[4] Yet what age scholar Margaret Gullette calls "our irrational fear of forgetting"[5] has made such deep inroads into our psyches that routine memory lapses provoke terror and diagnoses invoke thoughts of suicide. A 2012 Marist poll found that Alzheimer's had edged out cancer as the disease Americans fear most.[6] Why is our fear so out of proportion to the threat? Because in our modern "information society," no competence is more crucial than mental agility. Because the brain is where the self resides, so no fear is greater. Because the deepest terrors are the hardest to confront, making neurological decline a repository for our darkest fears about living into our nineties. And because in an ageist society, negative assumptions about late life, however inaccurate, tend to be accepted at face value.

THE MYTH THAT OLD AGE AND MENTAL INCOMPETENCE GO HAND IN HAND CONTRIBUTES TO DISCRIMINATION ON MANY FRONTS

The myth that "you can't teach an old dog new tricks" plays out punishingly in many arenas. Beliefs that older workers aren't worth training because they're slow learners and computer-illiterate are stubbornly persistent, despite high marks from employers on both performance and skills.[7]

That stereotype is at work when people speak condescendingly to olders who are attempting to access social, legal, or financial services. People may insist they "know what's best" for an older person, even when that person is perfectly capable of making their own decisions. Even limited impairment can be used as a rationale for coercing olders into relinquishing control of decision-making and assets. More trusting and often less tech-savvy older victims of financial abuse are often too ashamed to report it because of the stigma of mental incompetence. The fall from wise elder to gullible idiot feels mortifying.

We reinforce the association with constant nervous references to forgetfulness and "senior moments." I used to think those quips were self-deprecatingly cute, until it dawned on me that when I lost the car keys in high school, I didn't call it a "junior moment." Youngers forget stuff all the time too! Any prophecy about debility, whether or not it comes true, dampens our aspirations and damages our sense of self, especially when it comes to brainpower. That damage is magnified by the glum, widespread, and false assumption that, somewhere down the line, dementia is inevitable.

COGNITIVE DECLINE IS PROFOUNDLY STIGMATIZED

Homophobia marginalized people with AIDS the way ageism marginalizes those with dementia: worse than old is very old, and worst of all is very old and incurably ill. Add to that the tremendous stigma that accompanies mental impairment of any sort. It's a quadruple whammy if you take into consideration the fact that family members often feel stigmatized by association.

Eminent sociologist Erving Goffman defined stigma as an "attribute that is deeply discrediting" and that reduces the bearer "from a whole and usual person to a tainted, discounted one."[8] Small wonder that when it comes to Alzheimer's disease—the most common form of dementia—the diagnosis alone can have devastating effects on self-esteem and social life, and is typically accompanied by feelings of anxiety, depression, shame, and humiliation. Some people think Alzheimer's is contagious. The stigma is only beginning to diminish as public figures like Ronald Reagan and Glen Campbell have emerged as public faces for the disease.

Developing what neurologist Peter J. Whitehouse calls a "humanistic, ecological framework of brain aging"[9] would strip it of this stigma. Because there's no agreed-upon way to differentiate between Alzheimer's and normal aging, and none in the offing, in this framework cognitive decline becomes just part of what it means to be a human getting along in years. Whitehouse's early research into the pathology of Alzheimer's and related dementias led to current drug treatments, and a cure would be revolutionary, but over one hundred drug trials have failed so far. Because Alzheimer's is caused by several factors, including genetics, lifestyle, and chronic diseases such as diabetes and obesity, no single treatment is likely to halt or reverse its symptoms.[10]

Whitehouse subsequently came to see the promise of a panacea as a cultural myth promoted by powerful pharmaceutical companies, advocacy organizations, and private researchers with much profit at stake. Instead of defining brain aging as a disease and searching for a cure, Whitehouse argues that resources would be better directed toward preventing cognitive loss and helping people cope with it. A shift away from a pharmacological "fix" would help both people with dementia and their caregivers cope with this enormously difficult transition, and focus on quality of life for both. It would reduce stigma. It would help us see people with dementia not as "lost" to an incurable disease—and therefore lost to us—but as still present in various ways, with ongoing human needs for affection, connection, and expression. It would help us develop meaningful and dignifying ways to be with them.

Dementia is often worse to witness than to experience. In 2010 the UK Alzheimer's Society surveyed forty people living with dementia about their lives and experiences. The group included minorities, LGBTQ people, people with learning disabilities, and people with more severe dementia living in care homes—people, in other words, who faced additional barriers to advantage and inclusion. Their proxies, typically family caregivers, expected the assessments to align with the progress of the disease: As cognitive function diminished, so would happiness. But even as activities and socializing became more difficult, the people with dementia continued to enjoy their lives. They rejected the assumption that the disease was the most important thing about them. The report concluded that "Maintaining a good quality of life is perfectly possible following a diagnosis of dementia."[11]

Perhaps because of what she does for a living, geriatric care manager Claudia Fine has taken her mother's decline—fairly predictable and non–crisis laden from a geriatrician's perspective—in stride. "Dorothy loves being in the park . . . the leaves . . . likes the sound of the rustle. She motions upward, says 'the the, the the . . .'" Fine's sister-in-law experiences this wordlessness as an intolerable loss. Yet, Fine observes, "Dorothy's obviously very happy." Dorothy lives in a nursing home, but even people who are severely afflicted can live happily with their families for a long time, like my godmother, Anne. She had an insatiably curious mind and a well-thumbed library that ranged from Gorky to gardening in several languages. By the time she reached her late nineties, short-term memory loss had her on a three-minute loop, and it grew shorter all the time. It was wretched for her caregivers, and our conversation shifted from the real world to imaginary landscapes, but I was available to her and she to me.

Dementia can liberate. It wasn't until writer Sousan Hammad's grandfather was affected that he began speaking about his formative years in a small town in Palestine under the British mandate, making the memories available to his family.[12] Hammad wrote an essay titled "Islands of Amnesia," and the islands metaphor also comforted age scholar Margaret Gullette when her gregarious mother started to lose her memory in her nineties. "My mother, too, was a self—living, often contentedly, on islands of land in the abyss. I made a decision to live with her on those islands," Gullette writes.[13] Anne Basting, author of *Forget Memory: Creating Better Lives for People with Dementia* (the inspiration for the title of this chapter), urges caregivers to avoid exhortations to "remember," and points out that "creativity and imagination are largely untapped reserves of strength when dementia strikes."[14]

Diagnosed with Alzheimer's at seventy-four, country music legend Glen Campbell said he wanted to keep performing as long as possible and wanted the public to understand why he sometimes forgot song lyrics or repeated himself. His farewell tour is documented in a movie called *Glen Campbell: I'll Be Me*, and his song "I'm Not Gonna Miss You," won a Grammy Award in 2015 for Best Country Song. At one point in the movie, when he struggles for the words to the chorus of "Galveston," one of his hit songs, hundreds of voices come forward with, "I can still hear your sea winds crashing." Thus prompted, Campbell picks up with a smile and finishes the song.

That's empathy—a shared connection no less powerful between strangers in an auditorium than between lovers or parent and child. It enables us to see people who are cognitively impaired not as diseased or as victims but as fellow representatives of the human condition in all its diversity, never more so than late in life. The hard but necessary task for those who remain on shore is to change our expectations of our Dorothies (as Claudia Fine has), and to reassess what activities qualify as meaningful (holding a doll, perhaps, or pushing a shopping cart). We tend to see these activities as pathetic, or to dismiss them because they're not things we remember the person doing. It helps to focus not on what is lost but what remains, and to find pleasure wherever it resides, as Dorothy does in the leaves overhead. In her book *Making an Exit*, Elinor Fuchs describes the final years of caring for her self-absorbed mother, who developed Alzheimer's disease, as their best time together.

As we age we remain ourselves. This is no less true of those whose brains age neurologically faster than others, much of whose mental faculties remain even as memories depart, and who continue to contribute to their families and their communities. The most powerful predictor of identity change—the dreaded loss of selfhood—is not memory loss. It's the disruption of moral faculties (evidenced by behaviors like antisocial outbursts, pathological lying, and stealing). Other kinds of neurodegenerative changes—including amnesia, personality change, loss of intelligence, emotional disturbances, and the ability to perform basic daily tasks—don't cause people to stop seeming like themselves.[15] As Whitehouse observes, "Neurodegenerative conditions do not 'claim' older people, nor do they dominate them or degrade their humanity; they simply alter the manner by which we live our lives. . . . There is no such thing as an 'Alzheimer's victim,' no such thing as a total 'loss of self.' The disease is never bigger than the person."[16]

That said, Alzheimer's disease is a massive public health issue. It's the most costly disease in America, and costs are projected to skyrocket as people live longer. Federal funding for Alzheimer's disease received a boost in 2016, but at about $936 million remains a fraction of what the National Institutes of Health spend on HIV/AIDS, although more Americans are living with Alzheimer's.[17] AIDS research went unfunded until relentless activism forced change.

Activism is also called for in order to meet the tremendous challenge of caring for people with dementia. Families need help: access to practical, high quality, and affordable home and community-based services. Eldercare-related jobs will be among the fastest-growing occupations in the country over the next decade. Caregivers are overwhelmingly women, often undocumented immigrants, and women of color, who work long hours for an average wage of less than twelve dollars per hour because they are poorly trained,[18]—and who are ill-trained in part because of the low value of their tasks in an ageist society.

In the book *The Age of Dignity: Preparing for the Elder Boom in a Changing America*, activist Ai-jen Poo lays the groundwork for turning this intimate and important work into a stable and attractive career. A lifelong activist for women of color and workers' rights, Poo calls for a comprehensive state and federal policy that would make home care universally accessible, extend labor protections like unemployment insurance to care workers, and improve job quality and citizenship prospects for immigrant workers. The Program for All-Inclusive Care for the Elderly (PACE)—a joint venture of Medicaid and Medicare—is one such example.

SO WHERE THE HELL DID I PUT MY GLASSES?

Although we all know ninety-year-olds who remain as sharp as the proverbial tack, they're a minority. The other 80 percent of us will inevitably experience some reduction in faculties. Although changes don't strictly correlate to chronological age, memory-processing speed, verbal reasoning, and visuospatial abilities do decline. In particular, explicit memory (the ability to remember and recall names and numbers on demand) takes a hit, although the vast majority of olders never lose any other part of speech.

Most of us will have a harder time finding words and recalling proper nouns than we did when we were young, and remembering where we left the damn thing we went into the other room to fetch, if we could only recall what it was. Forgetting where your keys are shouldn't be cause for alarm, nor forgetting So-and-So's name (as opposed to not remembering what keys are for, or forgetting who So-and-So *is*).

Older people don't process information as fast either. Our ability to multitask diminishes and distractibility rises, making us more effective if we focus on one thing at a time. These are real losses that are embarrassing, unnerving, sometimes maddening. Strategies for dealing with them range from Post-its to intensive therapy. The brain is brilliant at reorganizing in order to compensate for the effects of aging and injury. My trick is to name the mission aloud when I stand up—though only if no one's around to hear me, I admit.

Difficulty planning and executing familiar tasks can signal deeper cognitive problems. If someone seems noticeably confused, she may have mild cognitive impairment (MCI), which affects between 10 and 20 percent of people sixty-five and up. Someone with MCI has measurable changes that friends and family notice— needing to take notes more often, for example, or being confused about the day of the week but recalling the year and season. These changes don't affect the ability to carry out everyday activities or function socially. Most people with MCI do not progress to dementia. They continue to operate in the world just fine.

The MCI label is problematic because the condition is ill-defined and possibly meaningless. Clinicians have called the Alzheimer's pharmaceutical industry into question for creating a new category of patients and consumers who may only be undergoing basic brain aging. This is part of the profit-driven trend to medicalize aging itself.

IN THE ABSENCE OF DISEASE, THESE BRAIN CHANGES ARE *NORMAL*

These neurological developments do not signal that dementia lies ahead. We exaggerate both their incidence and their severity, and stigma and ignorance amplify the anxiety. As with every other aspect of growing old, the trajectory of brain aging is different for every individual. The way people function depends largely on how they adapt to these changes.

Our ageist society pathologizes natural transitions, and our consumer society sells us remedies to "fix" them, like hormone replacement therapy, erectile dysfunction drugs, and facelifts. Our "hypercognitive" culture prioritizes brain function above all, as evidenced by a vast array of products—from Baby Einstein to Shakespeare ("Bard on the Brain")—that promise to treat, manage, and improve it. When cognition becomes another attribute to be maintained or enhanced, it can be another way of problematizing normal aging. Consumer culture frames "brain fitness," like physical fitness, as a goal to which all of us should continuously aspire. Yes, lifestyle choices are involved, but changes in cognition do not mean that we are deficient.

The trajectory of brain aging is different for everyone. The way we function depends largely on how we adapt to these changes.

Lots of octo- and nonagenarians are playing bridge and Scrabble or designing buildings and writing books, and accomplishing lots of other tasks that require skill and concentration at a level that leaves younger peers in the dust. The brain of a healthy older person can do almost everything that a much younger brain is capable of. Sometimes it takes a little longer. Other cognitive domains remain stable or improve.

70

THERE'S STUFF YOU CAN DO TO FEND OFF
COGNITIVE DECLINE

The muscular atrophy that sets in when people aren't physically active is obvious. What about mental activity? Are all the olders who are shelling out for "brain boosting" software and regimens being hoodwinked? Probably. There's no conclusive evidence that any of the raft of commercially available games, devices, or exercises have any protective effect. Much about the brain remains a mystery, including how memories are made, stored, and retrieved.

We've learned a lot, though. We used to think that neurogenesis, the brain's ability to grow new nerve cells, ended in early adulthood. A large and growing body of research now attests to the brain's ongoing ability to make new connections, absorb new information, and acquire new skills in the process. Even pathology can be overcome. Autopsies of people in their eighties and nineties who were cognitively fit often reveal extensive abnormalities, with plaque characteristic of advanced Alzheimer's. The theory is that they were protected by what neuroscientists call cognitive reserve: the ability to build and maintain extra neurons and connections between them. Later in life, this can provide a bulwark against brain disease and mental decline. It's strange to think that you could die with a brain riddled with plaque and never know it, but it's comforting.

Luck matters. Genes play some role, especially in early-onset Alzheimer's; genetic intelligence comes into play; and cognitive reserve correlates with higher levels of education. Evidence suggests that we can build or replenish cognitive reserve at any stage. In experiments conducted at the National Institute on Aging, younger rats that ran complicated mazes showed more neurogenesis than their older counterparts, but they all grew new nerve cells in the hippocampus—the center of memory and learning.[19]

How do we build cognitive reserve? By challenging our brains, maintaining social networks, and exercising. Like the body, the brain needs workouts to stay in shape, something Sam Adelo figured out after embarking on a second career as a court interpreter in Santa Fe. He grew up speaking Spanish and hearing a lot of Arabic and French spoken by his father's cousins who had emigrated from Lebanon, and he traveled widely as an attorney for Gulf Oil and Chevron. "While somebody's speaking, you're going through about nineteen cognitive steps trying to figure out how you're going to say it in the target language," Adelo explained. "You've got grammar, you've got terminology, you've got context. And you've got to make damn sure, because it's a court of law: a man's life or liberty is at stake." Using language the way interpreters do, he said, "is like exercising a muscle." He had no doubt that he continued to get better at it because he was continually learning, and bemoaned the tendency of his retired peers to "fix the old adobe" and then settle into a rut. "A lot don't even want to learn how to use a computer, for example. Don't just say, 'I'm going to get my Social Security check and my pension check and just lay back and look at the television.'"

Like Adelo, almost all of the older workers I interviewed had something to say about mastering new skills. A beautiful woman who proudly traced her ancestry back to the first Spanish settlers of Agua Fria, New Mexico, in the fifteenth century, Miranda Pike had worn many hats, including modeling, bookkeeping, and running her son's medical office. She was "green as a hornet" though, when a hostess position opened up at Tortilla Flats, a local restaurant. Her niece knew the manager and asked if he'd hire a seventy-year-old. His response was, "Can she do the work?" Pike liked the place, and when a bartending spot opened up, she said, "'I want the bar!' I only knew the basics, but I bought a book with the 1,700 most popular drinks in New York City, and I studied it." Pike figured that the owner expected her to "fade out," but she was behind the bar eleven years later.

Dabbling doesn't do it. Sustained effort is also key. The 90+ Study—the world's largest study of health and mental acuity in late life, conducted by the University of California Irvine's Institute for

Memory Impairments and Neurological Disorders (UCIMind)—has tracked more than fourteen thousand people aged sixty-five and up since 1981. Part of the study—the card sharks of Laguna Woods, an Orange County, California, retirement community—also belong to that 20 percent of Americans who live past ninety with no apparent cognitive decline, so scientists are studying them closely. Whether your goal is winning the next bridge hand or curbing climate change, having a sense of purpose in life affects cellular activity in the brain and increases its protective reserve. Not only that, the stronger the purpose, the more it adds to the reserve.[20]

It appears that not all mental activities are equal, and that a social component may be crucial. An unnerving finding is that making it to ninety without dementia doesn't get you home free; the odds continue to increase. A broader finding is that dementia may be less of a risk for people who devote significant time every day—three hours and more—to a mentally engrossing activity.[21] The key components are novelty, complexity, and problem-solving. So if you knit, don't stop at scarves; if you're visiting a foreign country, try memorizing the phrasebook; and if you need a purpose, help me end ageism.

BREAK A SWEAT

Physical fitness and mental fitness go together—specifically, regular, strenuous exercise, which pumps blood to the brain. For me this means walking (fast, not strolling), and I cling to the finding that only ninety minutes a week improves brain function. Diverse challenges are best, though, according to a blue-chip twenty-one-year study that looked at which recreational activities benefit the mind, measured against the onset of dementia.[22] Board games topped the list, followed by reading and playing a musical instrument. Frequent partner dancing reduced the risk by a whopping 76 percent—higher than any activity, mental or physical, studied by the Albert Einstein College of Medicine researchers.

Note the adjective *frequent*. Once every so often won't do the trick for any of these activities. Nor will rote repetition. The key is the split-second decision-making involved in leading or following or learning new dance steps or adjusting to changes in style or rhythm, which integrates several brain functions at once and builds neural pathways. It's also good exercise, makes people happy, and is social. Admittedly, the partner-free, minimally skilled jumping around that I love so much doesn't exactly fill the cognitive bill, but hey, it's aerobic. The optimal combo is regular movement that has a social component and involves learning new things.

Neal Gray had always mixed it up. An aviation ordnance man in the navy, he became an industrial designer, then a technical writer, and eventually a handyman at the Scituate Harbor Yacht Club. Also a former professional race-car driver, he drove a Subaru to work, but when it acted up he got behind the wheel of his sleek TVR sports coupe. A cheerful guy, it annoyed him when people commented, "'You drive to Boston? At night?' Like it's impossible for an eighty-three-year-old to do," said Gray. Most of the trips were to rehearse with one of three gospel choirs he belonged to. Gray was mastering several new songs for each, "and when Boston Pops comes along, we have to learn six or eight more." The memorizing, he said, "keeps the brain active and it keeps me young."

Gospel singing involved a physical challenge as well. "Sometimes you have to clap, and you also have to sway, and I have trouble coordinating things," said Gray. He attributed it to a ten-day bout with scarlet fever as a child. "I survived the highest temperature on record in Brookline at the time—a hundred and eight degrees!" And it took him quite a while to coordinate the movements. But he stuck it out, and he didn't stop while he was ahead. "One of our songs is called 'I Need You,' and we have two people that sign it, so I'm trying to learn the signings for the chorus. I don't have to, but I'd like to learn."

Gray had faced many hardships: money worries, multiple layoffs ("Every company that I worked for went down the tubes, it was amazing!"), and the wrenching loss of a beloved wife. At the same time, he personified the three key features identified in the MacArthur study[23] as predictors of strong mental function in old age: regular physical activity, a strong social support system, and belief in your ability to handle what life has to offer. Psychologists call this trait "self-efficacy": the confidence that you can achieve a given outcome, like that annoying little train that chugged, "I think I can, I think I can." Olders high in self-efficacy are more likely to believe that they can maintain or improve their cognitive skills. That boosts motivation, which encourages effort, which boosts confidence when they achieve the goal. The critical starting point is tuning out the cultural messages that we can't accomplish something, whether building a porch or mastering Mandarin, just because we're over a certain age.

THE AGING PROCESS ITSELF CONFERS BENEFITS ON THE WAY WE THINK

Especially in the emotional realm, older brains are more resilient. As we turn eighty, brain imaging shows frontal lobe changes that improve our ability to deal with negative emotions like anger, envy, and fear. Olders experience less social anxiety, and fewer social phobias. Even as its discrete processing skills degrade, the normal aging brain enables greater emotional maturity, adaptability to change, and levels of well-being. These are the neurological underpinnings of that happiness U curve.

That's what Penny Kyle found when she returned to substitute teaching. She felt more competent than ever in her Detroit middle-school classroom, even if the students believed her when she told them she was 104. "I'm older and I have more sense. If the kids don't want to do an assignment, I just say, 'Well, it's your choice. If you don't want to do it, just be quiet.' Before, I would say, 'If you don't do it, this is going to happen and this is going to happen.' They all come around and do it." Kyle's attitude toward the nature of the job also grew more philosophical. "Don't let it drive you crazy if things in the classroom don't go the way you think they should, 'cause there's only so much you can do as a substitute teacher," she counseled with a shrug of her narrow shoulders.

Call it knowledge, call it experience, call it wisdom. Natalia Tanner called it experience, and said that being in her eighties had made her a better pediatrician right across the board, "in clinical relationships, relationships with parents, friendships. As you mature, you get more philosophical. Things don't upset you like they used to. When I was younger I was gung ho. 'Mother, don't feed that baby that bottle!' and so forth. But now I'm more laid back, and I'm interested in the totality of the patient." Another physician, geriatrician Hilary Siebens, observed that her mental processes had changed over the course of her late fifties and into her sixties. "I'm still interested in new ideas and events of the day, but connections to events gone by also spring to mind. There's a unique, valuable perspective that this older mind brings to the work at hand."

Brain changes can boost creativity as well. After arthritis forced her to give up embroidery in her seventies, the renowned American folk artist Anna Mary Robertson Moses, better known as "Grandma Moses," took up painting. She lived to be 101. Coincidence? Not according to renowned geriatric psychiatrist Gene Cohen, author of the book *The Mature Mind: The Positive Power of the Aging Brain,* which describes unforeseen psychological development late in the life cycle, and untapped wells of creativity and intellectual potential. Cohen likened these empowering changes to "friendly metaphorical inner voices saying, 'If not now, when? What can they do to me?' This gives people comfort, confidence, and courage."[24]

A 2001 brain imaging study out of Duke University showed that while younger subjects relied predominantly on one side of the brain or the other (depending on the task), older people began to use both sides in a more synchronized way.[25] Cohen describes this as "moving to all-wheel drive. Any activity that optimally uses both sides of the brain is like chocolate to the brain. Art is like that." Best of all, you don't have to be a billionaire or a Buddhist to experience these changes. The aging process itself confers them on the healthy brain.

THE OLDER BRAIN HAS ACCESS
TO MORE INFORMATION

Aging brings cognitive benefits as well as emotional ones, although age bias makes them harder to recognize. When a word or phrase takes time to come to mind, the pause may reflect not decline but mental processes at work. According to a growing number of studies, the apparent lapse reflects the fact that older brains are sifting through the store of information accumulated over a lifetime, filtering, placing information in context. For most people, apparently, attention is gradually widening. More data points make it harder to retrieve the name of that movie you saw with what's-her-name, but distractibility may not be a bad thing. Olders may notice details or subtle cues or seemingly irrelevant information that could end up contributing to a better answer or solution than those from younger respondents, whose focus is tighter. Not only do olders know more, a wider worldview equips them to read moods, head off misjudgments, and navigate tricky situations more easily than younger people.[26]

Over the years, skepticism about the so-called "dotage curve"—aka age-related cognitive decline in healthy adults—has grown, along with the awareness that cognitive abilities peak at different points across the life span. A 2015 study in the journal *Psychological Science* analyzed a huge trove of scores on cognitive tests taken by people of all ages. It found that four types of proficiencies didn't fully ripen until people were in their fifties: vocabulary, math, general knowledge, and comprehension (a test that involved explaining why things are the way they are—for example, why communities have zoning regulations).[27]

Other evidence comes from data mining by a team of linguistic researchers at the University of Tübingen in Germany who were searching huge databases of words and phrases.[28] Since older, educated people have larger vocabularies than people who haven't been around as long, the experiment simulated the task an older brain confronts. It takes longer to find a word not because memory is impaired, but because it's a bigger job. The lead author of the study, Michael Ramscar, admitted that he'd started out a firm believer in the "dotage curve," but that the simulations mapped cognitive processes so accurately that it slowly forced him to acknowledge that he didn't need to invoke decline at all.

The ability to sift through information has benefits on the job. "They use words like 'wisdom' to describe the way I can distill and encapsulate what's going on in a group," noted Stuart Atkins, a behavioral scientist from Los Angeles who led sensitivity-training sessions for sales teams. Atkins found his problem-solving becoming "alarmingly quicker" because he could get right to the solution without being distracted. "I don't want anyone thinking that I am over the hill because I'm eighty-four. Good Lord, I'm at the peak of my talents!"

A better filter also makes it easier to figure out when to opt out. Unenthused about a training session at the Grand Canyon that had no bearing on her work as a parks department outreach specialist, Betty Soskin found herself gazing through the huge windows at the snow on the pine trees. "Every now and then the sun would come out from behind the clouds, and huge globs would drop to the earth. I was like a little kid in a candy store. I *knew* this was more important to me." Instead of feeling lazy or deficient, Soskin was elated to realize that she'd gotten in touch with "a new kind of filter that kicks in somewhere around the age of eighty. Anything that's not an emergency, or that can't be used in the next forty-eight hours, just goes right through," she said, bursting out laughing. "It doesn't even slow me down. The filter still captures all the good stuff." On her blog Soskin described this ability as "a well-earned asset that deserves to be studied as one of the benefits of aging."[29] The park ranger hadn't stopped using her brain; instead, she was trusting priorities learned over a lifetime and applying her attention more selectively. As she put it, "My eighty-six-ness was not to be denied."

WISDOM'S NEUROLOGICAL BASIS ·

A word comes to mind for this ability to assimilate and prioritize information: wisdom. It's a good way to describe the advantage that older people enjoy when it comes to combining real-time information with a significant store of general knowledge. I tend to call it experience, which time confers on all of us and which is not the same as wisdom, which is rare and remarkable. We recognize the wise child with a shiver, and we've all met plenty of older people who don't seem to have learned one interesting thing. So I'm leery of the tendency to bundle "wisdom" and aging together under shiny cellophane, and to bestow it like a factory-assembled gift basket upon anyone with gray hair. Yes, adolescents are tiresome in predictable ways, and life experience tends to make for more thoughtful decisions and meatier conversations, but it's a form of reverse ageism to assume that wisdom, like wrinkles, comes with the territory.

Psychologist Todd Finnemore came up with a definition I can live with, though, and it's one of many to be embedded in the neurology of the older brain. "Wisdom is the capacity to see circumstances as integrated wholes. As we age our capacity for integration increases. Older brains are more diversely wired and use many more connections than younger ones, because we've made so many associations over the course of our lives. Wisdom allows for seemingly contradictory ideas or events to exist in our minds with less dissonance. We can be angry with someone we love without losing sight of our connection, or be outraged by an idea without losing hope. We don't rush to the only truth because that's all that we know. Not all older people are wise, and aging does not inevitably or magically create wisdom. But through attention to experience, aging offers many chances to develop wisdom."[30]

People often pair wisdom with passivity, another reason I steer clear of it. I hadn't conceived of the term in a political context, though, until I read "Against Wisdom," an essay by University of Washington professor Kathleen Woodward in which she calls for "a moratorium on wisdom" as an ideal for the old.[31] Woodward argues that anger and wisdom are incompatible, and that to idealize the latter robs olders of a powerful catalyst for personal and political change. It's way easier to park Granny in a rocking chair off-site, especially when she succumbs with a smile, than to deal with what more she might have to offer or have the right to demand. We like our olders calm and cheerful. Strong emotions discomfit, and we're quick to downgrade angry to crotchety or irascible.

Woodward questions just how well that script serves most grannies, pointing out that idealizing wisdom in old age often serves as a screen for ageism. She cites an oft-quoted passage from the book *Senescence* by psychologist G. Stanley Hall, the first major study of what Hall referred to as the second half of life (now more like the last two-thirds): "Age has the same right to emotional perturbations as youth and is no whit less exposed and disposed to them. Here, as everywhere, we are misunderstood and are in such a feeble minority that we have to incessantly renounce our impulsions." A hallmark of old age, Hall declared, is "a new belligerency"—what Woodward calls "wise rage." Buttressed by comfort and confidence, anger has a place in the arsenal, as a rebuttal of the notion that we grow too old to learn or feel, and as a response to being silenced or patronized.

WITH AGE COMES CONTENTMENT: THE HAPPINESS U CURVE

When I first encountered the U-shaped happiness curve, I figured that some social scientist had cornered two octogenarians, handed them a chocolate bar, and popped the question. Olders, too, blink in surprise at this finding, having assumed their contented selves to be anomalies, just lucky I guess. It's not because they were wealthy or bionic. People didn't reach eighty without facing adversity and loss, often crushing. They had more health problems too. But they also reported far fewer of the kind of financial and personal issues that angered and worried younger respondents.[32]

The scholarship behind this finding is broad and solid, including a 2008 Gallup poll of 340,000 Americans aged eighteen to eighty-five and a three-decade University of Chicago study.[33] There were ups and downs in overall happiness levels, generally corresponding with good and bad economic times, and younger blacks and poor people tended to be less happy than whites and wealthier people. But those differences faded as people aged. This effect doesn't crop up because positive emotions are easier to process than negative ones: The positivity is most notable among the mentally sharpest olders.[34]

This is not the case for everyone, like my partner's mom, Ruth, who regularly apprised me that being ninety was very different from being sixty, "and not in a good way." Yet it also appears that the source of this happiness is internal, and, for the vast majority, inherent to growing old. Andrew J. Oswald, an economist at the University of Warwick who has published several studies on human happiness, noted that the finding that we can expect to be happier in our early eighties than we were in our twenties is driven "not predominantly by things that happen in life [but by] something very deep and quite human."[35] Carol Graham, an economist at the Brookings Institution who studies the economics of happiness, described her findings in similar terms: "[It's] something about the human condition." The survey data she analyzed showed the same U-shaped pattern, independent of objective life circumstances, around the world.[36]

Gender, personality, and external circumstances also contribute, but less than you might think.[37] Younger people think happiness occurs because of *things*, "but when they're older, people know that happiness occurs in spite of things," says Cornell University's Karl Pillemer, a gerontologist at Weill Cornell Medical College.[38] This is quite consistent with cognitive behavioral therapy, he pointed out, "and they've come upon [this belief] naturally." In other words, age itself confers very effective coping mechanisms upon ordinary people. "If you can't make happiness a choice, you're going to have a lot of trouble finding it," said Pillemer. The choice was often expressed in terms of a turning point, as in the case of a woman who

Age itself confers very effective coping mechanisms upon ordinary people.

grieved for two years over the death of her twenty-two-year-old daughter, and then made a conscious decision to pull herself out of her tailspin. Instead of worrying or holding onto grudges, she and her peers recommend savoring the small things, letting go, and practicing gratitude.

AN AGEIST LABEL: THE "PARADOX OF WELL-BEING"

However universal or particular the reasons, most people over eighty report being just as happy, if not happier, than their younger counterparts. Researchers who study aging and happiness have dubbed this the "paradox of well-being," a term that makes sense only in an ageist culture. Why else would "paradox"—a seemingly absurd or self-contradictory proposition that turns out to be true—be used to describe such an accessible and well-substantiated scientific finding?

What genuinely surprises about the happiness U curve is that it persists in the face of a culture that does so little to bolster the self-esteem of older people or help us find meaning in our advancing years. Massive social and cultural forces work against this trait, exiling olders into terrain where "keeping busy" is supposed to compensate for a dearth of meaningful roles and valuable cross-generational connections. No wonder people are surprised when they find out about the happiness U curve. "Life gets better on every level of what it is to be a human being except the physical, but nobody knows this, including older people, because the ageism is so intense in our society," writes Wendy Lustbader in *The Unexpected Pleasures of Growing Older.*[39]

Lustbader points out that in contrast to the doubts and insecurities of youth, growing older enables us to become more self-aware and confident, less fearful of being judged, and authentically happy. Not that life gets easier, but that it becomes easier to focus on what truly matters—and that makes it better. Just as an impressionist painting becomes coherent only at a distance, Lustbader points out, a lifetime is a journey whose full meaning only becomes comprehensible over time. This truth is inherently inaccessible to the young, to whom "sorrows in later life seem so relentless that . . . we conclude that old age must be a dire time, indeed. It is only later that we find that fresh life evolves out of each grief."[40] Continuous renewal may seem like a lot to hope for, but the benefits of these difficult transitions are real.

Henry Wadsworth Longfellow describes the transition at the end of "Morituri Salutamus":

For age is opportunity no less
than youth itself, though in another dress,
and as the evening twilight fades away
the sky is filled with stars, invisible by day.

Moving from poetry to pop culture, Jane Fonda tackles it too. In a talk for TEDWomen she rejects the paradigm of life as an arch that peaks at midlife and then degrades, and proposes a lovely new metaphor: old age as a staircase, "bringing us into wisdom, wholeness, and authenticity—not at all as pathology."[41] Like me (and Betty Friedan and so many others), she was taken by surprise by the promise and pleasures of moving past middle age. "And guess what? This potential is not for the lucky few. It turns out most people over fifty feel better [than when they were younger], are less stressed, less hostile, less anxious . . . even happier," Fonda says. As a celebrity with access to resources like personal trainers and business managers, Fonda belongs to the lucky few, but nevertheless, she adds wryly, "This is not what I expected, trust me." Her forties were filled with apprehension, "but now that I'm smack dab in the middle of my own third act, I realize I've never been happier . . . I realize that when you're inside oldness instead of looking at it from the outside, fear subsides."

Fear does subside, though typically only at the hands of time itself. *Imagine how much more manageable the fear would be if we become old people in training when we're young.* If people of all ages embraced this natural process. Aging means living, just as living means aging. What would happen if we rejected the equation of "old" with "unfortunate"? What if we challenged the depiction of aging as something that can—and should—be overcome by right thinking or right spending? The truth, as gerontologist Muriel Gillick writes in the book *The Denial of Aging,* is that old age is "far more complex, textured, and fraught with possibility."[42] We'd live longer, because attitudes about aging directly affect our health. We'd live better as well, freed of reflexive apprehension in our middle years and open to more varied, optimistic, and realistic narratives about what lies ahead.

PUSH BACK!

HAS WHAT YOU DREADED COME TO PASS?

If you don't buy it from me or from Longfellow or Fonda—odd bedfellows, admittedly—reflect on your own experience. A glance at any greeting card rack affirms that birthdays after thirty are for dreading. According to Ari Seth Cohen, the founder of the popular *Advanced Style* blog dedicated to women over sixty, "The people who have the hardest time with aging are the twenty- and thirty-somethings."[43] Maggie Kuhn, who founded the Gray Panthers organization in 1970 to lobby for ending mandatory retirement at sixty-five and ending the Vietnam War, recalled her thirtieth birthday as the worst of all. Kuhn, who lived in an intergenerational household, died at eighty-nine, and her motto was "Learning and sex till rigor mortis sets in."

I had a lot of fun in my twenties, a single woman beginning a romance with Gotham that has yet to pale. But would I want to relive those years? Not so much. "It's great to be young" can be as burdensome a stereotype as "It sucks to be old." Depicting the period when most of us are trying to carve out an identity and a livelihood as "the time of our lives" only casts a pall. Disasters characterized early adulthood for *The Guardian*'s Sarah Ditum: boy disasters, booze disasters, school disasters, and job disasters. None were actually calamitous, and they helped her figure out what to give a damn about, and when. "The pleasure of getting older is part getting it right more often, and part realizing that there's often no 'wrong' to be afraid of anyway. . . . So when I hear people bemoan another birthday, or squirm against acknowledging their proximity to middle age, I think: you doofuses." If Ditum learns as much from her forties as she did from her thirties, she writes, "I'll be proud of the wrinkles that show it."[44]

We dread big birthdays because of the cultural freight attached to them, but what do common sense and experience reveal? A friend recalled turning twenty-five and being told, "That's your last good birthday." Really? I turned sixty in the Grand Canyon, and it wasn't too shabby. Anyone else have any fun after thirty? There is no line in the sand, no crossover between young and old after which decline sets in. This imaginary threshold damages our sense of self, segregates us, and fills us with needless dread.

There is no line in the sand, no crossover between young and old after which it's all downhill.

An ageist culture bills our twenties as the peak decade: You better be having fun right now, because life's as fun as it's going to get! In fact, it's a tough time for almost all of us. Midlife, when we confront dreams shelved, risks not taken, roads not traveled, the disquieting fact that days lived are starting to outnumber those to come, turns out to be the hardest stretch. Rounding home, we make peace with the way we spent our time and enjoy the present as never before. These rewards may be less apparent early on, but they're no less real.

Contributors to a 2009 Pew Research Center report called "Growing Old in America: Expectations vs. Reality" assessed their lives more positively as they moved into their seventies and eighties.[45] Although health and independence markedly declined after eighty-five, the oldest respondents, eighty-five and up, were among the most sanguine. Good health, good friends, and a solid financial footing were the most significant predictors of happiness. Many older Americans come up short on at least one of these indicators, and the disastrous effect of the Great Recession on the retirement plans and financial security of the postwar generation has yet to fully play out. Expectations about the upside of late life tended to overshoot reality: People over sixty-five had less time for family or volunteer work than youngers anticipated. But many of the problems they expected to confront—memory loss, being unable to drive, feeling lonely or useless—were less common than olders reported.

QUESTION THE MAINSTREAM NARRATIVE

If I hadn't looked under the metaphorical bed, like a child looking for monsters, I'd never have questioned narratives like the one novelist and lawyer Louis Begley presented in a short essay called "Age and Its Awful Discontents."[46] Begley described his mother's and his own long lives, the early years forged in the hell of German-occupied Poland in World War II, and the later ones in comfortable New York City apartments. Begley acknowledged his "abhorrence" of the physical ravages of age and illness and the fact that the aversion predated his mother's decline in her last years. He attributed it to the dearth of examples of a happy old age, examples lacking not because family members aged badly but because all died young and violently during the war. "Unsurprisingly, dread of the games time plays with us has been a drumbeat in my novels," he explained. He couldn't let go of the past, and didn't want to, perhaps out of respect for family members who did not survive.

Begley's seems less a story about age than about the games that *history* plays with us. The "awful discontents" of his and his mother's later years pale beside the privations they endured during the war and its aftermath. Visited daily by her family, Begley's mother lived to ninety-four, "comfortably but alone," after outliving husband and friends, too proud to use a wheelchair for concert- and movie-going, homebound because she "couldn't get the hang of using a walker."

It is sad to outlive your friends, but it is not tragic. It is wretched to be homebound, but Begley's mother rejected the technologies that could have rescued her. She had her reasons. That was her truth, at least as seen through her son's eyes: an agonizing passage that he assumes awaits him as well. "Yet my body . . . continues to be a good sport," Begley observed at seventy-eight while suffering from nothing that a steroid shot couldn't remedy. Add a loving wife and children, financial security, engaging work, and a healthy brain to the mix, and I arrive at a roster not of the "awful discontents" suggested by his title, but at something close to its opposite.

The fact that that's not how Begley saw it is partly a function of his nature and his personal history. It also reflects the way American society equates aging with decline. Consider the stock photo *The New York Times* picked to accompany the story, which appeared in its Sunday Opinion section. Shot from behind, a white-haired, slightly stooped woman strolls alone in a park, eyes on the sun-dappled path ahead. It's intended to evoke "the bitterness and anguish of my mother's solitude" with which Begley concludes his essay. Is the woman in the photograph lonely, or simply alone? Depressed, or deep in thought? No telling. She's a blank slate on which to project our hopes or fears. Other than the sensible shoes, which lurk in my own future, she looks damn good to me.

CHAPTER FOUR

HEALTH, NOT YOUTH: THE OLDER BODY

"Are you going to put a lot about diet and exercise and health in your book?" asked my friend Paola. We shared a godmother in Italy and became fast friends over the course of many summer visits. Paola, a public health nurse, is active, but her husband, Enrico, is *sportivissimo* (super-athletic). At fifty-five he runs marathons and swims around distant islands while she and I yak on the pier.

"Nope. There's already so much information out there," I replied, braced for criticism. Almost every aging-related website foregrounds wellness. I took a deep breath and continued, "And I think the emphasis is a little problematic, as though if you do enough push-ups or eat enough fiber, you can put off old age indefinitely. It becomes a way of not dealing with it."

"*Esattamente!* That's just it," said Paola with a wry smile, looking fondly at her husband stretched out on a towel in his teeny Speedo. (The man looks great. He has no body fat. Plus he's tan and Italian.) "Enrico thinks he can exercise his way out of it. Of course time will catch up with him, and I'm afraid it's going to be even harder on him when it does."

Don't get me wrong: Health matters enormously to how we age, and there's much we can do to maintain it. Unless he gets hit by a motorboat, Enrico is likely to outlive his peers and outpace them as well. Following him up mountains will be great for Paola too. But an active lifestyle is just one measure of aging, and it's relative. One of these days, Enrico isn't going to be able to swim all the way to that island. His pace has already slowed, adapting to the inevitable diminution of physical capacity.

Enrico is a perfect example of the fact that while physical decline is inevitable, poor health is not. Attributing decline to age rather than illness perpetuates the negative stereotype of older people as frail and debilitated. Most are not: 64 percent of adults over the age of sixty-five report no limitation in major activities.[1] Nor does any single age-related condition affect most of them. Much as we fear illness, healthy aging does coexist with chronic illness and disability in a multitude of olders. Obsessing over health isn't healthy. Many of the oldest among us live well not by avoiding illness, but despite it. There's no clear divide between mobility and immobility, or independence and helplessness. Binaries serve us badly. So, as ever, does age denial.

THE GOAL IS TO STAY HEALTHY, NOT TO "STAY YOUNG." LONGEVITY IS A BONUS

One manifestation of age denial is that it keeps many people from making lifestyle choices that pay off in the long run. As composer and musician Eubie Blake famously put it, "If I'd known I was going to live this long, I'd have taken better care of myself." At the other end of the spectrum, exemplified by Enrico in his Speedo, is the idea that growing older can be prevented by exercise or diet, or overcome by anything but death. The delusion grows harder to maintain as

Age denial keeps many people from making lifestyle choices that pay off in the long run.

birthdays pile up, and makes ultimate reckonings ever more difficult.

Denial has social consequences too. The collective desire to "put old on hold" is slowing healthcare reform that will meet the needs of an aging America. In *The Denial of Aging*, gerontologist Muriel Gillick delineates the effects:

> *If we as a society continue to deny the realities of old age, we will squander our resources on ineffective but costly screening tests and on ultimately futile but expensive treatment near the end of life; we will not have enough money left over to provide beneficial care. If we assume that diet and exercise will prevent chronic disease, then we will fail to take seriously the need for a radically new model of medical care*

that is up to the task. . . . And if we put our faith in drugs to make us immortal, we will neglect to fund research into such prosaic conditions as macular degeneration (the leading cause of visual impairment in the American elderly) and osteoarthritis (the number-one medical problem in the elderly and a major source of pain and immobility), disorders that impair the quality of life of millions.[2]

The "war on cancer" medical model has long been to attack one disease at a time, which may buy us additional life without health— the worst of all outcomes. Consensus is growing for a more holistic approach: intervening in the aging process itself, in order to increase our active years and postpone disability and mortality. *Postpone*, not prevent.

THE PROMISES OF "IMMORTALITY SCIENCE" ARE EMPTY

Many of the things on which this culture bases self-esteem—taut skin, athleticism, sexual prowess—are transient. With their careful treads and slowed responses, older people remind us that the reprieve is temporary. Small wonder that the delusion that we can hang on to youth, and even maybe somehow dodge death itself, has such appeal. Every week seems to herald an "anti-aging" breakthrough on the horizon: the possibility of using stem cells to rejuvenate tissue, or mobilizing nanobots to patrol the body and repair cell damage, or lengthening telomeres, to name a few. (Telomeres are stretches of DNA at the end of chromosomes that shorten naturally with age each time a cell divides.)

Leading the pack are the proponents of radical life extension, who think that advances in biotechnology will soon be able to slow down or turn back the biological clock, and that my generation can anticipate living far longer than our parents. Many proponents believe that what biomedical researcher Aubrey de Grey calls "longevity escape velocity" is within reach: the point at which, for every year that passes, life expectancy will increase by one year, making life spans infinite.

The last century's unprecedented increase in human life span does indeed put us on new evolutionary footing. When Dutch gerontologist Dr. Rudi Westendorp spoke at New York's Mount Sinai Hospital about good health after eighty-five, he opened with a zinger: "There is no biological limit to human age. Mortality is plastic, as the biologists say." Gray hair and reading glasses remind us that the machine will eventually fail, "like a cheap car," as Westendorp cheerfully put it. Over time our cells become less able to repair themselves in the face of injury or disease. But although decline is inevitable, we have yet to reach the limit of our biological design.

Aging isn't genetically hardwired. We can affect our health outcomes. But as life expectancy rises, it becomes more and more difficult to increase it further. "This is a mathematical certainty," says demographer S. Jay Olshansky,[3] who explains the dangers of making linear extrapolations from biological phenomena with the example that by 2420 humans will be running a one-minute mile, at which point men will weigh 293 pounds and women 261. Following puberty, the risk of death doubles every seven years. This exponential rise is a biological attribute of our species, and many others. Longer life spans do not change the trajectory.

I'm all for biogerontology, the study of what happens to

"Anti-aging" = "anti-living."

our bodies as we age. Why shouldn't we profit from research into the biology of aging being conducted by companies like Google's Calico, especially since the grossly underfunded National Institute on Aging can't afford much of it? Until we understand what happens to our cells and organ systems far better than we do now, no health-promotion strategy will have much of an effect on average life expectancy and maximum life span. Extend our healthy life spans? Definitely a worthy goal. Delay aging? Absolutely. But *conquer* it? No combination of testosterone, terror, and technological wizardry can overthrow the second law of thermodynamics: systems decay over time.

Living and aging cannot be separated. Aging is not a disease. (Otherwise life, too, would be a disease.) Aging cannot be "cured." Aging means living. As Anne Karpf told NPR's Brian Lehrer, "You can no more be anti-aging than anti-breathing."[4]

AGEISM IN HEALTHCARE MEANS LESS TREATMENT, WORSE TREATMENT, AND OFTEN NO TREATMENT AT ALL

It's a common assumption that older people benefit less from medical treatment than younger ones, and it's incorrect. The benefits of treatment—including serious interventions like CPR, transplants, chemotherapy, and dialysis—are not age-dependent. More and more eighty- and ninety-year-olds are getting open-heart surgery and surviving at rates equal to much younger patients.[5] Of course, as with forty-year-olds, some are not good candidates. Decisions should be based on clinical need and the individual's overall health—heart, liver, and kidney function—and not ruled out on the basis of age.

In fact "no ailment should ever be written off as an 'old age' ailment," says gerontologist Mark Lachs, author of the book *Treat Me, Not My Age*. "Treating patients based on their age means you can miss very significant, treatable situations."[6] Yet doctors routinely do just that. In 2012, the year age discrimination in Britain's National Health Service became illegal, a joint report published by Age UK, a London-based charity, and the Royal College of Surgeons, showed some older patients missing out on vital surgery.[7] A follow-up report two years later found the problem far from over, with widespread variation in the rates of surgery, including for breast excision, gallstones, hernia repair, colorectal surgery, and knee replacements.[8] Patients over seventy-five missed out at a greater rate than those between the ages of sixty-five and seventy-five.

Perhaps because health professionals deal with people at the more debilitated end of the spectrum, they're more susceptible than the general public to ageist attitudes and more likely to assume that aging and disease proceed in lockstep.[9] When a friend brought his eighty-three-year-old mother in to the family doctor for a checkup—she was in a wheelchair after a stroke—the doctor greeted them by exclaiming, "Are *you* still around?" A lot of doctors don't want to deal with mortality—their patients' or their own.

What are the effects? Medical problems in older patients are frequently misdiagnosed or go undetected. Even when disorders are correctly diagnosed, treatment biases or lack of information can lead to a lower standard of care than for younger patients:

- Physicians and nurses often consider symptoms like balance problems, incontinence, constipation, and memory loss to be inevitable consequences of advanced age, instead of seeing them as treatable conditions.
- They're often dismissive—"At your age, what do you expect?"—instead of viewing aches or discomfort as symptoms that can be ameliorated. Geriatric pain patients are less likely than younger people to receive adequate treatment.[10]
- Findings suggest that physicians communicate better with their younger patients and are more open to their concerns, even though their medical problems are less severe. Older patients also get less time with doctors, especially during follow-up visits,[11] and harried hospital staff are less responsive.
- Physicians often fail to account for age-related changes in the way older bodies absorb medications, to check for side effects, and to consider the effects of being on multiple medications. This makes olders more likely to suffer adverse drug effects and to misuse prescription drugs. A staggering 124,000 Americans *died* of adverse drug interactions in 2014, and over 807,000 suffered what the FDA calls "serious outcomes" like hospitalization and life-threatening disability.[12] This disproportionately affects people over sixty, who take more than half of all prescription medications. One in six hospital admissions of people over sixty-five is because of an adverse drug event, a ratio that increases to one in three for people over seventy-five. These effects are little

studied.[13] Many olders, especially nursing home residents, are dangerously overmedicated.

- This bias is reflected in public policy. As of 2019, applicants for grants from the National Institutes of Health will be expected to include people of all ages or to justify age limits, but much research is privately funded and the guidelines don't mandate the active recruiting of older subjects. Inexcusably, even for studies of conditions that are most common in later life, exclusion rates are high.[14]

- The National Institutes of Health's Revitalization Act of 1993 mandated the inclusion of women and minorities in federally funded clinical trials, but not of people over sixty-five, although they take many more medications. People over eighty-five make up the fastest-growing segment of the population, yet the prototypical patient is a young person.

- Many doctors assume that their older patients aren't sexually active, and don't ask about sexual histories or routinely screen for STDs. Olders often have HIV/AIDS for years without being aware of it, because they mistake symptoms like fatigue, weight loss, and confusion for normal age-related aches and pains, and because both doctors and patients think of AIDS as a young person's disease.

- Secondary prevention programs, like routine cancer screenings, often overlook older adults, and many physicians fail to offer adequate preventive counseling to their older patients.

Ageist stereotypes about mental health are also responsible for the relatively poor quality of psychiatric care offered to older patients, and the high suicide rate among older people with depression. Most depressed older people have wrestled with the disease all their lives. Older people actually have lower rates of depression than the young or middle-aged, but it's more likely to go undiagnosed.[15] It's also common for depression-related cognitive deficits to be misdiagnosed as dementia. Psychotherapy is equally effective for all age-groups, but psychologists tend to underestimate the responsiveness of older adults as well as their capacity for self-reflection.

Older patients' attitudes can be part of the problem. Stoicism is the norm for the generation that grew up in the Great Depression, making many reluctant to seek medical care at all. Conditioned by internalized ageism, many expect to decline rather than recuperate. Few are confident enough to point out that their other eighty-six-year-old shoulder is holding up just fine, or to press for an aggressive intervention for the shoulder that isn't. Sexism compounds the problem; older women are less likely to speak up in a medical setting, less likely to be heard, and less likely to receive aggressive medical treatment.[16] Older lesbians fare even worse, and widely documented racial disparities further disadvantage olders of color.

Age inequities in medical care are what brought psychologist Laura Carstensen to the study of old age. A car accident at twenty-one landed her in an orthopedic ward for twenty months. Most of the patients were old, and the nurses gave her an assignment: to help keep her older roommates oriented. With these women for months, 24-7, she saw how differently they were treated. "I had physical therapists three or four times a day, I was being rehabilitated, and they weren't."[17] Carstensen went on to found the Stanford Longevity Center, where research shows that much change that was once thought to be irreversible and biologically based has more to do with how people perceive their futures.

One reason nurse practitioner Rachel Drolet was drawn to geriatric care was because she saw older patients being put into restraints more quickly than younger ones. "Patients are charted as confused and potentially 'harmful to self' simply because 'old people' are known to get confused more easily," she told me. The first symptoms of a physical disorder may be mental or emotional, and behavior changes should be treated as acute medical problems. Drug interactions and unrelated diseases in olders can cause dementia and delirium. Anesthesia can take a very long time to wear off, and older patients may stay confused for a day or two. Far too often, these symptoms are written off as a sign of "normal" cognitive impairment.

There's a lot we don't know yet. Older patients shouldn't necessarily be put on the same medical regimes as younger ones, for example. "Everything we learn about aging is more nuanced than we thought," says Carstensen. Take sleep, for example. "For a long time, it was textbook to say that sleep changes with age, and the older you get the less you need. People weren't separating out the sleeplessness from other factors like illness and arthritis pain. It turns out that you can treat sleep disorders in old people and they'll sleep just as much as the young." Difficulty sleeping can also be a symptom of depression, which is likewise treatable at any age.

Despite the fact that record numbers of Americans are living longer, there are fewer than seven thousand geriatricians in the U.S. (which translates to less than four per ten thousand people seventy-five years old and up), and the number is dropping.[18] (Geriatricians are doctors trained in the medical, social, and psychological issues that affect older adults.) This means that geriatricians will have to serve as educators and consultants for the physicians who are actually treating older patients. "Imagine you had cancer," suggests Dr. Christopher Langston, who analyzes this data each year for the Hartford Foundation. "Would you be happy if your primary care physician consulted with an oncologist, but you never actually got to see one? That's pretty much the situation we're facing."

The geriatrician shortage will become critical by 2030, when 20 percent of the U.S. population will be over sixty-five. Yet although every American medical school requires students to do a full pediatrics rotation, only 10 percent require coursework or rotations related to geriatrics.[19] Less than 1 percent of U.S. medical school graduates choose it. On average, geriatricians earn less than other physician specialties that require fellowship training. This is partly because office visits with olders, who require holistic care, typically run longer than average—a disadvantage in a fee-for-service, volume-based system.

Another disincentive? Geriatricians get no respect. Tell someone you work in the field and the standard response is "Why?" or a condescending "How good of you." Social workers, only 3 percent of whom concentrate in gerontology, hear the same things. That's because of ageism. When he went into the field, Dr. Samir Sinha was told he was wasting his talent. Now director of geriatrics at Toronto's Mount Sinai and University Health Network hospitals, Sinha blames institutionalized ageism for the geriatrician shortage: "A culture that devalues the old places little value on those who work with them."[20]

Internalized ageism on the part of patients perpetuates this prejudice: God forbid anyone find out you're in the care of a geriatrician! Age denial seals the regrettable deal. Consulting a geriatrician, as Dr. Atul Gawande points out in his book *Being Mortal*, "requires each of us to contemplate the unfixables in our life, the decline we will unavoidably face, in order to make the small changes necessary to reshape it. When the prevailing fantasy is that we can be ageless, the geriatrician's uncomfortable demand is that we accept we are not."[21]

Medical students also assume, wrongly, that practicing geriatrics will be depressing. Guess what kind of doctors report the highest job satisfaction, over and over? Geriatricians. And the happiest geriatricians have lots of patients over seventy-five and accept Medicare.[22] To what did the authors of a University of California, Davis study of more than 6,500 physicians attribute this? "In addition to the steady hours, encounters with inspirational seniors, and enduring relationships, this specialty is enjoying increasing demand as baby boomers retire." They then note, without irony, that "relatively poor Medicare reimbursements have led to shortages of geriatricians nationwide."[23] How about improving those Medicare reimbursement rates? How about using those job satisfaction numbers to address the image problem? How about debt forgiveness for geriatricians in training?

WE'RE NOT JUST LIVING LONGER, WE'RE STAYING HEALTHY LONGER

Sixty isn't the new forty, but it is a new sixty. More active lifestyles, healthier diets, hip and hormone replacements, all forestall or prevent the loss of function that was once an inescapable aspect of making it past middle age. No longer does American society divide into a fit, active younger generation and a significantly impaired older one. Only 35 percent of Americans aged sixty-five and up report hearing difficulties, and just 8.5 percent report significant vision problems[24]— figures that call into question the caricature of the stooped, squinting grandpa with his ear trumpet. Even among those aged eighty-five and up, only a quarter need help with daily activities like going to the bathroom, grooming, dressing, and feeding themselves.[25]

In Orange County, New York, adult caseworker Tim Murphy is seeing "a whole new generation of people who are approaching 100 years old and still living fairly independently in the community. It's kind of exciting for us." That doesn't mean these centenarians don't need assistance of various kinds. They've figured out how and when to ask for it, though, and actively negotiate their aging. They adopt and critique the treatments, technologies, and resources that have helped them live so well for so long.

Serious illness and disease tend to be concentrated toward the end of life. A public-health goal is to compress this period: to live disease-and illness-free for as long as possible. It's a basic index of progress, and it's why healthcare costs are highest at the end of life. Healthcare costs are *not* rising in proportion to the average age of the population—a common fallacy. Disability rates among older Americans declined in the 1980s and 1990s, thanks largely to education and better medical care, especially for heart disease, and have remained stable in the twenty-first century.[26] Some research, like a 2016 study out of Harvard University and the National Bureau of Economic Research, shows disability rates declining.[27] Although Americans are getting diseases earlier, we've gotten better at treating them, and people are managing the effects better. In other words, although longer lives mean spending more years with disease, "disability-free life expectancy" has risen faster than life span.

Healthcare costs are not *rising* in proportion to the average age of the population.

Researchers distinguish between necessary daily activities like dressing and using the toilet, and "instrumental" ones like light housekeeping and managing money. They also assess physical capacity in terms of the ability to walk a quarter of a mile or lift something moderately heavy. The incidence of such limitations is declining, and measuring their effects on quality of life is highly subjective. An athletic person might be devastated by not being able to climb stairs or a foodie utterly demoralized by no longer being able to cook, while others might easily adapt.

Health itself can be construed as relative. A twenty-five-year study published in 2008 surveyed 2,300 healthy men for as long as a quarter century.[28] When it began, in 1981, the subjects' average age was seventy-two. At the end of the study, 970 men had survived into their nineties. *This group suffered just as much chronic illness as the population at large.* The difference in quality of life as well as its duration correlated with five predictable and modifiable behaviors: not smoking, controlling weight and blood pressure, avoiding diabetes, and regular exercise.

AGING IS NOT A DISEASE

The biological causes of death are more predictable than they were in 1900. Thanks to clean water and antibiotics, tuberculosis and diarrheal diseases have given way to heart disease, cancer, and stroke. If we find a cure for those, we'll die from something else—but not of old age, because aging is not a disease. It was long equated with illness because studies were originally carried out in long-term care and nursing facilities, where bodies and brains were rarely stimulated and many subjects were indeed ill. As the century progressed, research from projects like the Baltimore Longitudinal Study of Aging, initiated in 1958, began to decouple the two. Scientists began identifying factors that contribute to healthier aging and developing interventions, like exercises that improve balance and muscle functions, to delay or prevent problems once strictly attributed to aging. Researchers now draw a clear distinction between "normal aging" and disease.

Medically speaking, aging is the continuous loss of physiological capacity, like immune responses and homeostasis, which increases vulnerability to the leading causes of death. (Homeostasis is the body's capacity to maintain a steady internal state, like glucose levels or body temperature. That's why olders so often bundle up against a chill.) Typically, our senses become less acute, skin gets dryer, lungs grow less elastic, we become more susceptible to hypertension, stamina and strength diminish, bones grow less dense, and we shrink along with the discs between our vertebrae. (Here's a silver lining: At eighty-six my friend Corinne is no longer in pain from a bulging spinal disc.)

Some ailments, like Alzheimer's, spinal stenosis, and arthritis, are indeed age-related. But many of the changes we attribute to age begin in childhood, and are affected by factors like obesity, poor nutrition, environmental conditions, social adversity, and even personality. This makes early intervention critically important, and is why the rising disability rate among younger Americans today, which is linked to complex factors that include obesity and unemployment rates, is cause for alarm. It's also important to keep in mind that the extent and rate of age-related changes vary enormously from person to person. Not only that, the variation between individuals increases with age. This means that the older we get, the less anyone can reliably infer from our chronological age about our health (or cognition, or language, or independent function). In other words, it's impossible to predict the health and well-being of an individual on the basis of their age. Some octogenarians have trouble walking around the block while others run marathons.

ILLNESS AND OLDNESS ARE ASSOCIATED. THEY ARE NOT THE SAME

Claudia Fine, a geriatric care manager, makes her living helping people cope with complex chronic illnesses, and she's frank about the challenges. "Getting sick and failing, both physically and mentally, is really tough, and it's tough for everyone around you. As we age these problems become more prevalent. But aging and illness are not the same." She encounters plenty of programs for older people, such as tai chi and computer classes—until their health begins to fail. "For some reason, we—families, practitioners, society—don't create goals for older people that we can feel good about." Instead of turning away, Fine suggests focusing on aspects that remain intact, supporting their strengths, and preserving the essence of who these older people are. "Because if we don't, then all we have left is the sickness."

Debility generally accompanies great age. Even so, that association says nothing about the likelihood of any given older person getting hurt or falling sick, nor of her odds of complete recovery—even if her doctor is skeptical or her children anxiously conferring in the hallway about next steps. If the government funded recreational programs and job training programs for robust and vigorous olders, their numbers would be greater. Instead, we have Medicare. This serves the highly profitable, illness-oriented status quo: not just the medical industry and the policymakers that advance its agenda, but much of the massive infrastructure, both public and private, that has developed to deliver goods and services to older people.

PEOPLE GET CHRONIC DISEASES, BUT THEY LIVE WITH THEM

Although I expected to encounter the occasional geriatric marvel whirring along in a Miracle Chair, I originally assumed that an active old age required being free of any impairment. Not so. The octo- and nonagenarians I interviewed hadn't escaped chronic or degenerative disease, but they hadn't let it overwhelm their plans or their psyches.

The first woman to qualify as a journeyman in the Hungarian Guild of Chimney Sweeps, Oven Makers, Roof Tilers, Well Diggers and Potters, designer Eva Zeisel was falsely accused of participating in an assassination plot against Joseph Stalin, and her experiences as a political prisoner in Russia figure in Arthur Koestler's masterwork *Darkness at Noon*. Zeisel emigrated to the U.S. and went on to become a master ceramicist and industrial designer. Nearly blind at one hundred from macular degeneration, she'd learned to use balsa-wood models to design with her hands. I watched her working on a big silverware commission for Bloomingdale's department store. Was it more difficult to work like that? Zeisel shook her head once, firmly. "The process—getting shapes out of the air—was always the same."

Mobility is relative. On a trip to Vietnam in 2013, my partner, Bob, and I encountered travelers from all over the world, most far younger than we were, and a few significantly older. Carol and Mathis were on the two-day boat tour we took of Halong Bay, north of Hanoi, where over three thousand limestone islands rise vertically out of the green water. A retired French professor and Holocaust survivor, Mathis was a baby-faced eighty-seven. Slightly overweight, he had arthritis and stenosis (my ailments!), and surgery on his cervical spine had impaired his balance, so he relied on a three-wheeled walker to get around. Mathis skipped a few excursions, but when lunch was served at the other end of a very long, very tippy, handrail-free floating walkway, he heaved himself and his walker over the side of the boat and made his way down it, as a bunch of young Eastern Europeans waited quietly and respectfully behind him. Back on the boat, he confided a deathly fear of the water.

Mathis and his wife (somewhat heavier, equally indefatigable) had come to Vietnam via Burma, where they'd rented a car and driver. That's not what they would have opted for had they been more agile, but it's not an easy country to get around and they had traveled the length of it. A week later we struck up a conversation with a woman at our hotel in Hoi An, a former French colonial trading center. Somewhere in their late seventies, she and her husband were Canadians who had been living in New Zealand for forty-four years. His curvature of the spine turned his face cruelly to the ground when he stood, but it hadn't kept them off the road.

They were at the tail end of six weeks in Vietnam, which they had thoroughly enjoyed except for the time she passed out in the Mekong Delta because of what turned out to be very high blood pressure, previously undiagnosed and nearly fatal. After a brief stay in the hospital in Ho Chi Minh City to monitor her medication, she was back on the road. "Drink plenty of fluids," she advised. When I commended her on her stamina, she told me she'd had a parasite in India and gotten salmonella on a felucca on the Nile that laid her up for a couple of weeks after her return. "Hard-boiled eggs, wouldn't you think that would be the safest thing in the world? Everyone who ate from the basket on our side of the table got it." "And here you are off again," I chided her. "Have you learned nothing?" "I've learned *nothing*," she confirmed, returning my high five with a grin.

Bob and I can scramble into an upper bunk with ease, and did on the train from Hanoi to Saigon, but eventually we'll reserve lower ones. Or a motorcycle with a sidecar. These people, us included, represent one end of the spectrum, both economically and in sheer adventurousness. Many olders with the wherewithal travel only in their golf carts, while many more without the means voyage only vicariously, via screen or printed page. Wheelchairs will be cooler after my generation fully commodifies them, and will go way more places thanks to the Americans with Disabilities Act of 1990. Many destinations will remain inaccessible. Hundreds of compromises lie ahead. If they're what it takes to get me out the door, I hope I'll welcome them.

DISABILITY IS HUGELY STIGMATIZED

It doesn't take much head-scratching to deduce that a tremendous amount of our apprehension about growing old is rooted in fear of becoming disabled. The same medical advances that have swelled the number of people who live with disabilities are keeping more and more of the rest of us alive long enough to join their ranks. Yet despite the fact that one-third of disabled Americans are sixty-five or older, we act as though olders never become disabled and people with disabilities never grow old. It's appropriate to resist the equation of aging with disability, but they also overlap in ways that are important to acknowledge because they undermine ageism and ableism and pave the way for collective advocacy. We have much to learn from the activists who reframed the way we see disability in the 1970s and '80s. They changed it from an individual medical problem into a social problem—bingo!—and then demanded integration, access, and equal rights.

Whatever their age, people with disabilities are saddled with both the condition and its social cost. Before we understood what causes disease, the afflicted were quarantined or shunned. Society has yet to catch up with medical science. Many of us still avoid people with disabilities, because they make us uncomfortable. Internalizing stigma can damage self-esteem and quality of life more than the condition itself. Shockingly, many olders refuse wheelchairs or walkers because the stigma is so great—even if it means *never leaving home.*

Many olders refuse wheelchairs or walkers because the stigma is so great–even if it means never leaving home.

Others devise ingenious work-arounds, like my friend Wendy's eighty-six-year-old aunt, who lives in a high-rise in Queens, New York. When they headed out, her aunt plopped her purse in one of those stand-up shopping carts, although they weren't going shopping. It didn't take long for Wendy to realize that she was using the cart as a walker—one that didn't look like a walker. When a leg cramp struck, her aunt hobbled over to lean against a bus stop till the pain eased. "This way people will think we're waiting for the bus," she whispered. This is a wonderful story about adaptability, and a wretched one about the shame of "looking old."

Even when he grew completely blind, my uncle wouldn't use a white cane, preferring to rely on the kindness of strangers and taxi drivers. After breaking a bone in her foot, a not-yet-forty-year-old friend also declined a cane, deferring to crutches because they signal "injured," not "old" or "disabled." Such is the long shadow of all those signs that depict hunched over people with canes. A doctor doing her geriatrics residency at Weill Cornell Medical Center described a seventy-eight-year-old patient with multiple sclerosis. "She's had real difficulty walking, keeps falling even in her own home, but she's *furious* when people offer her a seat." Did the doctor wish her patient would accept the offer? "Yes! And I see the same thing with people who won't use a walker."

How about hearing loss? Nearly 25 percent of 65-to-74-year-olds and 50 percent of those who are 75 and older have disabling hearing loss, according to the National Institute on Deafness and Other Communication Disorders, but fewer than one in three who could benefit from wearing hearing aids have ever used them.[29] Cost is one reason. Denial is another. Many older adults maintain that they don't have a problem, telling audiologists, "I hear what I want to hear." Ignorance is another major factor. Hearing loss is typically gradual, and since we can't perceive what no longer exists for us, many people remain unaware of it. Others assume that hearing loss is just a normal part of aging, so it can't be harmful. They're wrong about that. The ear plays a role in balance, and even mild hearing loss can triple the risk of falling. It's linked to depression and also to dementia. According to research based on the Baltimore Longitudinal Study of Aging, the greater the hearing loss the steeper the rate of cognitive decline.[30]

I had my hearing tested after learning that, partly because I wanted to resolve an ongoing "You're deaf"/"You need to speak louder" domestic dispute. (My partner has a beautiful low voice and speaks very softly. His mother was extremely hard of hearing, and every few minutes she'd ask, "What did he say?" I'd turn to him and say, "Tell your mother what you said." Ah, families.) My hearing is in the normal range, it turns out, although there's loss in the higher registers typical of my age-group. The first word on the test was "inkwell," which cracked me up; apparently the standard tests haven't been updated since World War II.

I'm glad I don't need a hearing aid, but I'll wear one when I do. I hope it'll work better than current devices, and maybe even become stylish. New hearing-aid models can be adjusted precisely through smartphone apps, which has enormous implications for bionic disability devices. They're also very inconspicuous, which will help get them adopted—especially if users actually hear *better* than their non-hard-of-hearing peers, which may well become the case. Hearing decently is part of being fully engaged in ordinary life, not to mention not being maddening to be around. The earlier the diagnosis, the greater the range of appropriate therapies—along with the social and cognitive payoffs.

GENES MATTER LESS THAN YOU PROBABLY THINK[31]

Long-lived ancestors are a plus, but they'll only get you so far, as I learned from geriatrician Robert Butler. "It's really never too late to reinvent yourself and to invent different health habits. Only about 25 percent of our health appears to be due to genes. Seventy-five percent is environmental or behavior," Butler told me. Although I've seen the number pegged at 30 percent, genes are far less important than I once assumed. Furthermore, the role of genetics diminishes across the life span as environment grows more influential. Many risk factors, including the likelihood of obesity, hypertension, and high cholesterol levels, are by and large *not* inherited. In other words, as the MacArthur Foundation Study of Successful Aging put it, "How we live and where we live has the most profound impact on age-related changes in the function of many organs throughout the body, including the heart, immune system, lung, bones, brain, and kidneys."[32]

Not that life is fair. Jeanne Calment, the longest-lived person on record, who died in 1997 at 122, had a sweet tooth, was fond of cheap red wine and rich food, and smoked until she was seventy-seven. Reflecting on his two best friends from college, Butler observed that the one who'd been a pilot in World War II and continued to sail and play tennis had also had the most physical problems. At that point, a phone call interrupted our conversation. It was the octogenarian's personal trainer.

It helps to be able to afford a personal trainer. And to have access to healthcare. And to be able to practice the basics: Don't smoke; control your weight and blood pressure; eat less sugar and more veggies; exercise regularly; get enough sleep. These behaviors make sense whether or not they lengthen lives. At any age, we can improve our health.

A 2010 feature in *The New York Times* called "Secrets of the Centenarians" was packed with the usual truisms, summed up by columnist and author Jane Brody as "the Three R's—resolution, resourcefulness, and resilience"[33]—and emphasized that genes played a relatively small role in longevity. What are those "secrets"? Exercise, moderation, and strong social and family ties. Lifestyle, in short. What struck me, as in my own interviews, was the variety of the sample. Some of these centenarians would be great dinner companions; others were numbingly dull. Some were physically average; others bionic. Hazel Miller was the one I'd like to share a meal or a road trip with. What was this pragmatic centenarian's secret? "You just don't die." Miller had always liked to dance, "but, as you know, after a certain age there are no men to dance with, so I started line dancing." That's resilience.

ATTITUDE HELPS

Instead of waiting around for men to materialize, Hazel adapted to circumstance in order to keep doing something she loved. Another centenarian attributed her well-being to the fact that "I'm blessed and I've worked on it. You've got to work, be cheerful, and look for something fun to do. It's a whole attitude."

New York Times reporter John Leland spent a year communing with the "oldest old," wrote a book about the experience, and called it *Happiness Is a Choice You Make*. He writes, "The title of this book comes from one of the first lessons the elders taught me, that even as our various faculties decline, we still wield extraordinary influence over the quality of our lives."[34] The lives of most of the olders he interviewed were severely constrained by ill health, poverty, and/or isolation. Yet all found a measure of happiness by focusing not on what they had lost but on the distinct pleasures that remained to them in the here and now.

Like good genes, an optimistic attitude conveys real advantages. Studies show that optimists live longer than pessimists, and surely they enjoy their added years more. But an awful lot of aging sites and gurus overemphasize the role of a positive attitude when it comes to "aging well"—a bit like the Beatles crooning, "All you need is love." This places the responsibility for their circumstances on the individual, and it also deflects attention away from the institutionalized disadvantages that make it harder to smile, or simply to endure. A sunny disposition may help people cope with ill-treatment, but it's no substitute for a remedy.

PUSH BACK!

KEEP MOVING: THE BIGGEST THREAT TO AN ACTIVE OLD AGE IS THE MOST REMEDIABLE

A presentation by geriatrician Joanne Lynne about the lame state of end-of-life care in America opened with the question, "How many of you expect to die?"[35] Lynn then offered three options: cancer; chronic heart or lung disease; or frailty and dementia. Her graphs depicting the end of life for each condition (the Y axis showing function, the X axis the passage of time), and her description of the toll each takes took her listeners, and me, by surprise. Cancer deaths are usually preceded by only a few weeks or months of steep decline. Chronic heart or lung disease is characterized by bouts of severe illness alternating with periods of relative stability at a reduced level of function. The third path, extended frailty possibly paired with dementia, involves a long, slow decline, most people's worst nightmare, and it awaits many older Americans. They are typically over eighty-five, and disproportionately female and widowed.

We don't know what causes dementia, so it's hard to prevent, although we know that positive attitudes toward aging protect against it, even in people genetically predisposed to the disease.[36] In contrast, the indicators of frailty (weight loss, weakness, fatigue, slowed walking speed, reduced activity) are easy to detect. Reliable tests exist, but it's rare for doctors other than geriatricians to conduct them. The loss of muscular strength as we age is natural and often goes unnoticed, but it can eventually translate into an inability to get out of the bath or up the stairs. A lifelong shower shunner, my mother had so many handles installed in her tub that it started looking kinky, but she grew too weak to haul herself in and out of it.

Staying physically active dramatically increases physical fitness, muscle size, and strength in older people, and enhances bone strength and balance. It's associated with improving, and even preventing, cognitive decline, and along with diet can remedy and even reverse many of the factors that contribute to frailty—regardless of how old you are or how late you start.[37] Even much older people, already frail, can see huge gains from modest interventions like walking more or doing simple weight-training exercises. Nor do olders have to work harder than youngers to maintain the same level of fitness. "It's never too late," says Dr. Lachs. "It's a little bit like seeing an iceberg off in the distance. If you make a one- or two-degree course correction, you can really avoid the iceberg altogether."[38]

KEEP THE "ORGAN RECITAL" SHORT

The "organ recital," as I've heard it called—the litany of aches and ailments that grows over time—doesn't have to hijack the conversation. I'll want an update about any major health issues my friends are facing, but I bet we can train each other to make it snappy. I met a woman who lived overseas but who made an annual pilgrimage to catch up with everyone back home. She'd remind her pals that she was coming to hear what was happening in their lives, not in their innards. When the organ recital began, she'd remind the friend that she wasn't a doctor and leave. "It took a few years, but I broke them of the habit!" she recounted with a grin. When it comes to your ailments, no one, except maybe your mom, is really all that interested.

At a conference, a journalist colleague asked each speaker how he or she felt about getting older. My favorite answer was, "There's a lump of pain, and it just moves around." I think of it as the "only one baby can cry at a time" theory of pain. That was my husband's deadpan declaration when we brought baby number two home from the hospital, and his two-year-old sister burst into tears: "Only one baby can cry at a time!" he told her matter-of-factly. It completely threw her for a loop, giving us enough time to head off the tantrum. If I sit for too long or move for too long or just have one of those days, I hurt, but if my back's bugging me, I hardly notice my knee. Only one baby can cry at a time.

I have to remind myself that pain is just pain, and that not all of it is age-related. My jock daughter and I were both diagnosed with patellofemoral syndrome a few years ago, and physical therapy fixed both of us. It's hard to keep that in mind first thing in the morning, when I lurch for the doorknob to help me straighten up. What my grandmother called stiffness my orthopedist calls stenosis, my acupuncturist calls qi stagnation, and my GP says is arthritis. I don't talk about it much to anyone else, because A) it's boring; and B) I don't want to give it more bandwidth.

The objective is to be able to keep doing the things I want to do. So far so good, although the goalposts are shifting. I used to whiz along on my bicycle, and now I'm in the slow lane. I still barrel along the sidewalk, and when I have to slow down I won't like it any more than Ruth Friendly did. "You feel like you're still fifty, sixty, sixty-five. Even seventy-five was fine," said the television producer, who drove in to the city from Westchester for a family dinner every Sunday. "We're walking along Riverside Drive and suddenly I have to say, 'Can you slow down?' That's not me; I don't like that," Friendly told me. It *was* her, though, and shorter steps weren't keeping her from an active social life and demanding job.

"I'm much, much slower physically than I was even two years ago," said teacher and documentary filmmaker George Stoney, at ninety-two. "Just walking out of my building I'm constantly being passed by all these other people. I haven't come to terms with that.

It irritates me all the time." That's not the only depredation, but he wasn't in denial about them. When a student evaluation complained about the professor's hearing, Stoney promptly bought hearing aids. Someone almost inevitably offered him a seat in the subway, and "Very often I'm glad to sit down," Stoney said. Me too, and it's silly to be offended. That's internalized ageism at work, although those cloying signs in the bus are no help. "Won't you please give up your seat to the elderly or disabled?" they say, complete with a condescending little heart. What they should say is, "Please offer your seat to anyone who looks like they might need it."

ACKNOWLEDGE THAT LIFE IS FINITE. IT FILLS THE PRESENT WITH MEANING

We all wake up a day older, and one of these days we won't wake up at all. The sooner we accept that, the better off we'll be. That's when we overthrow what geriatrician Bill Thomas calls the "tyranny of still": the delusion that everything will be okay as long as we're still working, still wearing heels, still running up the stairs—whatever our "still" happens to be. Because nothing stays the same. Why, asks Thomas, do we celebrate change and growth until late midlife, and then start commending its opposite? In order to assuage our all-too-human fears about aging and its inevitable end? To sweep our anxieties under the proverbial rug?

Denial does not soothe. "Fight aging!" is no calming mantra. Its power diminishes as the years add up, and that energy could be far better spent. Like two-thirds of the Americans surveyed in a Pew Research report on "Living to 120 and Beyond,"[39] I'm skeptical about the benefit of radically longer life spans and uneasy about the likelihood that they would be available only to a small elite. My main objection is philosophical: far better to struggle to come to terms with the inevitable transitions than to postpone that reckoning in frantic pursuit of biomedical bonanzas. Far better to pull our heads out of the sand and work with, not against, the inevitable. Not dealing with aging is a way of not dealing with living.

That was the problem with the *Today Show*'s perky title for an interview with geriatric psychiatrist Dr. Marc Agronin.[10] "Put your

Not dealing with aging is a way of not dealing with living.

fears about aging to rest." Hedging that bet, with no apparent irony, was a chyron across the bottom of the screen packed with dementia and suicide statistics. The same split personality was evident in Dr. Nancy Snyderman, NBC's chief medical officer. Pointing out that Baby Boomers are in fact going to die, she asked, "The question is, how do you embrace that second half of your life, and own it?" Great question, but her answer was problematic: "Live a big life, do it right, and slide out at home plate!"

What if all you've managed is a medium-sized life? What if you break your hip rounding third? Some of us will slide home in style and some will stagger; some of the former will be chain-smoking steak eaters and some of the latter virtuous vegans. There's no knowing how it's all going to turn out. We pay a price, individually and culturally, when we pretend otherwise, and an even higher one when we aspire to stasis and "agelessness."

THINK ABOUT WHO BENEFITS
WHEN AGE IS REDUCED TO ILLNESS

If older people seem preoccupied by their maladies and doctor's appointments, it's partly because an ageist society denies them access to many of the things that once gave their lives meaning. Olders collaborate, having been indoctrinated over a lifetime by cultural expectations of declining health, learned helplessness, and the media's depiction of older people as consumers of prescription drugs, anti-aging remedies, and not much else.

Reducing older people to bodies in various states of decay makes it easy to marginalize them. Focusing on pathology is also an effective way to get funding for research into specific diseases when holistic efforts might well be more effective. The research and treatment of Alzheimer's disease, for example, sustains an entire clinical empire, while the caregiver crisis goes largely unaddressed. Population aging is driving the rapid growth of illness-related products and services and is a major profit center for the pharmaceutical industry.

No longer economically "useful," many who are old nevertheless "produce something of great monetary value: illness," observes age scholar Margaret Cruikshank. "The business of the old is to be sick."[41] That won't change unless we challenge the reduction of old age to physical decline and reflect on whose interests that equation serves. Modern medicine defaults to expensive, profitable, and often legally mandated interventions, especially at the end of life. Health is seldom defined holistically, and few doctors have—or take—the time to investigate its nuanced relationship with quality of life for older patients who may be managing several chronic conditions.

Aging well, Cruikshank writes, "means knowing that late-life illness has both cultural and biological origins."[42] In other words, if your knee hurts, it's not just about how much cartilage has worn away and what can or can't be done about it. It's about what you think that condition says about you, and which interpretations you reject or embrace. If you hear, "What do you expect at your age?" it's about pointing out that other parts of you are holding out perfectly well—and finding a new doctor. Plenty of octo- and nonagenarians are vigorous right up to the end, although they don't register on the policy agenda, where sickness takes center stage.

If you hear, "What do you expect at your age?" find a new doctor.

REJECT AGEIST STEREOTYPES: THEY'RE HARMFUL TO OUR HEALTH

A growing body of fascinating research documents the link between people's perceptions of aging and their health and behavior. Yale psychologist Becca Levy has been measuring the effect of age stereotypes for over twenty years. Again and again, she and her colleagues have found that people with more positive feelings about aging behave differently as they age compared to those convinced that growing old means becoming useless or helpless.[43] Long-term studies show that positive attitudes toward aging are associated with better functional health and are more predictive of health status than socioeconomic status, race, and gender![44]

"Implicit interventions"—flashing positive age stereotypes in the form of words like "active" and "creative" on a computer screen too briefly for them to register consciously—improved not just self-perception but physical functions like balance.[45] Those with more positive views of aging do better on memory tests. They have better handwriting, which correlates with good health. They can walk faster. A report in the *Journal of the American Medical Association* suggests that olders with this positive bias are 44 percent more likely to fully recover from severe disability.[46] And they actually live an average of seven and a half years longer.[47] Those unable to overcome a lifetime of internalized ageism, on the other hand, were less likely to seek healthcare or to exercise, and died earlier.

A goal of public health and aging policy is "more healthy years, not years without health." Imagine the benefits to health and human potential of overturning ageist stereotypes before they distort self-image, shorten steps, and limit prospects. Think what a public health campaign that overturned ageist stereotypes would do to extend not just the life span but the "healthspan" of all Americans.

CHAPTER FIVE

NO EXPIRATION DATE:
SEX AND INTIMACY

Nowhere is ageism more sexist, and vicious, than in the domain of sexuality. Most Americans think that older people aren't sexually active, aren't interested in sex, aren't physically capable of it, and in any case aren't attractive enough to find anyone with whom to engage in it. Hence the repulsive stereotype of the "sexless senior." Homophobia renders the older LGBTQ population even less visible. Prudery, which crossed the Atlantic with the Puritans, helps make the subject taboo. As a result, the sexuality of older adults is under-researched, ignored, and belittled. The consequences for health, happiness, and self-image are far-reaching.

WHAT'S WITH THE "EW" FACTOR?

Wrinkly old people having sex? Ew! Why does the very idea invoke something close to disgust in so many? Sex makes us feel more alive in the moment than just about anything else, and the prospect of enjoying carnal pleasures to the end ought to please, not dismay. Our bodies change throughout our lives in remarkable and beautiful ways, especially if we're female, and usually show the passage of time less markedly than our faces. The difference between ages forty and fifty-five, say, or seventy and eighty-five, ought not to be any more off-putting than what happens between ages ten and twenty-five. Instead we internalize countless messages that older bodies, women's in particular, are undesirable, ugly, and even repulsive.

If people were to get comfortable with "senior sex," it would be transgressive. It would overturn the conventional notion reinforced by entire industries and millions of advertising dollars that sex is the domain of the firm of flesh and satisfaction measured in the duration of erections and number of orgasms. Disability rights activist Simi Linton came of age in a world that lacked sex education and reproductive healthcare services for people with disabilities and couldn't envision a need for them. So she became a sex educator, encouraging people to experiment with oral sex, or noses or toes, or whatever was within reach—"to use disability as an opportunity to think in new ways about sex and what is important to them," as she wrote in her memoir, *My Body Politic*.[1] Linton and her colleagues enjoyed rattling people by talking casually about the robust sexual lives of disabled people, and came to understand that it was radical to link the two because it challenged cultural norms around pleasure, desire, and sexual ability.

It's time to link age and robust sex lives too—the lifelong right to intimacy in all its forms—and to look at where these repressive norms come from. Barbara MacDonald and her partner Cynthia Rich co-wrote *Look Me in The Eye: Old Women, Aging and Ageism*, a seminal collection of essays on the intersection of sexism and ageism. Rich held that physical revulsion is no less than a tool for oppression. "The principal source of the distaste for old women's bodies should be perfectly familiar," she wrote. "It is very similar to the distaste anti-Semites feel toward Jews, homophobes feel toward lesbians and gays, racists toward blacks—the drawing back of the oppressor from the physical being of the oppressed." Unreasoned and fear-based, physical revulsion operates as "an instant check whenever reason or simple fairness starts to lead us into more liberal paths."[2]

The right to intimacy is lifelong.

"Marxist quackery," snorted my houseguest, Patrick. "It's about beauty. There's nothing more sensuously beautiful than an eighteen-year-old girl." This after flaunting his cred by describing a long and passionate affair with a woman decades older than he, and how lovely parts of her body were. This wouldn't have been a story worth telling, I pointed out, if it didn't counter the *Playboy* pin-up ideal.

Sexual chemistry is real and wonderfully arbitrary, and there's no need to apologize for its presence or absence. There's no such thing as the right to be desired. But as Rich observed, all marginalized people have heard that it's "natural" for others to be physically repelled by them. This repulsion connects all the "isms." Ageism just has a cutesy name for it: the *ew* factor. None of this stigma is "natural," and none of it is fixed. Challenging stigma threatens the social and political structures that maintain power relationships. Not that long ago it was considered unnatural for women to work outside the home, and for black and white people to be friends, let alone marry each other. When we see older people as beautiful, it undermines the commodification of youth culture.

We're surrounded by billboards and movies and TV shows and fashion magazines that fetishize the very young. But examples of older people, let alone sexually active ones, are few and far between. Only 27 percent of all women's roles in prime-time TV go to women over forty, where they're typically cast as victims: betrayed, abandoned, and abused[3]—although pivotal characters in television series like *Transparent* and *Grace and Frankie* may be turning the tide.

When it comes to the movies, according to a 2013 University of Southern California study, less than a quarter of all female speaking parts are for women aged forty to sixty-four (substantially fewer than speaking parts for men the same age), and people over sixty-five appear in movies significantly less than children do.[4] Another USC study found that less than 12 percent of the 1,256 speaking or named characters in the twenty-five movies nominated for best picture from 2014 through 2016 were aged sixty and up, giving rise to the hashtag #OscarsSoAgeist. Many were portrayed as impaired. Oscars so sexist and racist too: 77.7 percent of the older characters were men, 89.9 percent of whom were white, 6.1 percent black, and 2 percent Asian. Not one was Latinx.[5]

There's a term for these omissions: symbolic annihilation, defined in Wikipedia as "the absence of representation, or

117

underrepresentation, of some group of people in the media . . . understood in the social sciences to be a means of maintaining social inequality." Marketing and mass media greatly influence popular culture and the way we see ourselves. Absence reflects the distribution of power in society. Dismissing the physical and sexual presence of older people makes it all the easier to dismiss their ideas and well-being.

DERISION OR CONDESCENSION— IT'S NOT MUCH OF A CHOICE

At any age, adults have the right to seek out sex with other consenting adults without censure. But you wouldn't know it from the way the media, and pretty much everyone else, treat the subject. Discussing the movie version of *Fifty Shades of Grey,* an NPR host quipped, "You might find out that Grandma needs a safe word" (a prearranged code used in bondage and domination sex to end an activity), as though the possibility were laughably remote. Or consider the discourse around "cougars": women who like younger men. Here's a charming description from the crowdsourced Urban Dictionary: "The cougar can be anyone from an overly surgically altered wind tunnel victim, to an absolute sad and bloated old hornmeister, to a real hottie or milf (Mother I'd Like to Fuck)." Other entries testify to advantages of an older partner's sexual experience, independence, and generally having her act together. There's nothing wrong with being a confident woman in her sexual prime enjoying younger partners and making love instead of babies, as long as we claim it, but the scrutiny is intense and far from neutral. No one paid much attention to Demi Moore's sex life until she swapped Bruce Willis for Ashton Kutcher.

Men can get the same treatment, as in *The New York Times* review of the 12-12-12 concert to benefit Hurricane Sandy victims. Snarkily titled "The Music Is Timeless, but About the Rockers . . . ," reviewer Alex Williams sneered at the star-studded lineup, describing their "visible aging" as "tragic" and scolding them for not "keeping their clothes on" in public. "It's like hearing that your grandparents still have sex: bully for them, but spare us the details," he concluded primly. Yes, that's exactly what it's like. These rockers are in great shape, doing real good, and having a blast. If you can't handle it, stay home and keep quiet.

When "senior sex" makes headlines, coverage careens between condescension and downright nastiness. "Sleazy Geezer Society Meeting Now in Session" was the title of a *New York Post* column about Egyptian banker Mahmoud Abdel-Salam Omar's arrest on sex abuse charges in June 2001, which suggested that Omar bunked with fellow hotel-maid-attacker and "co-codger in crime" Dominique Strauss-Kahn while they awaited trial.[6] Omar and Strauss-Kahn deserved to be punished for being violent pigs, not for being north of sixty, but the media coverage suggested otherwise.

Fears of older sexuality run deep, and behavior that's ignored, even commended, among the young provokes invective at the other end of the spectrum. Older guys get labeled "creepy old men" for engaging in perfectly normal behavior like watching porn or admiring someone who's hot. It's a hurtful slur that's almost impossible to refute. People are creeps because they're creeps, not because they're over a certain age. This double standard can also

Condescension neuters.

protect, by desexualizing older men, but that's no improvement. A story about a man in his eighties in an Indianapolis drugstore cereal aisle, headlined: "Elderly customer stuns woman at Southeastside by groping, kissing her," provoked a debate on Facebook as to whether he should be slapped or applauded. A feminist friend in her forties weighed in with "Both, if I could go with that. Yes, this behavior was unacceptable, but I am happy to know his libido lives on." What would she have said if the fondler were her age? Condescension neuters, and age is no excuse for bad behavior. His was reprehensible.

Condescension also characterized much of the critical response to best-selling author Iris Krasnow's book *Sex After . . .* , which is about women's sex lives after pregnancy, divorce, infidelity, breast cancer, coming out, and menopause. The last category generated the most buzz, with much eyebrow-raising on the part of reviewers at the possibility that women in their seventies and eighties could be having the best sex of their lives. Krasnow paved the way for them by titling the chapter "Giddy Golden Girls." BuzzFeed published an excerpt from an interview with an eighty-eight-year-old who hasn't dated since her husband of sixty years passed away, but masturbates frequently, a salutary reminder of one way to keep the cylinders firing. Did the headline really need to describe her cohort as "Ladies in their golden years"?[7] Would *Jezebel*'s Lindy West have described anecdotes about fellatio and lubrication from thirty-year-olds as "darling"?[8] *Jezebel*'s title for the post—"Women in Their 70s Say They're Having Way Hotter Sex Than You"—presumes that none of their readers could be that old, revealing an age-constrained sense of sisterhood. Data about the sex lives of women in their eighties and nineties is largely anecdotal: Researchers haven't studied it because of ageism, sexism, and the general assumption that those sex lives don't exist.

"OLD IS UGLIEST FOR WOMEN"

That's Cynthia Rich's line.[9] She is a lesbian, but that confers little protection against heteronormative standards of female beauty. Her partner, Barbara MacDonald, pointed out that young women's alienation from older ones and dread at becoming like them was the result of social forces. "Your power as a younger woman is measured by the distance you can keep between you and older women," she wrote with brutal frankness.

Economists have a name—the "attractiveness penalty"—for the fact that women are judged far more harshly than men for "looking old." Women not only bear the brunt of the equation of beauty with youth; we perpetuate it—every time we dye our hair to cover the gray or lie about our age, not to mention have plastic surgery to cover the signs of aging. Susan Sontag famously called out the "double standard of aging," defining it as the social convention that aging enhances a man but progressively destroys a woman. "Women reinforce it powerfully with their complacency, with their anguish, with their lies," she wrote. "In protecting themselves as women, they betray themselves as adults." Ouch. It takes courage for women to follow Sontag's advice and "allow their faces to show the lives they have lived."[10] It's not that men get away unscathed. When Mick Jagger told musician George Melly his wrinkles were "laugh lines," Melly responded hilariously, "Nothing's that funny."

Judged to look old far sooner than their male counterparts, women compete to stay young. No judgment, I swear. But this punitive and expensive undertaking reinforces Sontag's double standard (not to mention ageism, sexism, and patriarchy), pits us against each other, and sets us up to fail. Does any woman reading this really believe she is a lesser version—less interesting, less fun in bed, less valuable—than the woman she used to be? If so, where does that message come from, and what purpose does it serve? What's the ultimate aphrodisiac? Confidence.

The price of defying convention is steep. Open any women's magazine and a hundred advertisements bellow, "How can you expect to be desired if you 'let yourself go?'" Ads and editorials tout every means possible—Spanx! Personal trainers! Liposuction!—to hang onto unlined faces and bodies sculpted for skintight fashions. Fertility notwithstanding, why on earth, asks critic Carina Chocano, do we privilege "the tragic, grotesque, totally unfair and yet unassailable ephemerality of a woman's so-called prime . . . over any evidence to the contrary? We expect women to submit to its incontrovertible veracity with equanimity and shame, and we expect men to be gracious about it and try not to gloat." Now that she's in her forties, Chocano understands how damaging it is to equate youth with worth and wonders why we don't push back. "I look back at this now—at how bad, how ashamed I felt for letting myself turn twenty-nine—and I can't believe how much of my youth I squandered on feeling old."[11]

Murder, She Wrote, which starred Angela Lansbury, was the eighth most watched program on television when CBS canceled it because its ratings were "skewing too old" (not enough viewers in the coveted eighteen-to-forty-nine-year-old demographic). Returning to the London stage at eighty-eight for the first time in nearly forty years, Lansbury said the transition had been less difficult for her in view of the fact that "I was playing older parts when I was terribly young because I wasn't a big screen beauty."[12] Casting decisions like these emphasize not only that beauty equals youth but that its absence equals old. How often do we hear "She used to be beautiful," as though age and beauty were mutually exclusive?

There's no harsher reminder of what wrinkles signify than when we size up someone attractive across the room and they don't even meet our gaze. This transition is especially painful for women accustomed to leveraging their looks and conventional allure. And visibility itself can provoke a problematic response. For example, a while ago a cute young guy came up to me at a dance club and told me I looked like Susan Sarandon. Then, instantly, his face clouded over and he blurted, "I meant it as a compliment." He wasn't saying that I look like Susan Sarandon. He was saying, "You look old and you look hot"—a message so rare in this culture, so apparently contradictory, that being compared to a smart, bodacious movie star in her sixties risked coming across as an *insult*. Small wonder that so many older women bail entirely on the messy, risky business of baring flesh and heart to someone new. It takes courage and confidence to refuse to abdicate, especially from sexual and recreational realms, and it's imperative to make space for those who have never been visible.

PEOPLE NEVER STOP HAVING SEX

Sex was indeed once the domain of the young. That changed when the Paleolithic Era ushered in longer life spans, and shifted a lot further during the twentieth century's unprecedented leap in longevity. Most of us haven't had much trouble letting go of the idea that sex is only for making babies. It's high time to shelve the companion idea that sex is only for youngers, and to look at the tunnel vision that contributes to it.

Young adults have sex. Middle-aged adults have sex. And guess what? Women who were sexually active at midlife *continue to have sex*—as do their partners! Older men probably keep doin' it in proportionately greater numbers. When AARP asked divorced sixty-plus men what they liked best about being single, 22 percent answered "more sex." Only 1 percent of divorced women that age agreed.[13] It would be very interesting to break out what's behind that discrepancy, including relationship status and cultural expectations, because women don't stop wanting sex after menopause. The quality does not decline. Both are ageist and sexist myths. Sex is good for us, and we get better at it.

How Old Is Too Old To Have Sex? was the title of a *Huffington Post* online discussion that I took part in in 2013. The question itself is profoundly ageist. We don't ask when people age out of singing, or quit eating ice cream; why on earth would we stop making love? We don't, of course, although sexual activity does decline with age. Wrinkles and creaky joints notwithstanding, older Americans are the fastest-growing users of internet dating services. Men are living longer, thanks largely to better treatments for conditions like heart disease and cancers that disproportionately affect males. Drugs like Viagra and Cialis give erections a boost. Olders are better off financially than they were a generation ago. The internet makes finding a partner more private and more likely. Mores are changing too. The same generation that would have banished a grandchild for "shacking up" is now moving in together in record numbers, and love late in life is looked at far less askance.

We don't ask when people age out of singing, or quit eating ice cream; why would we stop making love?

This activity is reflected in the incidence of sexually transmitted diseases among olders, such as chlamydia, gonorrhea, and syphilis. People age fifty and older account for an estimated 45% of Americans living with diagnosed HIV, and the number is growing fast.[14] They are less likely to be aware of their HIV risk factors, and less likely to receive an early diagnosis. Older heterosexual women are at particular risk, because vaginal thinning makes it easier to contract all STDs. If you're sexually active, use condoms, get tested, and ask the same of your partners. Bust your doctor if she doesn't address your sexual health and make the same recommendations.

According to a survey conducted by the *New England Journal of Medicine*, 25 percent of the respondents in the oldest age-group (seventy-five to eighty-five) were having sex, many several times a month, and a third of those were also giving or receiving oral sex.[15] Even in nursing homes, where sexual expression is typically discouraged and informed consent can be an issue, things can get frisky. Moving into an institution means giving up the comforts of home and, potentially, a great deal of independence and privacy to boot. It shouldn't mean forswearing a basic human right as well. This group's offspring, the postwar generation, is definitely not going gentle into *that* good night, thank heavens! From cradle to grave, no matter where we live or for how long, human touch remains essential.

DATING IN AN AGEIST WORLD

So what can we do to stay in the game? For starters, people reentering the dating pool after a death or divorce need to update their assumptions and expectations, as well as their profiles of course. Online dating has opened up a world of opportunities, and retirees are often in a position to be more flexible about travel and meeting people far away. In the past few years, dozens of sites have sprung up that cater to "mature" adults seeking everything from casual friendship to marriage. OurTime.com is a site for singles over fifty; AARP offers a dating service; eHarmony reports that the over-fifty-five demographic is one of its fastest-growing segments. It's also a good idea to join a large, general site or two, like OkCupid or Match .com, to expand the pool and the possibilities.

There's a lot of lying about age on dating sites—as well as about height and income and that not-so-recent photo—on the part of all genders. I've heard anecdotally that the first exchange when people meet is often an admission of all the stuff they fudged on their profiles. Most people shave a few years off because "It's the age I feel" or "That's how old most people guess I am," in order to get more hits from people they deem desirable. And a lot of men are seeking women younger than themselves.

Given our ageist culture, lying about age is understandable. People do it not because they're fundamentally dishonest but because they're afraid that the truth would eliminate them before they ever get a chance to meet you. But insecurity about age (or anything else) is the opposite of attractive. It's also what motivates people to post outdated photos, but why disappoint with how poorly you compare with that selfie instead of how well? Stretching the truth might make sense in the short term, but once you start lying, you've got a mess on your hands. Admit the lie and your date will be wondering what else you haven't come clean about. Keep quiet and things will get really awkward when a friend spills the beans or your date spots your driver's license.

One option is to tell the truth further down in your online profile, as a friend of mine does. Another is to fess up before you meet up, or over that first coffee. The best option, though, is to be honest from the get-go. If you don't get hits, age might not be the problem; have someone take a really great picture of you, and get some advice on what makes a profile stand out. If you see an amazing profile seeking younger women only, try sending a lighthearted note acknowledging the fact and asking if the person will make an exception. Most of the time, if two people connect and enjoy each other's company, it won't end up mattering. And someone too narrow-minded to consider the possibility, or deterred by a disparity in the "wrong" direction, probably isn't for you anyway.

I'd like dating sites to eliminate age as top-tier screening information entirely. People could ask as soon as they connect, via chat or in person. Would-be breeders could request a fertility write-up along with STI test results. (Men too. The incidence of birth defects and mental illnesses rises with the father's age, but when's the last time you heard a woman worrying about a man's sperm being past its prime?) If *all* profiles on a site deliberately omit age and age range up front, the question becomes moot and there's no inducement to lie. It's illegal to ask for age on a job application because it fosters discrimination. It has the same effect in the world of online match-making. Isn't a dating profile a job application of sorts? Why should age be any more acceptable in this context?

Norms around dating have become more egalitarian. Women don't wait around for the phone to ring the way nice girls did in the 1950s, and may do the inviting or take the lead sexually. That's a great fit with the self-awareness and assertiveness that age can impart. Desire and desirability are integral to how we feel about ourselves and operate in the world. Sex improves sleep, reduces the risk of depression, and bolsters the immune system, to name a few of its benefits. People who describe themselves as healthy are more likely to be sexually active, and a healthy sex life is a predictor of longevity. Sex not only makes us feel alive, it helps us live longer. As Joan Price, the diva of senior sex and author of the book *Naked At Our Age*, put it to me, "Despite what society and the media convey, senior sex isn't icky. We have no expiration date, sexually speaking. The only reason it stops is that we let it stop. Sexual pleasure is our birthright lifelong!"

This means claiming that birthright, and being as open-minded as the people we hope to meet. Stella Grey, a self-described "mid-life ex-wife" who writes about online dating for *The Guardian*, refused to meet up with a guy who looked cute and sounded interesting and straightforward, even for a drink, because she was twice his age. If the age discrepancy were truly her only reason, I wish she'd said yes. Age has little to do with shared interests, and if they'd had chemistry and gotten naked, I bet they'd have had a fine time. Because men tend to date younger women, straight older women are at a considerable statistical disadvantage in this arena. One remedy is to be more open-minded about whose company might be fun. Lots of fun.

Try not screening for age when you're looking for a match online. It's true that people need to have compatible interests and goals and lifestyles in order for relationships to work. Men looking to start families probably aren't going to date women over forty, and may skew considerably younger just to take the let's-make-babies pressure off. Older people who've been widowed or divorced and who want to remarry are likely to have better luck with suitors near their own age. It can feel safer and more comfortable to stick to people whom you know will share your cultural and historical reference points. But it's also very restrictive. Common interests often have little to do with age. Ever watch swing dancing, for example? Couples come in all sizes, races, and genders, not to mention ages. Unless we're astrologers, why assume that birth date is the key to compatibility? Can he or she drive a truck/pay the rent/love a cat/hike a trail/find Crimea on a map?

When OkCupid declared "Love Is Blind Day" in January 2013 and removed everyone's picture from the site for a few hours, they learned something that turned all the received wisdom on its head. Messages sent during that window were more likely to get replies, and people exchanged contact information at a higher rate—with people they'd never seen a picture of. No matter which person was better looking or by how much, the percentage that rated the date positively was constant. *Attractiveness didn't matter.* As OkCupid cofounder and data-cruncher Christian Rudder observed, "People make choices from the information we provide because they *can*, not because they necessarily should."[16]

EROTIC IS FOR OLDERS

No sexually experienced person would consider eroticism the domain of youth. Music and literature are full of examples. "They say combustion's for the youngsters, but they don't know nothin' 'bout

127

it," sang Bonnie Raitt in 2002. "Anybody's got trepidation about get-ting on in years, forget about it," she told the audience in New York's Beacon Theater, saying her fifties were her best years yet.[17] The blues in particular testify to a long tradition of people feeling sexual right up to the funeral. As age scholar Margaret Gullette points out, "Cultures truly interested in pleasure don't romanticize inexperience."[18]

In her late fifties, writer Joan Nestle announced, "Gray hair and textured hands are now erotic emblems I seek out." June Arnold wrote a novel called *Sister Gin* in which Su, a middle-aged woman, falls in love with a woman in her eighties, whose age in no way dims her desire. She comes to "lust after a final different dry silken life and so much grace and elegance from all the knowledge of the day . . . There is no more beautiful word in the language than 'withered.'"[19]

Remember novelist Louis Begley's grim assessment of the "aw-ful discontents" of old age? Only six months later I was surprised and pleased to come across "Old Love," Begley's paean to his wife.[20] He describes confessing to a friend at thirty-nine his love for a young woman and his fear that it would fade if her beauty did. "Might it be displaced by a sort of repulsion? For instance, when her skin with-ers and wrinkles, will I still want to kiss the crook of her arms, those arms that I so admire, and, if gallantry pushes me to do so, will I have to avert my eyes?"

Begley's friend sensibly pointed out that he and his love would change in tandem, and that his gaze, too, would evolve. Indeed, de-spite Begley's apprehension, the "handiwork of time" has enabled him to become more worthy of the "Lady in Question," and to love her, and much else about his life, more deeply as the decades passed. At eighty, instead of becoming the "monster of indifference" of his nightmares, he finds himself delighting in the ordinary in a thou-sand unexpected ways. And yes, at eighty he and the Lady in Ques-tion are still doing the deed, and finding just as much pleasure and meaning in it. Begley persists in envisioning a time "when we will be content and grateful for being able simply to hold each other in our arms." Perhaps, but I doubt it, and Begley has proved a lousy prognosticator.

Another writer, Grace Paley, movingly described her enduring desire for her husband of many decades:

> that's my old man across the yard
> he's talking to the meter reader
> he's telling him the world's sad story
> how electricity is oil or uranium
> and so forth   I tell my grandson
> run over to your grandpa   ask him
> to sit beside me for a minute   I
> am suddenly exhausted by my desire
> to kiss his sweet explaining lips.[21]

If these depictions of late-life passion seem odd, it's only because they're so unfamiliar. As more people join the ranks, a literature will surely emerge.

In 1978, in the same pages as Begley's essay (the Sunday *New York Times* Op-Ed section), the poet May Sarton questioned what young people really know about love, especially given their tendency to conflate it with sexual passion. Love in late life may be just as intense, she noted, but different because it is "set in a wider arc, and the more precious because the time we have to enjoy it is bound to be brief." Sixty-six at the time, Sarton enjoyed another productive seventeen years despite debilitating illness, and continued to form new emotional attachments, although sex was no longer in the picture. Even then, memories can provide a potent erotic charge. So can simple touch. A seventy-six-year-old friend of mine has had a fantastic sex life, but now lusts more for tenderness. As she put it, "You can be intimate with someone in so many ways." Widowed after fifty happy years, an eighty-two-year-old woman said holding hands was what she missed most. "Somehow it's just as passionate. That touch carries with it the weight of so many memories, and many are sexual." She figured younger people "would shake their heads and think, 'poor old soul, her sex life was probably not very good.' They would be wrong!"[22]

The keys to a gratifying sex life are keeping it a priority, embracing a broader notion of the forms sex can take, and rejecting the ageist voices that equate "older" with "undesirable." When we pull that off, those voices grow fainter and, for the bold and the fortunate, other narratives replace them. I don't love the "still" in the title of Deirdre Fishel's book and documentary, *Still Doing It: The Intimate Lives of Women over Sixty,* but I do love her call to arms: "Women over sixty are still doing it—it being whatever turns them on, from doing humanitarian work to buying a dildo, from climbing Machu Picchu to having the best orgasms of their lives. Sex is so much more than an act—it's a metaphor for being alive. . . . Women of all ages, stand up! Follow your passions! Fall in love! Get laid!"[23]

That does not mean that women *should* stay sexually active, or feel deficient if they abstain. There's no such thing as "normal"—at any age—and no single standard to which we should hold ourselves, especially as we grow more confident in our self-knowledge and diverse in our desires. There are myriad paths to feeling desired and cherished. If you don't feel like ramping up for sex any more, it's *totally* fine, as long as it's okay with you. This is a time to check in with yourself. Some women lose interest, and some men are glad not to be led around by their dicks anymore. It can feel great to turn that energy elsewhere—to let the whole thing go—if that's your choice. People can have satisfying intimate relationships in which sex is no longer important, or perhaps never was.

It's totally fine to let the whole sex thing go, if that's your choice.

Germaine Greer was just one of many feminists to call for women to celebrate old age as a time of liberation from the tyranny of the male gaze and the "shackles of sexuality."[24] Opting out can bring comfort, peace, and more time and energy to devote to people and pursuits that matter more, especially for straight women without partners. Millions of widows decide that caring for one mate to the end was enough, and settle happily into single lives, solo sex, and the pleasures of caring for children at a grandparental remove. Others are doing their part to put "GILF" into the lexicon alongside "MILF."

SEX CHANGES ALONG WITH OUR BODIES

In my twenties, I thought I was having the best sex ever and that older people weren't having any at all. Silly me. Those fast and frequent fumblings are not the memories I cling to. Sex centered on penetration, although its role in female pleasure is considerably exaggerated, but I didn't know that at the time. Both by choice and of necessity, sex and arousal change over time. These changes tend to be met with silence, panic, and meds. They can be addressed with pills, lube, and other medical products, each of which can be enormously helpful. In the long run it's even more important to look differently at what constitutes sex. Think slow, whole-body, playful.

Libido tends to diminish with age, and close to 40 percent of people over seventy report physical issues, primarily erectile issues for men and vaginal dryness for women. True erectile dysfunction is rare, but just about every man experiences erectile dissatisfaction—because his penis isn't performing the way it did at eighteen. It was a bad day when I was diagnosed with periodontal disease and vaginal thinning in the same morning. Floss and the yellow Listerine that tastes like kerosene are doing the trick above the waist, and an Estring—a silicone ring worn in the vagina that releases a low dose of estrogen—does the job below. Postmenopausal thinning and shrinking of vaginal tissue—terrifyingly dubbed *vaginal atrophy,* yikes!—along with reduced blood flow and less flexible pelvic-floor muscles can make sex excruciating for women. These conditions are treatable with lube and massage, although you don't hear much about that because the remedies are inexpensive and the market considered negligible.

Physiological changes mean recalibrating fundamental notions of what sex consists of. That doesn't mean trading down. What matters most is figuring out how we feel about our sexuality, what we need and want, and communicating those expectations and desires to our partners. Age and experience ought to make us better at that, and at deciding which accommodations feel right and which don't.

Getting hard (for men) and getting wet (for women) stop being reliable measurements of arousal. Action often precedes arousal, not the other way around. "Women who think they need to be in the mood to have sex might in fact need to have sex to be in the mood! In other words, just do it!" Joan Price advises. Older genitals need more stimulation to get aroused and more time to reach orgasm. People have to prioritize sex and remember to be sexual. It takes effort and work; it's a process. This isn't unromantic, it's realistic, and it's as true of tired parents of toddlers as it is of their parents and grandparents.

Men feel hugely vulnerable about getting hard, but sex doesn't have to involve erections, or orgasms. Nor do orgasms require erect penises. Women's sexuality is more broadly based in the body than men's, and more fluid. For most, intercourse becomes less important over time relative to kissing and intimate touch, another reason to reprioritize intercourse. As we age, focusing on arousal serves us better, women in particular. Masturbating is a way to stay sexually active and care for ourselves; it keeps nerves firing and tissues healthy, and can be private or a shared pleasure. Outercourse, an umbrella term for any kind of lovemaking that doesn't involve penetration, has a lot to offer. Lovemaking lasts longer. There's more space for communication. For new lovers, it's a way to build trust and learn each other's landscapes. For longtime lovers, it's a way to go back in time (remember dry-humping?) and to expand the repertoire. Women, too, often enjoy less goal-oriented sex, especially the 75 to 80 percent who have difficulty climaxing via intercourse. The shift in emphasis makes some women *more* orgasmic.

At any age, partners need to ask for what they want—or don't want—whether it's porn, or a sex toy, or kissing all afternoon. Keep lube handy, and don't be shy about reaching for it. Go down on her if your dick isn't behaving itself. Adapting to changing bodies can be a catalyst for erotic exploration. That's why many men and women with spinal cord injuries report more adventuresome sex lives, and why so many sexually active olders say they're enjoying it more than ever. Good sex requires knowing our bodies and expressing our desires. Life tends to makes us better at both.

BEAUTY AND FASHION ARE SOCIAL CONSTRUCTS—WE MAKE THEM UP

Compare the unforgiving spandex and short shorts of today to fashions in colonial America, where old age was not shunned but exalted. Relatively few people achieved it, and older men held the reins. They wore white wigs and stiff frock coats, and stockings that exposed their calves: styles that flatter the older body. No short shorts here! Styles changed, and will change again as markets and trends demand. The point is that fashion represents values that are malleable.

The enormously popular *Advanced Style* blog shows that style is anything but the domain of the young. The success of the book based on the blog inspired journalist Mireille Silcoff to write, "Scratch the surface of youth culture, and a kind of Eldertopia is revealed."[25] "I wear your granddad's clothes, I look incredible," say the lyrics of "Thrift Shop" by rap duo Macklemore and Ryan Lewis. *Fabulous Fashionistas*,[26] a TV documentary on Britain's BBC4 about six genuinely fabulous women with an average age of eighty, for whom fashion is a way of being fully in the world, went viral upon being posted to YouTube in November 2013. Comments and captions were all variations on the idea that a benefit of aging is the confidence to wear what you like instead of dressing to be trendy or to please others. That's the essence of collective resistance on the fashion front: rejecting the notion of "mutton dressed as lamb" and dressing to suit our shapes, our styles, and our senses of self.

Nonagenarian style icon Iris Apfel graced the cover of fashion magazine *Dazed* (formerly *Dazed & Confused*) in 2013, rockin' the look in Comme des Garçons' Rei Kawakubo. As Sarah Ditum commented in *The Guardian,* the trend upends some preconceptions in a modeling industry that encourages twenty-year-old aspirants to knock a few years off their ages. That's despite the fact that women between ages fifty-five and seventy-four spend the most on clothes. "We perpetually tell ourselves beauty is youth and youth beauty, and fashion is about beauty, so it must be for the young. That's a funny sort of disservice we do to ourselves, because the practical experience for a lot of women is that getting older is actually pretty wicked."[27] (As in "wicked good.")

Older models remain a tiny minority, but demand is growing, with Ellen DeGeneres as the face of CoverGirl, Diane Keaton fronting for L'Oreal, and the dames of *Downton Abbey.* Known for their provocative ads, in 2014 American Apparel used sixty-two-year-old, gray-haired Jacky O'Shaughnessy to model lingerie with the tag line "Sexy has no expiration date," and didn't Photoshop her neck and midriff into wrinkle-free perfection. The Helen Mirrens and Judi Denches of the world are forging a footpath that needs to become a highway.

PUSH BACK!

REJECT ANTI-AGING RHETORIC

The next time you see a product touting its anti-aging prowess, remember that what "anti-aging" really means is "anti-living." In my twenties I read an article in a fashion magazine that counseled smiling less so fewer marks of happiness would be etched on my face. Who wants to live in a world that discourages smiling? Yet that message has only gotten louder. The global market for anti-aging products and services surpassed $291 billion in 2015.[28] American girls are sexualized at age eight and ushered over the hill two decades later. In an ageist, lookist, and highly visual culture, worries kick in ever younger, with the mantra about cosmetic procedures becoming "intervention early and often," to freeze the blank face before it can tell any stories. Twenty-somethings are spending thousands on chemical peels and dermal fillers so the ring-bedecked hand in their engagement selfie looks appropriately plump and perfect.[29] To add injury to insult, with Kim Kardashian blazing a trail, beauty ideals are becoming more and more unnatural.

It's tempting to ridicule this absurd insecurity, but what really deserves our attention are the destructive cultural forces behind it. Sexism and capitalism, anyone? Who says wrinkles are ugly and curves unattractive? The multi-billion-dollar skin care and weight loss industries. You can't make money off satisfaction, but shame and fear create markets that advertisers and marketers exploit. We're being sold a bill of goods and paying the price, both in our wallets and in diminished confidence in our bodies as a never-ending source of pleasure.

UNSHACKLE YOUR VIEW OF ATTRACTIVENESS FROM THE PLASTIC "PERFECTION" PROMOTED BY THE MEDIA AND THE BEAUTY INDUSTRY

Age and beauty can and do coexist. "Farewell to Youth but Not Beauty" was the title of a piece in the Style section of the Sunday *New York Times*. The occasion was the launch of a new line of lipsticks from MAC Cosmetics inspired by Iris Apfel, recognizable by her heavy round glasses and trademark dark red and scarlet lipsticks. The new line sold out in just a few days, and my blog post about it reminded Kelly, a sex therapist who'd just turned fifty, of a book called *How Not to Look Old*. "It's full of tips like 'wear soft pink, shimmery lipstick, so it doesn't draw attention to your wrinkled mouth.' And it's true, it really works," Kelly commented. "That got me wondering at what point will I stop caring about not looking my age and just wear what I like?"

Maybe never. Maybe that would signal defeat, maybe victory. Kelly has since gone gray, and she looks gorgeous. That book *is* right about the lipstick, damn it. Sometimes I reach for a gentler color, and sometimes I reach for the red. It looks fantastic when I've bleached my whole head white, as I occasionally do. The goal? Quoting Margaret Gullette: "Enticements to look younger—like enticements to look whiter, or thinner, or anything other could finally be rejected as bigotry." It happened with "Black is beautiful," which was coined in the 1960s and became a rallying cry of the civil rights movement. The slogan was intended to validate African American culture and beauty by challenging the white/European aesthetic that dark skin and nappy hair and African American facial features were inherently unattractive, and to counter the practice of people with lighter skin attempting to "pass" as white. The practice of attempting to "pass" as younger is equally self-destructive, and challenging the notion that old = ugly is no more farfetched an ideal.

As feminist philosopher Amia Srinivasan points out, slogans like "Black is beautiful" and the "Big is beautiful" mantra of the fat-acceptance movement aren't intended only to empower. They challenge us to rethink our values. "The question posed by radical self-love movements," she writes, "is whether there is a duty to transfigure, as best we can, our desires."[30] No longer at *Jezebel*, Lindy West has described staring at parts of bodies she had always reviled on herself, like fat rolls and arm fat, consciously deciding to find them beautiful, and learning that it worked.[31] Want to change the way you see people, whether they're old or fat or trans? Work at it. Desire is not innate and it is not immutable. Seeing differently is a radical ask indeed, a collective act of reimagining and the work of a lifetime. It is both necessary and possible. Otherwise we perpetuate bias, oppression, and exclusion.

Seeing the face in the mirror as alien may be the most universal manifestation of internalized ageism. Instead of muttering, "What the hell happened?" how about taking a minute to recall some of the things that did happen, and how remarkable a lot of them were? That crease between nose and lip? Actress Frances McDormand grins as she credits her son Pedro for the one on the left side of her face, etched by twenty years of going, "Wow!" or "Oh my God."[32] Calling her face a map, she rejects the surgery that would erase her history.

My hands now recall my mother's on the steering wheel of her Chevy Bel Air station wagon, carting her four kids around. What's wrong with my knobby white knuckles? Absolutely nothing. Getting older has made me a lot more forgiving of my physical shortcomings, and that is *really* welcome. Buns of steel they ain't, but I look down in the shower at bits that once tormented and think, "Not bad!" I sure never thought I'd be going strong so long after my "sell by" date, and I'm hoping many more women come to the same conclusion. Men too.

Instead of detaching from our aging bodies, why not marvel at the way they change throughout the life course—or at least learn to accept it without censure?

Instead of shelling out for costly "remedies," why not call out the medical-industrial complex for medicalizing these natural transitions? Why not insist on non-frumpy fashions that flatter the older body—don't forget the shoes!—and reward those in the industry who use models of all sizes and ages?

Why not, above all, learn to look more generously at each other as well as at ourselves? In a piece in *The New York Times* called "The Case for Laugh Lines," Dominique Browning bemoaned the "weird, collective, late-onset body dysmorphia" that compels so many to freeze or ruin their faces with a needle or a

> **Why not, above all, learn to look more generously at each other as well as at ourselves?**

scalpel. Yet at the end of the piece she did a complete 180, reneging on any effort to make peace with those laugh lines. Describing herself as "a big believer in denial," Browning wrote, "It is too much to ask that we embrace our changing faces—that we celebrate our mother's beauty in our own graying hair, that we remember the joy that created those laugh lines, that we recognize our father's forehead in the way ours wrinkles when we are perplexed, or we catch a glimpse of our aunt's eyes when our own crinkle with delight."[33]

It's a tall order, yes, but hardly too much to ask. Why *shouldn't* we take pleasure in those associations, and the shared memories they represent? You and I can choose where we find beauty, and we needn't stop at twenty-two. "There's so much going on!" writes *Huffington Post* blogger Chuck Nyren about older women's bodies. Unlike their younger counterparts, which he describes as "unfinished, incomplete," older bodies offer "contours aplenty, shapes galore, curves, mounds, crannies, sections soft, hard, comfy to hold. . . . Afterward, you think about what you've missed, what you didn't quite get to. There'll always be something new to play with, pinch, brush against the next time."[34] Why does that seem so damn radical? If we can readily see beauty in weathered wood or a tulip exploding as its petals dry, why not in rounded bellies and smile-etched faces and work-worn hands? Sex never stops sustaining us, and beauty is everywhere.

CONSIDER A WIDER RANGE OF SEXUAL AND ROMANTIC POSSIBILITIES

Sexuality is less about appearance than we think. Scan our acquaintances for those who are sexually active and it's immediately apparent that prettiness is not the common denominator. Their lovers have responded to warmth, to interest, to sexual energy, perhaps to an invitation—which does mean risking rejection. Too often older women don't project sexual energy because they're worried about their imperfections. Of course men care about how women look, but they're way less likely to be thinking, "Gee, I wish her boobs were perkier" than "I'm about to get lucky!" Any woman for whom it's a priority can stay sexually active. The same is certainly the case for men. This is even more true in body-positive, non-heteronormative, non-monogamous circles.

Being more proactive does mean thinking differently, and it doesn't work for everyone, especially for straight women open only to monogamous, committed relationships with a slightly older, good-looking, successful guy who lives nearby—King Charming, that is. Women live longer and significantly outnumber their male counterparts, and nice guys who can drive at night grow ever scarcer. Relationships change over time in real and challenging ways. Partners age differently and at different rates, which can make it harder to continue to share activities. "Till death do us part" was a far easier promise to keep a century ago, when American husbands, on average, made it only to fifty-three and their wives not much longer.

That's a big factor behind rising rates of "silver divorce." Although the rate has stabilized or dipped for other age-groups, fully one out of every four people experiencing divorce in the United States is fifty or older, and nearly one in ten is over sixty-five.[35] While widowers are more likely to determinedly seek out new partners, women already know how to operate a washing machine and are often quite content to be on their own, with friends and family for company. Women tend to be better at seeking out interests to pursue. The pleasures of wine and cheese for dinner with Netflix for company are distinct. Many, widows in particular, wonder whether they really want another mate to nurse through man-colds and worse. Yet after a lifetime of Hollywood rom-coms and smugly coupled Valentine's Days, the single life remains a dismal runner-up for many of them, even the liberated and evolved.

Why not expand our notion of what's possible, and might even be a lifestyle upgrade? Consider a friends-with-benefits relationship, typically a fun, sexual relationship between two good friends, even if just to tide you over until something more serious comes along. It needn't mean last-minute bootie calls unless that suits you both; more casual relationships should still involve mutual respect, clear agreements, and safe sex. They have to make you feel good, and there's no reason to tolerate bad behavior. There's also no reason to let outdated norms about "sluttiness" and "faithfulness" stand in the way.

Be open to how compatible a much younger companion might prove to be. A big age difference makes men less likely to feel they have to compete in the tiresome ways that patriarchy dictates. "More than ten years younger?" protested my friend Valerie. "He wouldn't know who Eisenhower was." "How much time do you spend talking about Eisenhower?" I countered. She burst out laughing and said, "Point taken." Go out with him and be prepared for a "you go, girl" or two. Yes, it takes a bit of moxie, and sure, some people will look askance, but are they the ones whose opinions really matter? In online dating, pushback against the idea of "age appropriate" is being led by younger people, whose profiles now frequently say "I like older" or "No age limits." This is the same demographic calling out the racism behind statements like "not attracted to Asians" or "No black people." They're more likely to accept gender nonconformity too. And as Mike Albo reported for AARP, "For them, age is just another limit to shatter."[36]

Why shouldn't "friends with benefits" come in all ages—as well as more serious relationships? If you've ever wondered about what it would be like to have a lover of the same sex, maybe now's the time to find out. Does a healthy, fun, sexual relationship have to be exclusive? Why not consider having a lover with the same taste in movies and another with a great sense of humor, and maybe even a third whom you look up once a year when you're at the shore?

Consider sharing, seriously. The same culture that promotes ageism also promotes a restrictive, monogamous, heteronormative, child-producing model of relationships and families. Capitalism benefits from a society of isolated, independent consumers. Sharing doesn't mean cheating; polyamory involves multiple committed relationships, with all parties aware and on board. If that's hard to contemplate between the sheets, consider how much sense it makes when it comes to the more humdrum aspects of life, like caregiving. Mightn't it be nice to have chicken-soup duty only on Tuesdays, because others are also on the job? To share the worry and apportion the logistics? To bail on the standard all-or-nothing proposition, and contribute to a network that will support you in turn, should the need arise? And to not have to relinquish those solitary pleasures? There are many different frameworks for friendship, intimacy, and love besides the mainstream, white-picket-fence, King Charming, Hollywood scenario. Longer lives offer the opportunity to explore them.

Wherever we fall on the spectrum—men and women, trans men and trans women, straight and gay, bi and bi-curious, monogamous and polyamorous, older and younger—take heart! Let's use not just what's between our legs but our brains and imaginations to explore new ways of being intimate and giving pleasure to each other. To think more broadly as sexual beings. To act more compassionately and generously, especially toward ourselves, and take that personal and political awareness out into the streets. To think more critically about the culture that profits from our biases and is jeopardized when we join forces. Look carefully before we leap, and take a chance. The odds of being rewarded are far greater than the culture has brainwashed us to believe.

CHAPTER SIX

NOT DONE YET: THE WORKPLACE

Older Americans are damned if we work and damned if we don't. If we stay on the job, we're criticized for taking jobs away from younger people. (Economists call that the "fixed lump of labor" fallacy.) If we step off the treadmill, we're branded "greedy geezers" for sucking up more than our share of resources, letting younger workers support us, and leaving nothing in the pot for the next generation's golden years. (The old-age dependency ratio rears its ugly head again.) And we're damned if we're laid off, because experience is a liability in an ageist world. Ageism handicaps younger workers too. Millennials are criticized for having no work ethic and needing their hands held, and recent graduates with no track records face higher unemployment rates than older workers.

But once out of a job, workers like Arynita Armstrong have a much harder time finding another one. "They just see gray hair and they write you off," said the sixty-year-old from Willis, Texas, who'd been looking for work since losing her job at a mortgage company five years earlier. "They're afraid to hire you, because they think you're a health risk. You know, you might make their premiums go up. They think it'll cost more money to invest in training you than it's worth it because you might retire in five years. Not that they say any of this to your face," she added.

Also quoted in this front-page article in *The New York Times* was Susan Zimmerman, who said starkly, "If I break my wrist, I lose my house."[1] The sixty-two-year-old freelance writer in Cleveland worked three part-time jobs and had pieced together a regimen of home remedies that she hoped would keep her healthy until Medicare kicked in. In order to hold on to her house she'd had to start taking Social Security benefits early, which means she'll receive 30 percent less for the rest of her life than if she'd been able to hold off till age sixty-six.

Olders who find a new job make on average 20 percent less than they'd been earning—the biggest income loss for any age-group, according to the Bureau of Labor Statistics.[2] They're also more likely to have been laid off from industries that are downsizing and more likely to have some sort of disability that limits their options. Many never regain their former standard of living, not to mention their sense of personal and professional worth. Most will live for at least another two decades. Bankruptcies are booming among older Americans, more of whom—especially low-income households—are carrying more debt in larger amounts than earlier generations.[3]

Ageism prevents older workers from finding challenging work of which they're eminently capable, and relegates them to jobs that all too often neglect to take advantage of their skills and experience—Walmart greeters, say. Those who do get hired are increasingly funneled into what a 2016 study out of the Center for Retirement Research dubbed "old-person" jobs.[4] A mix of high-skilled service work (like managers, sales supervisors, and accountants) and lower-skilled service work (like truck drivers, janitors, and nursing aides), these jobs tend to pay 6 to 11 percent less than jobs that favor younger workers. Ageism also makes it harder for olders to find part-time and volunteer positions. Discouraged and diminished, many stop looking for work entirely. Many become economically dependent, contributing to the misperception that olders are a net burden to society, but it's not by choice.

AGEIST AND BASELESS STEREOTYPES STUNT WORKERS' PROSPECTS

Every day older job seekers confront myths about their skills, health, and capacity, according to which they:

- Can't master new skills: Older workers score high in leadership, detail-oriented tasks, organization, listening, writing skills, and problem solving—even in cutting-edge fields like computer science—especially if the new task relates to a preexisting skill or knowledge base.

- <u>Aren't creative</u>: It turns out that it's being in the same job for thirty years that squelches creativity. Put that person in a new job and she'll come up with new ideas. Mixed-age teams have been shown to be highly productive in areas that require creative thinking, like R&D and marketing.
- <u>Can't handle stress</u>: Experience equips older workers to put crises in context and ride out office drama. Patience helps too. Age confers coping skills.
- <u>Slow things down</u>: Younger workers can go faster but make more mistakes. Olders may go more slowly—it depends on the nature of the task—but value accuracy. It's a wash. Output is equal and is affected far more by motivation and effort than by age.
- <u>Miss work because of illness</u>: In fact, older workers are highly reliable. This myth reflects the erroneous cultural equation of age with sickness.
- <u>Can't handle physically demanding tasks</u>: Also frequently cited as a factor in hiring and training decisions, this liability is hugely overstated and absurdly outdated. Only a small percentage of jobs today require manual labor. Older workers do take longer to recover from workplace accidents but hurt themselves less often. As always, there's enormous variation among individuals. Health and experience are far better indicators of workplace fitness than age, not least in physically demanding jobs like firefighting and airline piloting.[5]
- <u>Are burned out</u>: "Waiting for that gold watch" is as outdated a cliché as the wind-up artifact on which it's based. The General Social Survey, a longitudinal study that has interviewed over fifty thousand Americans since 1972, shows that people over sixty-five are happiest in their work. "A lot of people think of people working in their sixties and seventies as trapped in their jobs," commented Tom W. Smith, director of the survey. "Most older workers work because they enjoy their jobs."[6]

In other words, not one of the negative stereotypes that older workers confront holds up under scrutiny. Research into their strengths, which is relatively scant, shows that olders are no less motivated or reliable than their younger colleagues, nor more vulnerable to family responsibilities. Only one stereotype—that on average, they're less likely to engage in career development—has any empirical support, a finding that almost certainly reflects the fact that almost all training programs are geared toward younger employees.

Not one of the negative stereotypes that older workers confront holds up under scrutiny.

When it comes to actual job performance, older employees trounce their younger colleagues, according to Wharton professor Peter Cappelli, coauthor of *Managing the Older Worker.* "Every aspect of job performance gets better as we age," said Cappelli. "I thought the picture might be more mixed, but it isn't. The juxtaposition between the superior performance of older workers and the discrimination against them in the workplace just really makes no sense."[7] Historian David Hackett Fischer also found that, in many jobs, performance improves with age. "Workers over sixty and even over seventy are absent from work less often, have fewer accidents, work more harmoniously with others, are judged by their supervisors to be more dependable, show better judgment, and are generally superior to younger workers both in the quality and the quantity of their output," he determined.[8] Social scientists have found this to be generally the case in Europe as well.

When well-placed and well-managed, older employees are enormous assets to enterprises of all kinds. Given the central task of modern life—creating and exchanging complex information—a deep knowledge base is more valuable than ever. Veteran workers also tend to bring valuable experience to the table, as well as honed interpersonal skills, better judgment, and a more balanced perspective.

145

FOR MANY, WORKING ISN'T OPTIONAL

How are older people supposed to remain self-sufficient if we're forced out of the job market? Many workers of all ages have trouble making it from paycheck to paycheck, let alone saving for retirement. The notion that those on the older end of the spectrum are at liberty to choose whether or not to retire feels almost quaint, like the presumption that mothers of small children return to work on a whim rather than to make ends meet. Many are on the hook for their kids' college tuition or caregiving expenses for their parents, or both. The traditional pension plan has been largely supplanted by 401(k)s, which are vulnerable to the vicissitudes of the stock market, and only about half of American workers participate in an employer-based retirement plan.[9] For the postwar generation, relatively few years remain in which to recover financially from the Great Recession, and many Baby Boomers were already vulnerable. Only around 50 percent have saved enough to meet basic retirement needs into their eighties and nineties, and half don't think they'll be able to retire at all. This is certainly one reason that employment rates among people sixty to sixty-nine are higher than ever before.[10]

How are older people supposed to remain self-sufficient if they're forced out of the job market?

According to the U.S. Census, the poverty rate for Americans over sixty-five has been increasing since 2015, because of higher medical expenses among the near poor and because Social Security is lifting a smaller percentage out of poverty, 9.5 percent.[11] The National Council on Aging describes over 25 million Americans aged sixty-plus as economically insecure—living at or below 250 percent of the federal poverty level (FPL). The FPL is a meager $29,425 for a single person.[12] One stroke of bad luck can spell disaster for these older Americans, who are grappling with the rising cost of housing and healthcare, dwindling savings, food insecurity, and inadequate transportation. More accurate measures of economic well-being, including the Wider Opportunities for Women's Elder Economic Security Standard Index and the Institute on Assets and Social Policy's Senior Financial Stability Index, show millions of older adults struggling to meet their monthly expenses, even though they're not considered "poor" because they live above the long-outdated FPL. Two-thirds of single Social Security recipients aged sixty-five-plus depend on Social Security for 90 percent or more of their monthly income. Benefits in 2017 averaged just over $16,968 a year for retired workers—not exactly "greedy geezer" territory.[13] (Without Social Security income, the Department of Labor estimates that 15.3 million people aged sixty-five and over would have fallen below the poverty line in 2012, close to quadrupling the number in poverty.)[14]

The situation is significantly more dire for women, who are even less likely to have enough money saved for retirement. They're more likely than men to leave and reenter the workforce, leaving them with significantly lower Social Security benefits. They live longer, and they earn less. The effects of the gender wage gap—eighty cents for every dollar earned by male counterparts—start early and add up over time. They are further compounded by race and class, with African American women typically making only 63 cents, Latina women only 54 cents, and Native American women only 58 cents for every dollar paid to white, non-Hispanic men.[15]

Many women end up in poverty for the first time in their lives as they age into their eighties, if not before. According to a 2013 report from the National Women's Law Center, about 2.6 million older women live in poverty and 733,000 in extreme poverty, surviving on as little as $5,500 a year, or $458 a month. Among women sixty-five and older, poverty rates were particularly high for those who lived alone and for black, Hispanic, Native American, and foreign-born women.[16] Providing older Americans who cannot support themselves with decent lives will require huge social and economic shifts. It is ageism, first and foremost—the lower value this society accords its older citizens, especially those who are not white or male—that stands between us and the necessary commitments.

IT'S FAR MORE THAN THE INCOME
THAT MAKES A DIFFERENCE

Americans tend to equate working with making money, and it's hard to focus on other issues if there's no bread on the table. But having a job contributes to well-being in many other important ways, all of which matter as much to olders as they do to everyone else— women, queer people, people of color, people with disabilities— across all ages and classes.

I learned this early on, when my research focused on people over eighty in the workforce. Dr. Robert Butler founded the National Institute on Aging, and one of the things his researchers there discovered was that people who have something to get up for in the morning actually live longer and better, "as long as they have a decent and enjoyable job, which of course is not always the case," as he pointed out. In addition to a paycheck, work confers a sense of purpose, of belonging, and of social connectedness—the things many retirees say they miss most. It's easy to understand the ongoing desire to continue to work and to contribute to society.

For older men, work is often the primary source of identity and social contacts. Bill Banneker's busy professional life as a Seattle real estate broker helped keep loneliness at bay after he lost his wife. When it came to coping with the death of her first husband, "work got me out, gave me something to hang on to," television producer Ruth Friendly told me. "Work worked." It's also a cornerstone of self-esteem. Over her husband's objections, Penny Kyle got her teaching certificate renewed at Wayne State University after raising three boys. "When I started to work the second time, I just felt good getting up in the morning, being in the rush hour traffic. I had a better opinion of myself."

Natalia Tanner was the first African American woman to attend medical school at the University of Chicago and the first black pediatrician in Detroit. Which—racism, sexism, or ageism—had posed the biggest hurdle? "I think age," said Tanner. "Most people think that when you're my age (eighty-five), you're debilitated in some way, mentally or physically." Although olders are constantly fighting that perception, skills in use stay sharp. There's a strong positive association between employment after age sixty and cognitive performance. Most of this is intuitively obvious, one reason my original focus on older workers shifted to ageism itself.

Mental and physical health are deeply interrelated, and many of these men and women embodied what researchers call the "healthy worker effect": the consistent tendency for the actively employed to have lower rates of illness and injury than the population at large, at any age.[17] As a kid, lighting designer Imero Fiorentino used to go see Arturo Toscanini conducting the NBC Symphony Orchestra live. "He would walk from the wings stooped over, small steps, but when he got up on the podium, he moved like a kid! I find myself doing the same thing," said Fiorentino. "I save my energy, but when I get in the studio, I move like the speed of light."

Work we love can actually keep us alive. Fanita English was semi-retired from her career as an acclaimed psychoanalyst when she was badly burned in a kitchen accident. She left the hospital with Oxycontin and Vicodin addictions that she hid even from her daughter, and moved into an assisted-living facility in San Mateo. "I came here to die," she said. In the spring, the phone rang. It was the very proper director of an institute in Germany berating her for dropping off the face of the earth. "'You're in the June program.' And click." English suddenly thought, "Well, maybe I can make it in June." She went cold turkey from the painkillers, made the conference, and picked up her career where it had left off.

I met almost fifty workers in their eighties and nineties who did everything from cutting hair and waiting tables to coaching singers and running PR firms. Story after story confirmed the myriad benefits of employment, social contact above all, and the capacity to remain professionally capable and engaged in late life. We pay a huge price, individually and as a society, because so many people are prevented from doing so.

OLDER WORKERS *DO NOT* TAKE JOBS
AWAY FROM YOUNGER ONES

The reasoning that older workers necessarily profit at the expense of younger ones seems logical, and people of all ages and political persuasions buy into it. "I am appalled at older workers who hang on to their jobs so they can live lavish lifestyles, while young workers trying to support families are left with lack of advancement or even laid off because they don't have tenure," wrote "Disgusted in Columbus, Ohio" to Dear Abby.[18] Forget lavish. As Abby pointed out in her response, many people are working longer simply to survive.

Summarily laid off at sixty-seven after twenty-two years as a bench chemist for a hospital equipment company, Peg Whittemore figured there was no point in objecting. "Companies will look for people who are getting to the end of their career agewise, because they can probably bring someone else in who can do just about the same thing for about half the salary," said Whittemore. "It was a shock of course. And yet you know there's a good logic for it." Not necessarily. New workers and older ones typically have different skill sets. Older workers are indeed likely to command larger salaries, but inexperienced hires need to be trained, which is expensive, then they're likely to ask for raises, and turnover is higher. Retaining older workers reduces turnover costs, which increase significantly when the move is unexpected.

Nor do older workers typically clog the promotion pipeline. According to a 2016 report by the Associated Press–NORC Center for Public Affairs Research, for example, 58 percent of people age fifty and over who planned to keep working also planned to switch careers or employers.[19] When older workers do stick around, of course it can affect the upward mobility of younger workers. Academia, where jobs are few and tenure guarantees permanent employment, is a case in point. It's not easy to balance legitimate seniority—the greater knowledge and experience of older employees—with the ambition of younger ones to rise through the ranks. Instead of working toward equitable solutions, though, companies exploit the problem by pitting older and younger employees against each other, as early twentieth-century manufacturers did with workers of different races or nationalities and as Walmart and Amazon do today with union and nonunion employees. In an ageist and capitalist society, where corporate profits come first, these tactics go unchallenged.

The problem is structural: There aren't enough jobs. Here's an analogy from poverty expert Mark Rank, who compares economic rank to a game of musical chairs with eight chairs and ten players. Who's most likely to stay standing when the music stops? The slower and less adept. That explains only who loses, though, not why there are losers in the first place. That happens because of the way the game is organized: There are too few chairs. Being old or young or disabled puts people at higher risk of joblessness and poverty. But the underlying issue is the failure of economic and social institutions to provide enough "chairs" for everyone who needs to sit down.[20] High unemployment rates aren't a "too many old people" problem; they're a labor market problem.

The amount and nature of work is not fixed. Otherwise the expansion of the female workforce in the twentieth century would have put hordes of men on the street, for example, but it didn't. If the job market is strong, which is a big if, workers of all ages benefit. Having more salaries generates more tax revenue; seasoned talent is valuable; and it's not a zero-sum proposition. Older people are job creators. According to a 2012 Pew Charitable Trust report, "Evidence suggests that greater employment of older persons leads to *better* [emphasis added] outcomes for the young—reduced unemployment, increased employment, and a higher wage."[21] It's not only that older workers don't crowd out younger ones; they also increase employment among the young in many ways. As bigger earners, they can afford to buy more products produced by the young. They may be business owners who employ younger workers. And of course they pass along valuable skills.

An aging population also means unprecedented opportunities for innovative kinds of jobs that involve intergenerational collaboration. Older workers are typically better at seeing the big picture and can draw on institutional knowledge, while youngers are likely to have an edge when it comes to spotting new trends and integrating technology. Every generation points fingers at the one that preceded it, but an ageist culture fosters competition instead of encouraging collaborations that benefit employers and workers. And although younger people are usually less affected by age discrimination in the workplace, it's in their enlightened self-interest to fight it. Distant though it may seem to a college student, age forty, the age at which legal remedy becomes available, isn't that far off.

Pitting workers against each other also fails the commonsense test. It's not as though our lives and financial obligations are contained by generational moats. Children inherit. Grandparents exhaust their savings, or help with tuitions. A Social Security check makes everyone in the household more financially secure. People with steady incomes help unemployed family and friends stay afloat. Independent of age and biology, tribes and networks support us all.

Pitting younger and older workers against each other also fails the commonsense test.

AGE DISCRIMINATION COSTS COMPANIES, AND IT'S ON THE RISE

There's a grim lesson to be learned from American slavery. The market price of slaves peaked at age thirty-five but remained high into their late seventies, evidence of their lifelong value in the labor force.[22] Modern-day age discrimination affects productivity and profits. When olders are forced out or encouraged to accept early retirement, companies lose some of their best workers and irreplaceable institutional memory. After Hurricane Sandy devastated the East Coast in

October 2012, what saved New York City hundreds of millions of dollars and brought the subway system back to life extraordinarily fast? The historical knowledge of Metropolitan Transportation Authority engineers and track workers and carpenters, many of whom had spent their entire working lives keeping this vast system running. Meanwhile, youngers mobilized Occupy Sandy, helping families dig out after the storm and carrying food and water up twenty flights to olders trapped in high-rises without power. Companies and communities need this full range of skills and abilities.

An organization that does not discriminate (on any basis, including gender, race/ethnicity, age, favoritism, sexual orientation, religion, and language) isn't just a better place to work, it's one that works better. As David C. Wilson wrote in the *Gallup Business Journal*, "When older workers face discrimination, everybody loses."[23] If their workplace is age-diverse, older workers are the most likely to be happier overall, and the most loyal. Enlightened employers understand the value of an intergenerational workforce and want staff members who can easily connect with customers in all demographics. (This isn't to imply that younger employees should handle tech accounts while olders sell condos in Florida. Female customers don't require female salespeople nor Asian people Asian ones, and it would be foolish, not to mention illegal, for employers to assume otherwise.) Smart managers don't want to come up short when a project calls for a range of talents and backgrounds, and know that an age-diverse team is most likely to deliver it.

My BFF Virginia, an expert in workplace diversity, told me about the "shoe test." Look under the table, and if everyone's wearing the same kind of shoes, you've got a problem. Diversity isn't just an abstract idea or an ethical marker. It makes us more empathic and broadminded, reflects the world around us, and better equips us to participate in global culture. Smart and ethical employers know that, although far too many need reminding that age, too, is a criterion for diversity.

Even if companies don't care about age bias, it puts them at risk for lawsuits, which are on the rise as older Americans increase in number and seek longer careers. The workplace is where many people, men in particular, first become aware of age discrimination which the U.S. Equal Employment Opportunity Commission (EEOC) defines, broadly, as "treating someone (an applicant or employee) less favorably because of his age." Whether it involves hiring, promotions and raises, or layoffs, age discrimination in employment is illegal. Women experience more of it, and earlier. (Seventy-two percent between the ages of forty-five and seventy-four think people face age discrimination at work, compared to 57 percent of men in the same age range.[24]) The EEOC is fielding an increasing number of claims as Baby Boomers enter their sixties and workers at the top of their game find themselves being shown the door and unable to open a new one.

Fifty years ago, Senator Claude Pepper introduced the Age Discrimination in Employment Act (ADEA) to challenge the stereotype that older people are worth less than younger people, and therefore not entitled to the same fundamental rights. It's that basic. Passed in 1967, not long after the Civil Rights Act, the legislation was part of that decade's wave of antidiscrimination measures. It differs from the others, though, as well as from the Americans with Disabilities Act of 1990, because ADEA cases don't allow compensatory or punitive damages. It was intended to protect both employees and job applicants over forty, a standard established almost a century ago, in 1929.

Although a multigenerational workforce is the way of the future, job seekers are reporting discrimination kicking in significantly earlier. A TV sitcom called *Younger* debuted in March 2015. It follows a newly single mom who revitalizes her career by passing herself off as a twenty-something. She's forty. Her peers have been getting Botox and hair transplants in Silicon Valley, where in 2007 Facebook CEO Mark Zuckerberg famously told an audience at Stanford University that "young people are just smarter." In a *New Republic* article titled "The Brutal Ageism of Tech" by Noam Scheiber,

San Francisco cosmetic surgeon Seth Matarasso, who says he's the world's second-biggest dispenser of Botox, described a patient base that had morphed from sagging spouses in late middle age to guys saying things like, "Hey, I'm forty years old and I have to get in front of a board of fresh-faced kids. I can't look like I have a wife and two-point-five kids and a mortgage."[25] That's grotesque.

The Bay Area's extreme obsession with youth is no more palatable than the standard-issue bias against people with dark skin or a vagina or who use a wheelchair. Yet it wasn't until people at the top of the food chain—smart, skilled, straight, well-paid, nondisabled white guys in their thirties—experienced discrimination for the first time that ageism in tech began to garner some well-deserved attention.

NOT THAT AGE DISCRIMINATION IS EASY TO PROVE

Although discrimination in hiring is probably the most common form of workplace discrimination, it's the least understood and it's hard to prove. Unfortunately, when it comes to age there are many ways to discriminate with great subtlety. Detection is elusive, prosecution even more so. And when times are tough, labor market disruptions make it more difficult to discern actual discrimination from cutbacks that affect olders and youngers equally.

Even as age discrimination is becoming a high-profile issue, it's gotten harder and harder to win a lawsuit. The most recent setback was a 2009 Supreme Court ruling, *Gross v. FBL*, that older workers must show that age was the decisive factor in their firing, not merely a contributing factor—effectively increasing the burden of proof and establishing what *The New York Times* called "an ultrahigh hurdle."[26] That's a higher standard than the standards for a race or sex claim, which are spelled out in the 1964 Civil Rights Act, at which time Congress was reluctant to include age as a protected category. Because of this ruling, hundreds of cases have been dismissed. "Many people also seem to agree . . . that unlike racism, which is inherently wrong, there is something natural about the old making way for the young." So observed journalist and lawyer Adam Cohen in a *New York Times* op-ed piece titled, "After 40 Years, Age Discrimination Still Gets Second-Class Treatment."[27] "To be rejected on account of old age may or may not feel the same as being rejected on the basis of race or sex," Cohen concluded. "But it is clearly unjust and dehumanizing, and the law should take it more seriously than it does."

Justice Sandra Day O'Connor set age apart, writing that old age "does not define a discrete and insular minority because all persons, if they live out their normal life spans, will experience it." This makes ageism and its consequences harder to isolate. But as Margaret Cruikshank points out in *Learning to Be Old*, not only do older persons constitute a minority of the general population, there's no comfort in the fact that they escaped unfair treatment when they were young. All discrimination is inherently wrong. The fact that anyone can become its victim does not make ageism more excusable. The right to work as long as we are able is a fundamental one. Invoking Anatole France's comment that equality before the law means that sleeping under a bridge is equally forbidden to the rich and to the poor, David Hackett Fischer writes, "A free society must recognize the individuality of its members; it must respect their differences as well as their similarities. It must attempt to enlarge their autonomy by promoting freedom of choice—freedom to choose work or retirement."[28] We need to support those who want to work longer, and also support those who cannot, along with their care partners.

The tide may be turning. In March 2017, a bipartisan group of senators introduced a bill written in response to the 2009 Supreme Court ruling and designed to make it easier for workers to prove they were victims of age discrimination.[29] A few weeks later, the EEOC won a landmark judgment for $12 million, its largest age-discrimination case in three decades, against Texas Roadhouse, a national, Kentucky-based restaurant chain. (Among the evidence the agency presented were job applications from thirty-eight restaurants in twenty states, on which company officials posted yellow stickers with comments. Besides "Old 'N Chubby" they included "OLD," "little older lady," and "middle age . . . Doesn't really fit our image.")[30] Affirmative action is mandated by the federal government if women or minorities are underrepresented. Why not apply it to older workers as well?

FOR BETTER AND FOR WORSE, "RETIREMENT" IS BECOMING OBSOLETE

During the Industrial Revolution, early retirement became a mark of achievement. As lives grew longer, people chose to work less. Societies that could afford it were considered more advanced. A comfortable retirement was a sign of social status. Near riots in France in 2010 at the prospect of raising the retirement age attest to the staying power of this social construct. Yet in view of longer healthy lives, the needs of the next generation, inadequate savings, and the benefits of ongoing engagement, the aspiration to retire at the traditional age of sixty-five is ill suited to an aging world.

A later retirement age suits people with good health and work they like, but not those hungrily eyeing their La-Z-Boy recliners or those whose jobs have taken a physical toll. Retirement is often a necessity for those Americans who spent decades on assembly lines or in coal mines. Today, though, the vast majority of older workers are employed in the education and health sectors, which can be less physically demanding. Social Security no longer penalizes those who continue to earn. Workers who delay collecting Social Security (up to age seventy) receive "delayed retirement credits" that increase their benefit when they do retire.

The concept of fixed retirement at a certain age is nearing obsolescence. More older people are staying in the job market and expanding the definition of "working age" in the process, a welcome development. That was true before the economy tanked, at which point four out of five Boomers had already declared their intention to keep working and earning in retirement—if it can still be called retirement.[31] Some older workers never step down from full-time employment. At the other end of the spectrum, many are laid off or forced to retire and can't find new jobs. Yet others retire, then return to the workforce. Or retire and pack their schedules with volunteer activities. The vast majority aspire to a work life that bridges the gap between career-building and collapse—a meaningful, part- or flextime way to continue to contribute, whether at home, at church, in the office, or in Sub-Saharan Africa.

A postretirement career, once a contradiction in terms, has gone mainstream. Encore.org's Marc Freedman has popularized the phrase "encore career" and declared the nature of what it means to grow older in America to be "under radical revision. For a long time the dream in this country was liberation from labor. Now it's becoming a dream around the freedom to work."[32] Encore careers are designed to help people transition from the corporate sector to meaningful work in areas like education, the environment, and public service—fields that satisfy an often long-deferred desire to make the world a better place. It's a great model for experienced professionals.

Self-employed professionals enjoy a huge advantage in deciding when to step down and on what basis. The first female resident in ophthalmology at the Manhattan Eye, Ear, and Throat Hospital, Eleanor Faye built a remarkable legacy in the field of low vision—the rehabilitation of people who are visually impaired. Faye stepped down from surgery in 2002, at age seventy-nine, after a very successful cataract operation. "I was walking on Sixty-Fourth Street toward my office, and I suddenly said to myself, 'That's the last case I am going to do. I've had a stellar career, and I'm going out when I'm still on top.'" As competent as ever, Faye has been happily assisting her associate and taking care of her patients' postoperative needs ever since. Likewise physician Billy Kyle, who figured he'd done enough operations and wanted a less hectic life. He kept his hand in doing general practice, though, because, he said, "I think if you don't use it, you lose it."

Harold Burson set up shop after dispatching an employee to the New York Public Library to look up all the listings under "publicity" and "public relations" in the 1947 Yellow Pages. It listed over five hundred people, "and a lot of them were newspaper reporters like me, or men who'd been public information officers for some military unit." Burson figured there was room for one more, and founded what became one of the largest public relations companies in the world, Burson-Marsteller. At sixty-seven, "absolutely at my peak," Burson stepped down as CEO, but continued to work a thirty-five-hour week as chairman emeritus. At eighty-seven he remained an immensely valuable employee, and his clear-eyed pragmatism continued to stand him in good stead. "Since I'm no longer the CEO, the one thing I have to do to retain my position is to keep my mouth shut," Burson explained. "I watch people make what I think are mistakes and say, 'They'll learn from it.' That's an art, a real art, 'cause this is my baby that they're sticking pins into."

Faye, Kyle, and Burson are the success stories, the olders who went out on their own terms and catapulted confidently into a satisfying next stage. Few people have as balanced a sense of their options as Burson did, not to mention his autonomy. Many who retire continue to identify themselves with jobs they once held because of the status they conferred, and many underestimate the less obvious benefits of having somewhere to show up on a regular basis. Social scientists asked a whole cohort of decently compensated early retirees from a German company a simple question: Would you like to go back to work? An average of a year into early retirement, 85 percent said yes. As Ursula M. Staudinger, director of the Columbia Aging Center, put it, "It turns out that it's very hard to estimate the value of work before we lose it. And it's probably true across industrialized nations."[33] Respondents missed the social contacts and the structure of their day-to-day routines, but were also very specific about what type of work they wanted, and about the need for more autonomy and shorter shifts.

Accommodating older workers benefits all workers.

Many older Americans are unprepared, both psychologically and financially, for the transition from employee to retiree. "I think many people do more work to plan a trip than they do to plan their retirements," said retirement expert Stan Hinden, whose plans unraveled when his wife was diagnosed with Alzheimer's.[34] Life can get in the way of the best-laid plans. Longer lives complicate matters further, because people are going to have to work longer to fund them. Whether by choice or out of necessity—which may coincide but often do not—Hinden and other older workers are reversing historic retirement trends. People who are the same age can function very differently, and capacity should trump chronology. That variation, of course, makes it even harder to wield the blunt instrument of public policy fairly, and the shifting landscape of retirement doesn't help.

Neither does the fact that companies need to plan well and spend money in order to accommodate older workers. Accessibility is key, and requires installing equipment like electric doors and ergonomic furniture. When these are available to everyone, all workers benefit; that's why it's called universal design. It reduces the stigma associated with needing "special" arrangements and becomes "normal." Other potential accommodations, which likewise benefit other employees, include workplace wellness programs with geriatric mental health components; absenteeism management programs that support caregiving for people of all ages; and employer support for end-of-life discussions and planning.

Along with being respected and having their contributions valued, older workers want to be able to adapt their roles and responsibilities. According to the Sloan Research Network on Aging & Work, their top priority is workplace flexibility, defined as some choice and control on the part of employees and their supervisors over when, where, and how work gets done. Phased retirement is a middle path that allows reduced work hours, more flexible work hours, and maybe even collecting retirement benefits, all in exchange for a smaller paycheck.

Yet few companies have implemented the workplace modifications and flextime arrangements that would best fit the needs of a graying workforce and enable them to make the most of it. Much workforce policy, in both government and the private sector, is oriented toward the full-time employees, despite the fact that contract and part-time jobs are becoming more the norm for *all* workers. Many pension plans and Social Security regulations effectively disallow gradual retirement options, although the AARP Best Employers for Workers over 50, and the Sloan When Work Works Awards show the potential of win-win solutions, especially for those with caregiving responsibilities, when it comes to workplace flexibility. Workers with more control over their schedules report higher satisfaction and better work-life balance. Companies with formal flexibility programs retain current talent, increase productivity, and gain a recruiting tool.

UNPAID WORK IS WORK

Almost all older men and women are productive in the larger sense of contributing something to society, working without pay for churches, hospitals, charities, schools, and other organizations, or helping friends and family with childcare, office and housework, and carrying out a thousand other tasks outside the formal workforce that save money or help others earn it. Olders are also an enormous source of consumer spending and economic productivity. Much of this contribution goes unrecognized.

The distinction between paid and unpaid work is important, but both have value. The omission of unpaid work from our national accounting contributes to the widely held belief that olders don't carry their weight financially—a belief that the MacArthur Study of Successful Aging calls "wrong and unjust in several ways: the measures of performances are wrong; our society doesn't count a great deal of productive activity; the playing field is not level; older men and women aren't given an equal chance for paying jobs; and millions of older people are ready, willing, and able to increase their productivity, paid and voluntary."[35]

Measures of productivity need revising, not least because they omit much menial, unpaid work done by women. As Dr. Butler had to explain to me early on in this project, just taking care of yourself is being productive, "because no one else is taking care of you. Of course if you're paying somebody else to take care of you, you're offering them employment." Paradoxically, as Margaret Cruikshank points out, older people may be engaged in the most demanding and absorbing tasks of their lives—creating a new way of being in the world—"but it won't be called 'work' unless it's paid."[36]

Lots of seventy-year-olds look in on their eighty-year-old neighbors, and eighty-year-olds on their ninety-year-old pals. Jim Lizzio lived right around the corner from where he was born in 1916, in lower Manhattan's Little Italy, and he was the go-to guy for countless neighbors in his high-rise. "Most of them are alone, crippled, can't walk," he explained. "It's 'Jimmy, get me some milk.' 'Jimmy, get me stamps.' I enjoy doing that." That's if he's not at his job as a maintenance man for an offtrack betting office, or visiting a pal in the hospital, or bringing a little something to a cousin in the nursing home. Even Lizzio's doctor had a hard time believing that he was ninety-three. "You've never met a person like me," he informed me with a grin.

True enough, but just about everyone I talked to knew someone like Jimmy. Even the more typical of the oldest old, with a daunting number of functional limitations, continue to be a source of family recipes and lore, graduation presents, and inspiration. Making a life is as important a task, and as or more difficult, than making a living. What makes it a good life toward the end is as individual as everything else about us. For some, it's being in the world like Jimmy; for others, it's repose. Movingly describing her father's transition from tool-and-dye designer to college student, writer Joyce Carol Oates pointed out that he'd gone from a "life of sheer utility" to one of "contemplation and appreciation." The wildly prolific Oates aspired to the same. Rejecting the view of an artist friend who "didn't want to live if he couldn't be productive," Oates reasoned that surely at some point it becomes enough to admire the books and plays and films and cultural works that others continue to create.[37] Supporting the arts is "useful." Cooks need eaters, authors need readers, humans need art. None of these activities are passive; all involve exchange.

PUSH BACK!

EDUCATE YOURSELF ABOUT AGE DISCRIMINATION

Learn what age discrimination looks like. The signs can include being quizzed about your retirement plans or treated differently from younger colleagues—like being excused from training programs or passed over for a promotion for someone less qualified, for example. Does your company have a pattern of hiring only younger people, even if the boss is your age or older? If you're being harassed, take detailed notes of times, witnesses, and places it occurred. They're evidence.

Know your rights, and your employer's. Don't keep quiet if you encounter a problem. If a change in health or medications makes doing your job harder, ask for accommodations—right away. If they're reasonable and you can still do your job, you're protected under the Americans with Disabilities Act. If you think you've been discriminated against, you need to file a charge with the Equal Employment Opportunity Commission or your state/county/city agency before you can sue. Check out city and state deadlines online. When in doubt, check with an employment lawyer in your state.

DON'T USE AGE AS AN EXCUSE

It's maddening to be told that we're "too qualified" for a job, or that an advanced degree is "a bit intimidating," especially in view of the experience that older job seekers bring to the table almost by definition. Why isn't hiring someone who can do an outstanding job for the money the best business decision? At best, the interviewer is being lazy and failing to take the whole person into consideration. In any case, he or she is biased. That doesn't make it okay, however, to blame being north of forty for a lack of prospects. Skills, wardrobes, and attitudes all need to be kept up to date. Being physically fit helps counteract the misperception that older workers are less productive and energetic.

A wealth of websites and organizations are dedicated to helping people find that "encore career," especially in the nonprofit sector. Organizations like AARP and the National Council on Aging offer programs to train older workers and help Boomers navigate the next phase. Show you're not a technophobe by including your LinkedIn URL on your résumé, or mentioning something you came across on the employer's Twitter feed. Don't know how Twitter works? Open an account—it's free—and start following people. I'm no natural, but Twitter has brought some key opportunities and connections my way. If you're behind on computer and software skills, go back to school. Many institutions offer online courses, but don't pass up the chance to meet people in person; networking is critical at any age. Be open to opportunities that seem unlikely, and willing to consider a position at a lower salary if it gets you back into a field that suits you. Consider part-time or short-term consulting and contract work, where there's less discrimination in hiring. Volunteer. It'll sharpen skills and provide new contacts.

CHECK YOUR OWN BIAS

If you don't like working for someone who's much younger than you, work on coming to terms with it—just as men had to do as women bosses became more common. (The same applies to a younger employee who feels uncomfortable managing someone his dad's age.) Age alone doesn't qualify or disqualify someone to be a supervisor, and someone young enough to be your grandchild could have plenty to teach you.

SPEAK UP IF YOU ENCOUNTER AGEISM IN THE WORKPLACE

In September 2015, Anne Hathaway joined the roster of Hollywood stars who have complained about ageism. "When I was in my early twenties, parts would be written for women in their fifties and I would get them," she said. "And now I'm in my early thirties, and I'm like, 'Why did that twenty-four-year-old get that part?' I was that twenty-four-year-old once. I can't be upset about it; it's the way things are."[38] I wish Hathaway had taken a page from Maggie Gyllenhaal, who went ballistic—and viral—five months earlier at being told that she was too old at thirty-seven to play the lover of a man who was fifty-five. Not just too old to be an object of desire, too old to get hired.

Age discrimination will indeed be "the way things are" until we raise our voices to challenge it. We need to work, we want to work, and it is our right, as set forth in the United Nations' Universal Declaration of Human Rights: "Everyone has the right to work, to free choice of employment, to just and favorable conditions of work and to protection against unemployment."

Because of ageism, employers consistently use age as a liability and set workers with decades of productive years ahead adrift. "It would be great if correcting that were as simple as changing a law," wrote Contributing Editor Eliot Cose in a *Newsweek* article titled "Why It Makes No Sense to Fire Older Workers."[39] "Instead, we face the more daunting task of changing ourselves." Well put, except for the "instead." Both tasks are necessary in order to overturn the barriers that older workers face, whether they're film stars or food servers.

A massive shift is already underway in the nature of work and how it is distributed. Most of the occupations that employ large numbers of workers—jobs in transportation, retail sales, and construction, for example—are easy targets for automation. Millions of people will join olders in becoming unemployable through no fault of their own. Where will the money come from to buy goods and services that are no longer produced by human labor? We need to think now about how to avert a dystopian future and develop new banking and barter systems, "smart cities," sustainable ecosystems, and solutions that work for all of humanity. Incorporating a third generation, and even a fourth one, into the workforce is only one component of solving this problem. It's going to require all hands on deck.

CHAPTER SEVEN

LONG LIFE IS A TEAM SPORT: THE INDEPENDENCE TRAP

My best friend, Virginia, has two daughters. She also has siblings and a huge network of loyal friends. Not to mention me, her BFF and co-proprietrix of the Home for Superior Women. That's where we plan to end our days, once all the men are dead, with a select cadre of other women, if anyone else meets our selective and arbitrary criteria. Nonetheless, what's her biggest fear about growing old? "Besides the wattle on the chin? I think it's being alone," Virginia says. "You know, by myself in an apartment somewhere living off cat food and television." Virginia has no cats. She concedes that the scenario improves a lot if she has Wi-fi. She also concedes that it's not rational. Yet the specter of spending our last years with only cats and TV for company haunts many of us.

ISOLATION CAN BE UNSAFE

Virginia and I can afford to locate the Home for Superior Women out of the reach of rising waters, unlike seventy-six-year-old Avgi Tzenis, whose house in Sheepshead Bay, Brooklyn, was wrecked when three feet of water and sewage swept through with Hurricane Sandy in October 2012. Tzenis had been widowed in 2012, after years of nursing her husband through dementia. Six weeks after the storm, she was still in the cold and dark without any idea how to pay for repairs. Hers is a story about poverty and infrastructure collapse and climate change, but also about the perils of social isolation.

About a third of people seventy-five and older live alone.[1] Almost half of women over seventy-five live alone.[2] Those numbers are double-edged, telling stories of self-reliance on the one hand and vulnerability on the other. Older adults who live alone feel more financially strapped than those who live with others, and somewhat more isolated.[3] Many studies show a connection between social isolation and higher rates of elder abuse. Because of ageism, social services for adults are grossly underfunded, with far too few resources allocated to ensuring that these olders are safe, warm, fed, and looked in on. Remember the European heat wave of 2003, when almost fifteen thousand people died in France alone?[4] Mortality was highest among the very old, specifically people who lived alone, didn't require medical care, had no immediate family, and stayed in non-air-conditioned apartments as cities emptied for France's hallowed August vacation period. Many bodies went unclaimed for weeks. Most of the victims of Chicago's 1995 heat wave were older too. Distinguishing between a natural disaster and a social one, sociologist Eric Klinenberg wrote, "Hundreds of Chicago residents *died alone,* behind locked doors and sealed windows, out of contact with friends, family, and neighbors, unassisted by public agencies or community groups."[5]

SOCIAL NETWORKS HELP KEEP US HEALTHY

Researchers have found all kinds of correlations between ill health in late life and feelings of being left out, isolated, and lonely. When Laura Carstensen was recuperating in that orthopedics ward, what did she notice besides lower standards of care for older patients? That the matriarchs with grandchildren on their laps recuperated far better than those who had few visitors. Olders with regular, meaningful social contacts are less likely to land in the hospital in the first place, whether from hip fractures or heart attacks, and less likely to die there.

The MacArthur Foundation Study of Successful Aging found a strong correlation between better physical function and emotional support, no matter what form it took. After a heart attack, Silicon Valley entrepreneur and octogenarian Dave Davison got involved with the Cardiac Therapy Foundation, a support network that puts recuperating patients together—"and none of them have died of heart disease," he reported. That evidence of a mind-body connection is anecdotal, but it makes intuitive sense. So does the finding that older people who remain engaged with their community are less likely to become cognitively impaired than those who don't get out and about. Isolation in itself is a risk factor for dementia, and some research says perceived isolation—feeling lonely—may be even more detrimental to health. It's a risk factor for depression and makes people less likely to look after themselves.

Although older people are more socially active than the stereotype suggests, especially if social connection is defined broadly, our circle of friends does tend to shrink as we age. Networks atrophy when we stop going to the office every day. We might move out of the home where we raised kids and away from its connection to neighbors and the community. Old friends pass away, as do spouses and siblings. "One of the terrible things about getting to my age is that my old friend Leonard is no longer here," lamented documentary filmmaker George Stoney. "Lora is in a wheelchair. Betty, my companion from the last thirty to forty years, is now, as I say, sinking into yesteryear. She's not sure that I'm George, and that is very hard." Stoney was grateful that his professional and social lives had always commingled, and that his teaching work offered a way to meet young people, including his filmmaking partner of the last decade.

Part of the trimming of the social circle is conscious, because olders tend to spend their limited time with fewer people who matter most. "It's important to use the time you have wisely," lighting designer Imero Fiorentino advised. "The present time is all I have left. I'm not sad about it." He'd stopped having casual lunches, instead contacting people he'd known over the last forty years to "put a cap on our experience together, but not in a sad way. It is a wonderful reliving of my life." That was how Fiorentino maintained key connections. A number of studies show that friendships tend to improve as people age, with olders enjoying closer ties to friends and family than most younger people, and fewer distressing relationships.

Davison felt that an important component of aging well was investing significant time in a small number of people. The person who came to mind was a guy he'd known and loved for a long time, who'd been widowed and then diagnosed with Alzheimer's. Davison visited often, until conversation was no longer possible, as did a lot of his round-robin tennis partners, who also socialized on the court. "The tennis wasn't all that good, but the conversation was tremendous," he recalled, and the friends functioned as a very informal support group. Members died, if not of heart disease then of what Davison called "other old-age problems," but they didn't die alone. Perhaps they lived longer too. A growing body of research shows that loneliness not only makes older people unhappy, it also makes them more vulnerable to illness and disease.

IT HELPS TO BE A FEMALE

Strong social-planning skills made Davison unusual for an older man. My dad, too, was highly sociable, and had a lunch or dinner date almost every weekday during the nine years between my mother's death and his own at eighty-four. (I think it helps to be a gossip.) My partner's dad, on the other hand, made it to ninety-five without ever picking up the phone to ask a pal to meet him somewhere. He was lucky to have a wife who managed their social life, although the names in Ruth's iPhone contact list dwindled to very few indeed.

Comparing contented widows to woebegone widowers on the *New York Times* "New Old Age" blog, Anne C. Roark wrote, "In a strange twist of fortune—some might call it poetic justice—age can bring with it something of a reversal in gender roles. The rise of an old girls' network, friends and family who see women through a lifetime of transitions, often contrasts sharply with the decline of the professional associations that secure young men's places in the world but offer little support or solace in later life."[6] The rise in "gray divorce" is leaving more women single, and their exes with fewer friends and less contact with family and community. Old age gives many white men, accustomed to outnumbering others in the office or the bar, their first taste of being in a minority (although this will become more common as the U.S. population continues to grow less white overall).

No doubt solitude and loss of status contribute to suicide rates three times higher among older men who aren't married. They're more prone to substance abuse, eat less well than their female counterparts, and are less likely to seek medical care without a wife to pester them. Higher divorce rates and lower birth rates in their children's generation mean that Baby Boomers have fewer grandchildren and smaller extended families than the oldest Americans now, which makes social networks more important than ever. So, men in relationships, take note: Don't leave all the care and feeding of your social network to your partner.

My manager at the Museum of Natural History figured hearing my talk would be good for her husband, who was turning fifty later that year and none too happy about it. The two discussed the talk nonstop over dinner, and Karen was a little taken aback by the message Richard had taken the most to heart. "I can go to an old people's home," he said brightly.

"What about tottering into the sunset together?" she asked, slightly crestfallen.

"Oh, I still want to do that," he assured her. "But if you die first, I can go to an old people's home." They're one of those couples in which the wife is the social planner. I'm sure Richard's deepest fear is losing his Karen; it's a very happy marriage. But on its heels was anxiety about ending up alone, living off saltines. The takeaway Richard had glommed onto was that he needn't dread the communal alternative. When we can control some of the circumstances, change itself helps keep us mentally and physically agile.

In hindsight, most people are glad they made the move into a retirement home, especially widowers who acknowledged that they'd been at risk of isolation and appreciated the new friendships that accompanied the move. Options are many, and the industry is growing fast. The term "assisted living" encompasses a bewildering variety of facilities, from small family-operated homes to large complexes. They typically provide meals, transportation, exercise, and help with daily activities like bathing, dressing, and grooming.

Nursing homes provide twenty-four-hour skilled nursing care, and their residents have more rights and are better protected by federal regulation. Nursing home use has been dropping for two decades, even among people over eighty-five, primarily due to the expansion of home and community-based services and residential care. There are good nursing homes and there are grim ones—often those run for profit. Like prisons, it's a growth industry. Staff are often underpaid and/unregulated. Unsurprisingly, the unhappiest residents are those who are lonely and abandoned, problems that reflect dismal economic and social priorities in the culture at large.

A relatively small number of Americans over sixty-five (less than 2.5 percent) live in institutional settings, 1.3 million of them in nursing homes.[7] Yet the prospect unsettles. The giant Miami Jewish Health Systems operation, where Dr. Marc Agronin is the mental health director, looks like a low-end Disney World hotel, and I'm pretty sure all that teal and taupe and ersatz Chippendale would send me over the deep end. Deep breath. Open mind. Agronin tells many moving stories of friendship and intimacy flowering in those linoleumed hallways and urges us to be less fearful and more imaginative. Referring to the widespread and prejudiced assumption that life in an "old-age home" must be wretched, he writes, "The true failure here is not old age; rather, it is the failure of our own creativity and willingness to conceive that life up until its last moments has its own ways and meanings." We don't know what it's going to be like until we get there, and it's likely to be different from what we now assume.

STAYING IN OUR HOMES CAN ISOLATE—
AND SEGREGATE

As the postwar generation starts squinting at what comes next, aging in place is gaining momentum. This movement—a range of policies and programs aimed at expanding community care for older people—enables people to live out their lives in their own homes, as most of us firmly aspire to do. For those who can afford them, options range from custom-built, pedestrian-friendly cohousing and villages with shared facilities, to "virtual" communities in which neighbors pool resources to cover anything from housekeeping and home care to cultural events and dog walking.

These setups work when supports are available in the form of household modifications to accommodate disabilities; home-delivered meals and other social services; neighbors and friends from church or mosque or temple who will check in; technology-enabled health-care delivery practices; and professional caregivers as necessary. People with fewer resources are more likely to rely on informal networks. If your goal is to live at home as independently and for as long as possible, start investigating local resources and supports now instead of waiting until "something happens." What community programs for older people are available? How's the public transportation? Who might be available for various sorts of assistance? Above all, does aging in place mean aging *in community*? Social connections contribute more than health or wealth to a good old age.

My partner's parents set a remarkable example of living life on their own terms, but as the last of their peers passed away, the same choices left them almost completely isolated. They paid no attention to our periodic suggestions that they consider moving to assisted living while able to take advantage of the facilities and make new friends. Luckily for everyone, their apartment was walker- and eventually wheelchair-friendly and easy to get to for home health aides, takeout delivery guys, and us. In 2017, at ninety-five and ninety-three, they died peacefully at home, eight days apart.

What many of us fail to consider, or refuse to, is the prospect of being homebound and spending our last years with only an aide for companionship. As Radical Age Movement founder Alice Fisher writes, "Aging in place works until it doesn't." Her dad had dementia and used a wheelchair, and emergency room visits were frequent, but Medicaid paid for an aide twelve hours a day, and her parents were able to stay in their Long Island co-op—until Hurricane Sandy compromised or eliminated all the services they depended on. Fortunately, the couple found a place at the Hebrew Home in Riverdale, New York, where Fisher's mom spent the happiest year of her final decade. "She made wonderful friends, joined in activities, began going to synagogue on Friday nights, went on shopping trips, and began to care again about what she wore and how she looked."

Fisher's dad lived in a separate part of the facility for people who need 24/7 care. Alice and her sister dreaded leaving him the night their mom died of congestive heart failure at ninety-one. Seeing that they were having a hard time, a nurse came over and pointed out a group of people hovering nearby. "They're just waiting for the two of you to leave," she gently informed them. As the two sisters waited by the elevator, they could see each of his floor mates come up and tell their dad, each in their own way, how sorry they were. "As we watched the aides help them form a circle around Dad, I turned to my sister and said, 'He's not alone.'"[8]

The nonprofit Hebrew Home is highly rated.[9] Models are changing in response to demand from the postwar generation, just as that generation changed the culture when it came to childbirth. As geriatrician Bill Thomas wrote in his book *Second Wind*, "When they came along, cigar-chomping obstetricians used to strap women down with leather restraints and pull the baby out. When the boomers got done with 'em, there were natural births, family birthing centers, midwives, lactation consultants."[10] I stole the "team sport" reference in this chapter's title from Thomas, who developed the Eden Alternative, a humane model for nursing homes that has provoked a culture shift in long-term care. The organization treats staff the way they'd like staff to treat the residents. Eden Alternative homes have plants and animals and children and nice communal spaces, and doors that close onto private rooms.

Olders who seek out communities for people aged fifty and up choose to be around people who share the same historic and cultural references—who remember Woodstock and Sputnik and Beatlemania. That's easy and comfortable, and it often works nicely. But age segregation makes our worlds small, and it's a huge problem in the United States. One study asked people over sixty with whom they discussed "important matters." Fewer than one quarter named people under age thirty-six.[11] My son's fiancée spent her summers at her grandparents' houses in rural Poland. The graveyard was next to the church, and everyone congregated in the town square. After emigrating to Chicago at age fourteen, Agnieszka looked around her new country and wondered, "Where are all the old people?" Contact with people of all ages dismantles age bias and benefits old and young alike.

I have a horror of the communal, but I'm just going to have to get over it.

We are social beings, and we're meant to live in community. I have a horror of the communal, but I'm just going to have to get over it. I don't know how Eden-like the Home for Superior Women will be, but the hallways will have to accommodate the thunder of little feet, and if I break my hip stumbling over a tricycle, so be it. I'm trying to look down the road, as are many of my fellow children of the sixties, who are rejecting the quarantine of the "old-age home" and experimenting with different forms of communal living. Just give me a door I can close.

The lousy economy is making the long drive to the suburbs less desirable, as does the isolation inherent in car-dependent lifestyles. Multigenerational living has become more common during the recession, as young people move back home after college and grandparents help out with childcare. Innovative solutions are cropping up all over the place, like Kansas City's Pemberton Park, the first apartment complex designed specifically to support grandparents raising grandchildren under age twenty-one. We can learn from all of them and see what solutions emerge as time passes, needs evolve, and the market responds.

WHAT MAKES IT SO HARD TO ASK FOR HELP?

Since social connections are key to a happy and healthy old age, why are so many older Americans isolated and lonely? Many factors are at play, of course, from lack of transportation and age-segregated housing that makes it harder to make younger friends to changing family demographics, all buttressed by ageist thought and practice. The overarching reason, however, is cultural, and deeply American.

In this country no myth is more powerful than that of rugged individualism: the notion that success and independence are paired, and that relying on others signals not just physical frailty but weakness of character. That myth serves us poorly, especially people with disabilities and older people, two increasingly overlapping circles on the Venn diagram of life.

Dignity and freedom of choice are and remain critically important, of course. Yet the way we grow old is governed by a whole range of variables, including environment, personality, and

The myth of self-sufficiency demands optimism without end, downplays life's challenges, and shames us when, inevitably, we fall short.

genes, compounded by class, gender, race, luck, and the churnings of the global economy—over which we have varying degrees of control.

What happens when we can't hoist a suitcase into the luggage rack anymore, or drive at night, or drive at all? When we can't hear the instructions anymore, or read the directions, or understand them? When we can no longer make it to the bathroom, or even heave ourselves out of bed? A culture that idealizes self-reliance amplifies those anxieties and silences questions about the structures that strand us. (Where's the *low* luggage rack? How come there's no bus? Why no large print, or audio assist, or person to ask? Why should diapers at the end of life be any more shameful than at the beginning?) This culture demands optimism without end, downplays life's challenges, and shames when, inevitably, we fall short.

THIS MYTH OF SELF-SUFFICIENCY TAKES A TREMENDOUS TOLL

This ethic of individualism serves the proponents of small government, who conveniently ignore the role of services paid for by their fellow citizens in making many of them wealthy. This ethic has systematically eroded communitarian values and sanctioned the U.S. government's abdication of responsibility for its vulnerable citizens. The effects can be seen in decades of concerted efforts to shrink the welfare state and public assistance programs, even though exactly the opposite is called for if the country is to meet the enormous challenge of caring for its older citizens in the years to come. As long as those challenges are ours to shoulder alone, there's no point in addressing, or even identifying, any of the larger factors that make it hard for people to navigate the transitions of late life.

Consider the terrible story of the Crabtree family. Jim Crabtree's wife developed early-onset Alzheimer's at age fifty-six. For six years Crabtree's parents were able to watch her during the day, but his eighty-four-year-old dad was experiencing cognitive problems, and his mother, eighty, suffered from severe arthritis. In May 2013, Crabtree's father shot both women and himself while his son was at work. Crabtree told NBC's Maria Shriver that it was a great gift from his father, since it "ended my Alzheimer's and elder care issues at once" and since the three who died were all "ready to go."[12]

NBC's only comment was that caregiving is tough. What does that say about our society? Imagine an alternative scenario: decent, affordable healthcare, subsidized caregiving, and help from a team of social workers, friends, and neighbors. That support would have gone a long way to help Jim Crabtree's family cope and spare them this horrific end. His mother's only illness was *arthritis*. Stories like these have even healthy middle-aged people wondering whether suicide—or, say, triple murder—will be the ethical alternative to asking for help. Those are lethal forms of internalized ageism, and they handily serve the American government's twenty-first-century austerity program.

THE IDEALIZATION OF INDEPENDENCE FEEDS THE MYTH OF "AGELESSNESS"

Growing older means relying on others, from a stranger's help with a heavy door to the full-time assistance of a live-in caregiver. The alternative is denial. Since people in an "ageless" society don't become dependent, there's no need to fund the support they might require. Who's left holding the bag?

- <u>Women</u>: A society that views caregiving as a private burden rather than a shared necessity disadvantages women, who perform the vast majority of this unpaid or underpaid work. It's unfair, it's exhausting, and it limits women's participation in professional and public life.
- <u>The nonrich</u>: The ninety-nine percent of us who cannot afford the extraordinary expense of hiring qualified people to help with everything from errand-running to bedsore-preventing.
- <u>Ultimately, everyone</u>: Affluence confers enviable protection from many of the vulnerabilities of old age, but only up to a point and only for so long. None of us is solely responsible for the way we age, all of us will need help, and everyone benefits when responsibilities are distributed and solutions shared.

Many people with chronic illnesses and disabilities, or simply over "a certain age," do indeed require economic assistance, but the fact that it's seldom by choice is rarely mentioned. Discrimination and physical barriers are enormous hurdles not of their making. They are denied autonomy, and it is held against them, especially against those whose disabilities are not obvious. Millions of older Americans need financial help for a host of reasons other than disability, including high unemployment, housing costs, and the elimination of pensions and decently paying blue-collar jobs.

Small wonder that most people's overarching worry is becoming a burden—to our community, our doctors, our families. Burden—"a word that carries its small-government politics inside it like a bomb," as Margaret Gullette trenchantly observed in *Agewise*.[13] Decent government-subsidized pensions, healthcare, and caregiver programs would sure lighten the load. After all, the commendable intent of subsidies like those is to support the personal autonomy of the recipients.

Clinging to an unrealistic ideal of self-determination also makes a good death more elusive. It compounds despair when treatments fail, and it makes dying yet another arena in which to test our competence. Paradoxically, as geriatrician Muriel Gillick points out in *The Denial of Aging*, the same insistence on individual choice leads both to futile therapy to prolong life and also to requests for physician-assisted suicide to shorten it.

Another paradox: If we wish to stay in charge to the end, we're going to have to figure out who could help us implement key decisions. Autonomy requires collaborators. Establishing and nurturing those relationships makes a lot more sense than fetishizing self-reliance. A third, overarching paradox: For the vast majority, death is a concatenation of unpredictable events, control over which is elusive at best.

Autonomy requires collaborators.

NO ONE IS EVER TRULY INDEPENDENT

Humans are social animals. We come into the world utterly helpless; as teenagers, our peers are all that matter; it's hard to build a career on our own terms; we live in a world shaped by collaboration of mind-boggling complexity on every scale; and in late life, nothing matters more than relationships. Every human interaction involves reciprocity, from buying gum at a convenience store to changing the diaper of a baby who'll grow up to be someone who might one day change ours. Yet that interdependence goes largely unacknowledged in modern industrial societies, except when someone gets hurt or falls ill.

Typically, the proportion of those contacts that remains voluntary gradually shifts. Of course we seek to control as much as possible and for as long as we can, from small decisions about what to wear or eat to larger ones about where we live and with whom. But circumstances will change, and the longer we cling to the delusion that we can manage these transitions on our own, the less prepared we'll be. Most of us will need all kinds of help well before the end, although not nearly as much as all the horror stories about "living too long" would have us believe.

Socialized to envision that only shame and loss accompany the decline of physical and mental agility, we find these transitions pitiable. Spending time with people who are ill, incapacitated, or dying is a good way to demystify and defang those circumstances. Pity might seem kind, but it infantilizes, ties the tongue, distances, and is often misguided. My kinesthesiologist was flooded with it when he reencountered an old family friend at a wedding. Now in his

The sooner we trade the self-sufficiency trap for a more communitarian, age-integrated, mutually interdependent point of view, the closer a truly all-age-friendly society becomes.

late eighties, the friend had been a local wheeler-dealer and an avid golfer, and Dr. Z was dismayed to find him hunched over a walker. Gesturing at it and braced for the worst, he asked, "Other than this, Sam, how are things?" With a big smile, the old friend responded, "I can do everything except walk!" In the book *Endnotes: An Intimate Look at the End of Life*, gerontologist-in-training Ruth Ray describes falling in love at forty-two with an eighty-two-year-old man in a nursing home who was severely incapacitated by Parkinson's disease.

Despite these physical and social constraints, which they navigated together, his was "the best loving she had ever known."[14]

If you feel you're controlling the course of your life, "then old age is an affront, because it is a destination you didn't choose," John Leland points out in *Happiness Is a Choice You Make: Lessons from a Year Among the Oldest Old*. "But if you think of life instead as an improvisation in response to the stream of events coming at you—that is, a response to the world as it is—then old age is more another chapter in a long-running story."[15] The sooner we trade the self-sufficiency trap for a more reciprocal, communitarian, age-integrated, mutually interdependent point of view, the closer a truly all-age-friendly society becomes. All those handicap-accessible ramps and elevators and curb cuts have helped far more parents with babies, travelers with bags, injured jocks, and burdened shoppers than people with physical disabilities.

"Age-friendly" urban and community initiatives are gaining traction around the world, in recognition of the fact that people stay healthier and more active in places that offer good-quality public transportation, food markets, and work conditions. A designated "age-friendly city," New York requires new housing developments to include low-income units. Suppose the city also required 10 percent of the units to go to olders, provided adequate public spaces where all residents could mix, and mandated universal design throughout? Age-friendly communities aren't just wheelchair- and walker-friendly, they're gurney- and skateboard- and stroller- and bus-passenger- and delivery-guy- and tired-person-friendly. Let's call these programs what they are—*all*-age-friendly. Let's acknowledge the need for helping hands, and reach for them gratefully and without shame.

PUSH BACK!

CALL OUT THE WAYS IN WHICH CAREGIVING UNDERVALUES AND EXPLOITS WOMEN—AND DEMAND CHANGE

Caregiving is a tender, beautiful, enriching part of being human. Women do two-thirds of it, perhaps looking after both kids and parents, or later on sandwiched between parents, grown children, and *their* children—what I call the "club sandwich generation," because thanks to the longevity revolution, four living generations are becoming commonplace. This wouldn't be a problem if this important work were valued, decently paid, and optional. It's none of those things. There's plenty of lip service about the selfless people who do this important work, but little protection from its economic, personal, and professional consequences.

Home care is one of the fastest-growing occupations in the U.S. These jobs are disproportionately filled by poor women of color, many of whom are undocumented immigrants. The nature of the job reinforces hierarchies of race and class. As anthropologist Elana Buch observes, home care workers are expected not to call attention to their labor, "sustaining elders' sense of independence by obscuring their reliance on others." Facilitating their employers' choices and decisions "takes precedence over workers' abilities to sustain their own lives and households."[16] Only one third of home care workers get health insurance through their jobs, and most have to rely on some kind of public assistance. As a legacy of racist employment laws, home care workers were not protected by the Fair Labor Standards Act, which guarantees minimum wage and overtime pay to most workers, until 2015.

Most of us do this work part-time for free. Hispanics and African Americans spend more time caregiving and have greater responsibilities than their white or Asian American peers. This takes a tremendous toll on work lives: As *The New York Times* put it in

2017, "Women's lower wages and family responsibilities have always batted them in and out of jobs—and in and out of the labor force—far more frequently than men." It's harder to get back into the labor force if you dropped out to care for someone. It's hard to find a job with the flexible schedule that caregiving demands, which makes it more likely for caregivers to end up working part-time jobs, often for lower wages, and without benefits like pensions, sick leave, and healthcare. Many give up: Since 2000, in stark contrast with working women in developed nations with comprehensive family support policies, American women's participation in the labor force has decreased.[17] Many draw on their own savings and income while looking after others, further jeopardizing their own retirement security.

What turns caregiving into a burden? Going it alone, without supports. The stress, especially if you're looking after someone with Alzheimer's or chronic illness, can take a tremendous toll on health and relationships. When demands become overwhelming, it's really hard for people—whether parents, children, lovers, or dear friends—to do what only we can do: preserve the relationships that sustain and define us, and make people prefer the care of those we love.

The current system takes for granted that family members can and will take on caregiving, as millions of us do, tenderly and willingly. The burden is likely to grow as care becomes more privatized. You can see this playing out in the booming aging in place movement. Many programs are innovative and worthy, but they're likely to have an unintended consequence: growing responsibilities for "informal" care partners—i.e., family members. Typically women, because more women step up to these duties—staying home with a sick kid or driving a parent to doctors' appointments—and because the person who earns most is the one who keeps working full-time, which is usually the man because women get paid less!

The sexism is obvious: The system privileges men over women at every turn. The ageism is clear: The very old and very young need the most care, and an ageist culture values them less. Ageism and sexism converge to make women more vulnerable over time: There are more of us, and we need more care because we live longer, are less healthy, and have less money.[18] Make noise about this!

SEEK OUT CONNECTIONS

Humans are tribal, and it's not easy to reach across lines, class in particular. My friends come in all ages but almost all are white. Social circles often narrow as we age, and it's important to forge and maintain a network that extends beyond family and best friends. As TV producer Ruth Friendly was well aware, this requires forethought. "You've got to lay the groundwork and become part of some organization you like and that can use your talents, because you're not going to do it when you're eighty." Look for multiple ways— whether as worker, spouse, volunteer, or care partner—to connect with the world and stay in contact, even if (perhaps especially if) you're an introvert.

Reaching out can feel like a stretch, but YWCAs and senior centers and supermarket bulletin boards all offer possibilities. Join a gym. Take a class. My friend Isabel's Meetup knitting group members include older African American women and purple-haired goth teens, and crafters of all stripes strike up conversations with her on buses and benches. Clubs or teams are a good way to meet people who share interests that may have developed later in life, or that we finally have time to pursue.

The cavalier instruction to "find your passion" has always irked me. What about people who work to live, or who have yet to find themselves through scrapbooking or saving feral cats? Court interpreter Sam Adelo had the best take on this that I've come across: Everybody's knowledgeable about something. "Draw on that know-how to help someone who *needs* that help," he recommended, whether a grandchild, a neighbor, or a virtual acquaintance. What's essential is that each party find value in the exchange. When ecologist Kate Zidar started planning a survey of ocean plankton, she looked up one of her former graduate school professors for advice on methodology. When they met up he mentioned that he'd been invited to teach a science class in a Korean university via video chat but had no idea how to set it up. Kate is a whiz on a computer. They bartered a training agreement, and a friendship was rekindled.

Only during the last century or so did people start asking advice from anyone *other* than the oldest person they knew. As repositories of knowledge and traditions, older people are natural models and advisors for younger ones—as long as they're worthy of the role and choose it freely. Youngers have plenty to teach older people, too, when we find ways to be in their company and are willing to listen.

Relationships, after all, are what give our lives meaning. We don't love less as we age, obviously, or love fewer things, or love less deeply or less well. We never outgrow the need for companionship, and it never fails to sustain us.

USE THE INTERNET

The internet is an indispensable way to access news and information, connect with friends and family, make new friends, and forge community of all types. Social networking sites like Meetup and Facebook help people find others who share an interest or activity. It's not an either/or proposition; people who use social networking sites like Facebook also have more active social lives offline. Inexpensive video technology and storage sites like YouTube give people a new way to tell their story and get feedback, and not just from the grandchildren. My father worked with Buckminster Fuller and enjoyed tracking the work of his acolytes online. It deeply engaged him and ensured a steady trickle of geeky visitors dropping in to talk about the remarkable inventor. Ruth, my partner's mom and a bookseller, Skyped prospective customers on her iPad to show them her wares, making her unusually wired for a nonagenarian. I resisted her entreaties to join Words With Friends, but she had six or eight games going at any one time with no help from me. Asked on her seventieth wedding anniversary what was the most remarkable invention she'd witnessed during her lifetime, she answered, "My iPhone."

Learning the new language of technology is challenging, especially since few devices are designed with older users in mind, and no one can keep up with the pace of change. When a photo-messaging app called Snapchat came on the scene, I was relieved when a classmate of my son's mentioned that he hadn't bothered to download it. I'd jumped to the ageist conclusion that of course he was using it simply because he was in his twenties. Gaps emerge incredibly fast; it's not uncommon for siblings only a few years apart to favor different social networking apps and platforms. The way our grandchildren communicate will mystify their parents in turn. It's up to each of us to find middle ground, to make new connections and sustain the old ones in whatever way makes sense.

Internet usage tends to drop off after age seventy-five, and older Americans have been slower to migrate to the digital realm than their children and grandchildren. Class plays a big role, with the use of digital tools and services highest among those who are wealthier and better educated, and far lower among those who are older and less affluent, many of whom have issues with health or disability. But by 2018, two-thirds of Americans age sixty-five and up were using the internet, up from only 14 percent in 2000, and that percentage continues to grow.[19] Despite these trends, the mindless, ageist, and sexist meme persists that older people, especially women, either can't or won't use newfangled technology. Tired of hearing people say stuff like, "Just explain it like you would to your grandmother," or "That's so simple my grandma could get it," Rachel Levy, a mathematics professor at Harvey Mudd College, set up a blog called *Grandma Got STEM*.[20] (STEM is an educational acronym for Science, Technology, Engineering, and Mathematics.) People share stories and remembrances about tech-savvy older women, and they're terrific.

We can be our own worst enemies. There's plenty of internalized ageism in the assumption on the part of older people that they're too old to learn how to maneuver in a wired world, or don't want to bother. My mom, who typed hundreds of long and entertaining letters over the years, claimed she couldn't get the hang of e-mail. Pia Louise hosts a radio show called *Living Portraits*, and requires her guests to participate via Skype or Google Hangout. "I feel people my age, fifty-plus, should keep up with technology. Instead I find they respond that 'they have no need for it,'" she wrote. "Yikes! What do you think?" Here's my response on my Q&A blog, *Yo, Is This Ageist?*

> *Because it applies to all guests, your policy isn't ageist. It's your prerogative, and probably a technical necessity. Plenty of people over fifty are new-media savvy, though, and it's ageist to stereotype them as technophobes or stuck in their ways.*
>
> *On the broader question, keeping up with new technology helps people connect across geography and generations—always a good thing. When people in my baby boom cohort don't text, it irritates me. But I sympathize with an octogenarian friend who doesn't want to text her grandchildren, saying, "I want to hear their voices." I hope they call her every so often, and also that if one of them offers to teach her to text, she won't say, "I have no need for it."*

I struggle with my own technophobia, and don't like to admit that my IQ plummets thirty points when I have to figure something out on my computer. My first and doubly ageist impulse is to see if I can rope someone younger into helping me out. But I'm trying, because it's integral to my social and professional life, and because I don't want to be relegated to the sidelines of an increasingly wired world. These needn't be one-way exchanges. Editor Nancy Peske increasingly relies on her teenager and his best friend for help with certain skills she doesn't have time to acquire, "and they're more visual than I am," she notes. "But I teach them big-picture things with tech and information they otherwise wouldn't learn for years, so it's an even exchange."

Getting together online is no substitute for actual "face time," of course, although Apple's or Skype's simulacrum is a great way to check in on faraway friends or family, especially when moving around is difficult or the travel expensive. The important thing is to sustain existing connections, be open to new ones—especially across generations—and to actively solicit them.

MIX IT UP WITH FRIENDS OF ALL AGES

In the U.S., nonfamily relationships tend to be age-homogenous. According to Cornell gerontologist Karl Pillemer's informal comparison of scholarly articles about cross-generational friendships, Americans are more likely to have a friend of a different race than one who is ten years older or younger than they are. A study of people over 60 found that of the people with whom they discussed "important matters," fewer than one-quarter were under thirty-six; if relatives were excluded, the number dropped to 6 percent.[21] That's a real problem. Age gaps jump out at me, an occupational hazard, although like other differences they usually recede the minute people make actual contact.

There's no reason so-called generation-gap friendships can't be every bit as close as any other kind. Age doesn't predict shared values or interests any more than it predicts how people vote: Gender, race, income, and wealth are all much more significant. People who like NASCAR or archaeology or poker or tango don't age out of those lifetime interests any more than people stop being drawn to working with kids or rescuing whales or playing the piano. Think of something you like to do, be it drawing or cooking or going to concerts, and find a mixed-age group to do it with.

Relationships across age gaps may require more effort to initiate, and differences in physical capacities and communication styles are real, but these boundaries are more permeable than we tend to assume. They broaden perspectives and banish stereotypes— that olders lead boring lives, for example, or that kids are hopelessly self-centered. While friends of any age enrich our lives, younger ones are more likely to be physically active, which is a bonus. Life experience makes olders a good source of career or romantic advice, while youngers offer a pipeline to popular culture and new digital domains. Contact engenders curiosity and empathy. Having older friends makes it easier for kids to imagine being old themselves someday, and easier to connect with olders as the surfers and hitchhikers they once were and as the planners, lovers, and dreamers they remain.

SUCK UP TO YOUR KIDS (OR SOMEONE ELSE'S)

Well into the twentieth century, people died not that long after their last child left home. (In 1900, the average U.S. life expectancy was forty-seven.) Now, in an unprecedented shift, parents are likely to have twice as much time with their adult kids as they spent with them as children. Longer lives and fewer children are transforming the traditional "family tree" into what sociologists have dubbed the "beanpole family," stretched vertically across time but with few members in each generation. Fewer siblings, aunts, and cousins, but related to more living generations. More shared history, more cross-generational relationships, exhausting and exhilarating.

When support goes both ways, whether emotional or tangible, everyone benefits. Support includes everything from offering childcare or a ride to the store to lending a car or advice or a sympathetic ear. It's great to be connected to grandkids; it's good for kids, too, and it insulates them against ageism. These relationships are natural in traditional cultures where extended families share a roof and grandparents contribute, help oversee family life, and enjoy more respect. They're harder to establish and maintain in an ageist culture, but they can play an outsized role in shaping values and interests, and may even catalyze careers in medicine. Explaining why people become geriatricians, Dr. Rosanne Leipzig of the Mount Sinai School of Medicine told me, "Everyone goes in because of a grandmother." Dr. Robert Butler, to whom this book is dedicated, was raised by his grandparents.

I'd better stay in my kids' good graces, especially if I'm going to stick around long enough to see *them* into grandparenthood. I'm mindful of another lesson from Dr. Pillemer. The unhappiest people he interviewed for the Cornell Legacy Project were those who were permanently estranged from a child. Grandparental rights are often poorly defined, so even if your kids don't need the free childcare it's important to stay in touch. If you can afford it, subsidize family visits. Respect your kids' schedules and priorities.

Not everyone is part of a family, let alone a functional one. Many find "families of choice" outside biological and marital ties, like filmmaker George Stoney, who in mid-life was "kind of adopted" by a family separate from his own. One of the grandsons lived with him in his apartment in the West Village, and Stoney has shared their place too. Relationships like these take luck and foresight and imagination. I hope I'll be able to wipe my own butt to the end, but I'm going to need help shoveling and schlepping, and I want to be able to cast a wide net. An ex's kids, foster kids, godchildren, friends' kids, the kids next door or down the hall—they're all contenders as long as the interest and affection is mutual. Intergenerational friendships can bear fruit for decades, and in completely unexpected ways.

REPRESENT!

Getting out of the house is good for both body and brain, but inertia is tempting, and all the more so when excursions mean busting out of age silos. Except for simulcasts of the Metropolitan Opera, my partner, Bob, and I are often the oldest people in the room, and often by decades. We don't like it, but we don't want to stay home just because we'll stick out. I think of it as affirmative action, which God knows is necessary in this age-segregated society.

A few years ago, at a huge, outdoor DJ fest called Electric Zoo,

Bob and I were plenty conspicuous. The friends we went with were in their mid- to late thirties, but the median age barely topped twenty. Most of the neon-garbed club kids paid us no attention at all, some did visible double takes, and a few even asked to take their pictures with us, which was kind of creepy but mainly friendly and well-meaning. And we often get big smiles or high fives from youngers hoping to be out on the dance floor when they're that ancient.

Our affinity for electronic dance music makes us unusual, but we'd have more company if more people took more chances and stopped restricting themselves to venues that attract only people in their age cohort. I'm not a good dancer and fret about looking foolish, but no one ever went to her grave saying she wasted too much time dancing. If we'd stayed home we'd never have tweaked some of these kids' notion of what their parents could be up to, and we'd have missed out on a very good time. We also made two good friends who were in their late twenties. Real friends. "We're *real friends*," said a woman who came up to me after my very first talk. She was referring to a guy in his twenties whom she'd met through her daughter and who also loved an English rock band named Muse. The woman felt she'd missed out on a wild youth, discovered rock music in her fifties, and became an avid concertgoer, usually alone. She was brave, and she was having a blast—and in a less ageist society, it wouldn't call for courage.

Not to turn this happy groupie into Rosa Parks, but that's how desegregation happens. People with the most at stake—olders, in this case—step up and step out. They *stop conforming*. The open-minded welcome them, and incremental social change takes place. Dance floors and rock concerts are examples at one end of the social spectrum. What about hitting a trendy restaurant even if you'll be the only gray head in the room, or opting for Airbnb even though older travelers tend to default to hotels, or exploring a neighborhood that skews young? Only if the prospect genuinely appeals, of course.

The point is not to act artificially but to test ourselves a bit, by challenging the status quo, keeping our worlds from shrinking, and doing our part to age-integrate them.

Philip Roth's novel *The Dying Animal* describes the affair of a professor in his sixties with a former student in her twenties. "Far from being youthful . . . ," he writes, "you feel even more than you ordinarily do the poignancy of her limitless future as opposed to your own limited one. . . . You note the difference every second of the game. But at least you're not sitting on the sidelines." Exactly. I don't condone sleeping with students, but I do recommend taking chances. At a minimum, lessons will be learned, and fun just might be had. The hard part is getting in the water. Some people will be snarky, like the bouncer outside a club on a frigid February night, where we were shivering in line with a bunch of friends celebrating a fortieth birthday. "Step up, Grandpa," he said to my partner.

Bob went over to him and said quietly "I get that you think it's cute to call me 'Grandpa,' but I don't like being noticed mainly for my age, especially in this context. It feels something like what I imagine it might be like for someone to call you the N-word."

The bouncer thought it over, nodded, said, "I got it."

"I *am* a grandfather, by the way," Bob added, "and proud of it."

Everyone learned something.

Weddings are one of the few times in North American culture when all ages make it onto the dance floor, and it's one of the reasons they're so fun. Why should olders cede the space? Or people with disabilities? "Dancing is the public expression of pleasure and freedom, and shouldn't be restricted to people on feet, or people who are young and thin and popular, or people who can perform all the moves," said disability rights activist Simi Linton in her documentary, *Invitation to Dance*. The dance floor at the party after the movie opening was filled with wheelchair users.

In Latin America, it's not uncommon to see grandmothers

with babies in arms shake it in the streets with everyone else. All ages mingle in the milongas of Buenos Aires to learn or teach the tango. In North America, cultural expectations are different, but that's no reason to leave them unchallenged—in daily life, if not on the dance floor. My dentist's receptionist, who's somewhere in her fifties, was invited by a woman in her building to her thirtieth birthday party. She chickened out at the last minute because of the age gap, and was surprised and flushed with regret when the birthday girl said, "We really missed you!"

Sometimes being with younger friends makes me feel younger, and sometimes it makes me feel ancient. It's complicated for them too. I know they're thinking, "I hope I age as well as Ashton," and also thinking, "I hope that never happens to me." Both are true. It's important to show up at that birthday party, not only because segregation impoverishes our lives but because the exchange of skills and stories across generations makes sense in so many arenas, from kitchen to conference room, from learning a language to mastering a sport, from art to astronomy. The list could go on forever, because it's the natural order of things. In the United States, ageism has subverted it, impoverishing youngers as well as olders. And when people aren't visible, whether ghettoized or homebound, whether by choice or reluctantly, so are the issues that affect them.

DECOUPLE IDENTITY AND CAPACITY

Even when shame is held at bay, even when help is adequate and freely offered, it's hard to negotiate relinquishing control. Especially as they head into their eighth or ninth decades, people worry, not without reason, about being whisked off to an institution if they encounter any difficulties managing on their own. Polarizing conflicts—between guilt and gratitude, dignity and disgrace (especially around toileting), giving in and taking charge—accompany fraught transitions. Age slows us down. It can feel as though everyone else, juggling work and commutes and other caregiving responsibilities, is in a hurry. It can be simpler to abdicate responsibility and agree to go along with the idea that whatever living arrangement a child forcefully suggests will keep us safe. It can be simpler, too, to take responsibility, by taking away a parent's car keys for example. Better to first talk honestly about these shifts in power. However uncomfortable, these discussions are essential to maintaining identity and self-esteem on the one hand, and mitigating guilt and resentment on the other. Trained mediators can help. Reciprocity sustains relationships, whether between lovers, neighbors, family members, or care partners and patients.

More accustomed to accommodating changes not of their making, women may have an easier time with some of these transitions. When I can't unscrew a bottle cap, I'm not embarrassed to open my front door and ask the next passerby for help. Strapping youngers often have a hard time opening the damn thing too. (Don't get me started on the need for universal design that would eliminate these mundane but maddening problems.) In his book *Aging Well*, George Vaillant describes a seventy-eight-year-old woman whose advanced emphysema left her unable to go shopping, use public transportation, climb stairs, even make her bed. How did she cope with this ever-shrinking circle of independent activities? The woman explained that she had to consciously acknowledge and grieve each loss of function. "Then it was easier."[22]

Acknowledging rather than denying is key. Reflect on what has already headed south, be it near vision or night driving. Part of coming to terms with such losses is to acknowledge the need, at first occasional but growing ever less so, to ask for help and to accept it. It helps to shift focus from controlling a circumstance to managing it, or perhaps managing the people in actual control. That huge task means reconfiguring both our relation to the external world and much upon which our internal sense of self is based. A few years ago I landed in the emergency room with a serious kidney infection, and the thought flashed through my head that I shouldn't let my kids see me so debilitated. "Who am I kidding?" was the next thought. They're grown up. I need them. This might

Asking for as little help as possible for as long as possible is shortsighted, and it limits and exhausts.

be the first time they'd find me in the hospital but it was unlikely to be the last. It was time for all of us to begin nego-tiating the inevitable reversal of roles. Most people strive to re-tain their identity by asking for as little as possible and resolutely resisting help. That strategy is understandable, but it's shortsighted and it limits and exhausts.

Clinging to self-reliance also fails to challenge the way society views the old and the "imperfect." When physical capacity dimin-ishes, self-esteem often follows suit. If disease or injury moves us into a category that we once pitied or feared, it's human nature to turn those feelings on ourselves—or to deny them and resist this difficult self-appraisal. No longer able to walk very far, Bob's ninety-four-year-old Uncle Eddie refused to use a walker (and forget about a wheelchair!), although this curtailed a lifetime of travel. The abil-ity to move on his own and stay vertical remained fundamental to his identity. The only way to change such a mind-set is to separate ego from body, whether as pudgy teenager or hobbled nonagenarian, as people born with disabilities learn to do early on. The challenge is to continue to see ourselves as beautiful, capable, and fully present, and to insist that others respect us on those terms.

In *Life Gets Better: The Unexpected Pleasures of Growing Older*, Wendy Lustbader eloquently addresses the need to accept that we will need help. "Courage in late life has a lot to do with letting go," she writes. "Especially when illness exposes us to need, we may enter an unnerving time of appraisal."[23] Limitations demand flex-ibility and improvisation. Compromises can seem intolerable at first, but learning to balance self-care with assistance and to accept it with dignity can bring unexpected benefits. Lustbader tells of an avid reader who was told at seventy-one that she was losing her central vision and that it was incurable—my worst nightmare. (Okay, my second worst, and now e-readers have bright screens and big type.) She grieved hard and long. Then she had a book giveaway party and was surprised when three friends offered to visit weekly to read aloud to her. She keeps three books going at a time, and she loves these sessions. Just as importantly, so do her readers. "Reader and listener, giver and receiver, became indistinguishable."[24] Recalibrations like these are a dance between pushing back and letting go. When others are involved, the process can be richly collaborative.

Even small acts, which might at first seem demeaning, can help us regain a sense of control of our lives. Influence over even very limited circumstances can be of real benefit. In a landmark 1976 study, psychologist Ellen Langer gave houseplants to two groups of residents in a New England nursing home. One group was charged with tending the plant, and also given input into their daily schedules. The other group was told that the staff would care for the plants, and they weren't given any choice in their schedules. Eighteen months later, twice as many of the olders in the first group were alive as in the control group. In the same vein, when nursing home residents received help with a jigsaw puzzle rather than just being encouraged, they rated the task as more difficult and performed less well. When their competence is questioned, people become more dependent and develop learned helplessness. Little by little their identity and autonomy erode.

No matter now well intentioned it may be, offering help based on the assumption that an older person is less competent than a younger one is ageist. Ask first, in a neutral way that makes the offer easy to accept or decline. Dependence needn't mean powerlessness. It's different from true incompetence, a distinction that mitigates what age scholar Margaret Cruikshank calls "age shame." Learned helplessness can actually kill, while having a choice is hugely significant. Dr. Atul Gawande frames this in terms of remaining the writers of our own stories, and having them reflect our characters and our deepest needs. The dying, he writes in his invaluable book *Being Mortal*, "ask only to be permitted, insofar as possible, to keep shaping the story of their life in the world—to make choices and sustain connections to others according to their own priorities. In modern society, we have come to assume that debility and dependence rule out such autonomy."[25]

We can change that. Just as age is better viewed as a spectrum than as an old/young binary, so, too, with self-reliance. Seeing it as a dichotomy (dependence/independence, giver/receiver, passive/active) reduces myriad human exchanges to one-way transactions, when in fact they are complex, nuanced two-way transactions that involve mutual risk and reward. Too often, we forget that. A speaker at a conference I attended asked the audience, "Who likes to receive help?" A few hands went up. "Who likes to help others?" The room filled with raised hands.

Not being in control of a situation is not the same as being helpless. Autonomy exists only in relation to others. A paradox described by Dutch gerontologist Jan Baars is that it can be possible, even necessary, to accept someone else's power in order to be autonomous. Suppose someone with limited mobility has someone drive him to an appointment, for example.[26] If the driver is serving the disabled person by carrying out his request, who's the autonomous one? Situations like this are complicated to negotiate and involve high levels of mutual trust and communication, even among trained professionals. Things get even trickier when somebody *decides* to let others make decisions on his or her behalf.

Transactions like these show that the concept of self-reliance inevitably extends beyond the individual. Dependency and self-reliance are not mutually exclusive. The formal caregiving system turns us into either employers or consumers at the end of our lives. Conventional attitudes and institutions leave few good options. Weaving our way out of the self-sufficiency trap involves forging, reconfiguring, and valuing a web of informal relationships, based on need, ability, mutual interests, friendship, and barter of all sorts.

ASK FOR HELP. ENCOUNTER "MODEST DELIGHT"

As Baars notes, self-respect is vulnerable and relies on mutual support; it falters if not validated by those around us. There's more back-and-forth than a square dance and no caller to say when to swap. Transactions are unscripted and complex, especially between strangers. Even so, there's pleasure for the taking. In 2005, when I moved to a Brooklyn neighborhood with a median age of around twenty-three, I said to myself that it would be time to move when I could no longer hustle up the subway steps as fast as the kids. (Remember I'm Not Ray? This was during Stage 2, or "Look How Great I'm Doing!") Since then, I've realized that I could let the hipsters pass, or help me with my bags, and that it would be good for both of us.

I hadn't put it to the test until not that long ago, though, when I was heading to the airport after work and schlepping a suitcase along with my purse and computer bag. My back was already protesting. What exactly was I waiting for? So when I got to the subway I asked an amenable-looking guy to carry it down the steps. There are three separate sets of stairs, and I forced myself to ask each time. Each time I was rewarded with a big and genuine smile.

I posted it on Facebook to make it real: "Asking was harder than carrying the damn thing, and I'm actually proud of myself. And I think it made my helpers feel good." Once I'd clarified that I already possessed a bag with wheels, ergonomic satchels, cleats, carabiners, etc., it turned into a very interesting thread about swapping the giver/taker binary for a complex, two-way exchange.

"Not until very recently did I realize that when the person bagging my groceries asks if I want help to my car I can say yes without shame," commented Terry Finn. An actor—she dated my ex-husband before we met (that's how far back we go)—and

Facebook has rekindled a wonderful friendship. "Struggling with keys, my giant fucking purse and an ungovernable shopping cart is not only silly but terribly unattractive (a criminal offense in West LA). Plus, I'm sure the kid is thrilled to get out of the store for five minutes."

Asking empowers.

Betsy Martens, a video producer and activist in Chicago, chimed in next. "Asking for help has always been hard for me, no matter what the age. I'm working on it now, though, and finding it empowering. Of course, first I have to trip someone with my cane." She was kidding about the tripping, but the cane was real; she'd recently had hip surgery.

More from Terry: "Another kind of 'letting go' today while walking past a new tenant moving in to my apartment complex. Watching the struggle to get a coffee table from the truck to the door, I realized I couldn't help. Always having been proud of my physical strength, I was the first one helping the mom with the stroller down the subway stairs or anyone struggling with an unwieldy burden. Now I see I can't really do much beyond holding the door or just getting out of the way. Even if I still had superhuman strength, I don't think anyone would be comfortable with a white-haired lady huffing and puffing her way through the hall with a box of their unproduced screenplays."

"I've always thought of myself as physically strong too," I admitted, adding "I'm all for the kind of discomfort that dislodges people's preconceptions." The notion of a "white-haired lady" with superhuman strength appealed, although it wasn't particularly helpful in coming to terms with a somewhat unwelcome shift in identity.

"All right, all right, step aside, you amateurs," wrote Fletcher Barton, a writer and friend from college days. "As Ashton knows, I have an incurable progressive muscle disease (I'm a Jerry Lewis kid), and when it comes to asking for help, I *know*. Prove it? Okay, often as not when somebody's done helping me, they thank *me*! Sounds unbelievable, I know, especially given my surly bitch interpersonal style, but the inventor of applied positive psychology, Martin Seligman, discusses just such a thing in one of his books, *Flourish*, saying essentially that after lifting his bridge partner in and out of the car he felt a surprising, deep human connection. Another positive psychologist, Barbara Fredrickson, has written a book, *Love 2.0*, saying such passing moments of connection can generate valid episodes of love. Everybody should be crippled! All right, it's not a prerequisite for happiness, but anybody who plans to get old should read these books. Even this far along, life surprises."

Photographer Sari Goodfriend jumped in next, calling this "one of the funniest and most insightful comment threads I've read on FB on a topic I think about regularly, having sustained a back injury recently and having always been like Terry and jumping in to help and use my small person strength. But I have realized that people do like to help. It's just a matter of giving them the opportunity."

Back to Fletcher, to "duck in again and clarify my post . . . The takeaway isn't that it feels good to help the handicapped, though it might, but that there is a way to ask for and accept and appreciate help that leaves the helper grateful too. It seems magical, really, and it's probably quite rare and requires practice and tweaking. Nor of course will it work with all helpers. But it's worthwhile to keep in mind, as we march toward needing to ask more often, and rather than dread, the prospect of at least occasional victory brings a modest delight." What a perfect turn of phrase. Fletcher now uses a motorized wheelchair or scooter to get around, as will some of the rest of us in due course. The dance between strangers is different, both simpler and more complicated, arguably all the more moving, reminding us of our common humanity and the fact that no one actually goes it alone.

A further, marvelous paradox is that asking empowers. Sociologist Meika Loe describes this process many times over in *Aging Our Way*, her five-year study of how thirty of the "oldest old" (ages 85–102, in this case) meet the ever-increasing challenges of living as independently as possible. Many manage their own care, hiring and firing paid assistants as necessary, and also provide important assistance to friends and neighbors. Most spend the majority of their time alone, but also reach out to a network of friends, relatives, and assistants for help with shopping, transportation, and caring for their homes and themselves, as well as for company. "Perhaps the most profound, even ironic, lesson from their stories is this: asking for help enables autonomy and control—as long as it is on the elder's terms," Loe wrote.[27]

As these octo- and nonagenarians scaled back and asked for help from family and friends, they constructed a safety net that enabled them to retain control over most aspects of their daily life and also improved its quality. Asking for help gave them power over their circumstances and made their helpers feel generous and important. Intuitively, this does not surprise. Imagine allowing that awareness to inform our choices, and enabling common sense and communal good to trump misguided pride and embarrassment.

For each of us, the terms and power dynamics will shift. I've got time to practice. The goal is to give and to receive with grace. What is grace? Ease in acceptance, dignity in the face of difficulty, gratitude without resentment. Vulnerability, openness, even transcendence. We know it when we see it, and it lifts us up. People *like* helping, and it ought to be just as uplifting to be on the receiving end, especially when assistance is freely offered, as between strangers. When someone offers me a seat on the subway, I accept with a smile unless I'm getting out at the next stop; it's a gift and a courtesy, as would be obvious in a non-ageist society.

The key, it seems to me, is to embrace the idea that needing help is no more shameful at the end of life than at the beginning. That's the way it is in other cultures, after all, where from cradle to grave people openly rely on and acknowledge the help of others. Maggie Kuhn, the visionary activist who founded the Gray Panthers and who was always firmly focused on intergenerational solutions, said it best: "Interdependence is the truth of our lives."[28]

As Kuhn knew well, the myth that we can go it alone is promoted by powerful interests. The Gray Panthers advocated for "fundamental social change that would eliminate injustice, discrimination, and oppression in our present society."[29] There's little place for those who move slowly, or perhaps not at all, in a society that turns its back on those who fail to age "successfully" by looking and moving like younger people. Overturning the dual stigmas of age and disability will require institutional as well as personal transformations. In their demands for equal treatment, equal access, and equal opportunity, the civil rights and disability rights movements show us the way.

CHAPTER EIGHT

THE BULL LOOKS DIFFERENT:
THE END OF LIFE

Aging is life itself, which is what makes it so damn interesting. Dying is a distinct biological process that occurs only at the end of all that living, as anyone who has witnessed a death can testify. But an ageist society conflates the two, which is why bookstores have shelves labeled "Aging and Death," and why you can get a graduate degree in "Older Adult/End of Life Care." Part of the conflation is just human; old people are indeed reminders of mortality. It comes as a shock to realize that we're past the midpoint of our lives, even when it's long past, which is a function of age denial. Returning from her thirty-seventh college reunion, my friend Susan wrote, "I was stunned to discover how far along we are on the big curve to death."

As a child, I was terrified of dying. In midlife, it seemed obvious that the prospect of the Grim Reaper's knock would grow ever-more oppressive as it grew more imminent. So I was bowled over to learn that the older people are, the less they fear dying. I can't say I'm unafraid, but I feel a lot better about the prospect, partly because I have more insight into the role culture plays in shaping our anxieties and our options.

Fear of dying is human. Every society and individual struggles to come to terms with it. It's why we have religion, and Mozart's Requiem. Fear of aging, on the other hand, is cultural. The way older people are treated varies considerably in different societies. They enjoy respect in East Asian cultures where the Confucian tradition of filial piety still holds sway, as well as in Mediterranean cultures where many generations live in proximity—as long as global capitalism has not eroded these traditional beliefs and structures. If the proverbial boat were sinking, members of those societies might reach for the parent instead of the baby. The past has value, they reason. You can have more children.

The point is not that one ethic is better than another, but that they're culturally defined. In a youth-obsessed society, people yoke aging to its inevitable end. We project our fears. We grossly underestimate the quality of life that the old enjoy, and often its value as well. Consider a study conducted at four university hospitals of 1,438 seriously ill patients aged eighty and up. Researchers asked whether the patients would rather live a year in their present condition or have less time in excellent health. They also asked the patients' surrogate decision makers, often their children, how they thought the patients would answer. Surprising their surrogates, most of the olders said they'd trade only a month or less for better health, and 40 percent were unwilling to relinquish any time at all. Interviewed a year later, the olders were even less willing to exchange time on earth for excellent health.[1]

A different study measured the self-assessed quality of life of 498 cognitively intact people aged eighty and up soon after a hospitalization, along with four "domains of health status": their physical capacity, ability to perform daily tasks like eating and bathing, psychological distress, and pain. The results were highly variable. Some people with the highest physical capacity rated their quality of life as lousy, while others in far worse shape, including 51 percent with severe pain, rated it as good or better.[2] The researchers' conclusion? Making assumptions about the quality of life of older people based on their health alone is a mistake. So is generalizing about what matters to them and why.

THE BULL LOOKS DIFFERENT

The philosopher William James dubbed the illusion that we can ever know what another person is experiencing the "psychologist's fallacy." In a talk on end-of-life issues at Baltimore's Johns Hopkins University Hospital, Dr. Thomas Finucane put this in a way that really stuck with me. His mantra was a Mexican saying: "The appearance of the bull changes when you enter the ring." The matador's point of view is different from the spectator's.

The bull looks different.

Behind Finucane was a chart that represented women in labor, with the x-axis depicting the number of centimeters dilated and the y-axis the point at which they requested anesthesia. The line ascended in a steady diagonal; women started out set on natural childbirth, but more and more changed their minds as their labor progressed. Another data point from the doctor: Right after the accident that paralyzes them, most quadriplegics say they don't want to go on living. A year later, 60 percent rate their quality of life as good or excellent.

Two other stories told by the doctor also stuck with me. One was of an extremely straitlaced woman who was struck by a form of dementia that robbed her of all propriety. She told dirty jokes, lifted her skirts, flirted with her grandsons. There was no doubt that the woman, if compos mentis, would have chosen death over this mortifying incarnation. There was also no doubt that she was having a fine time, which made the transition easier for well-meaning friends and family to accept.

One more story. A man drank. He drove. He told his wife that if he were ever incapacitated he would absolutely want her to pull the plug. He crashed his car and suffered major brain damage. After a year of rehabilitation, he remained completely paralyzed, barely sentient, able only to blink. His wife dutifully reiterated his wishes to his physicians, and the medical ethics team sat down at his bedside. Did he know who he was? Yes. Where he was? Yes. What had happened to him? Yes. Did he want to die? No answer.

The life force is *strong*.

The bull looks different.

The sight of an old woman hunched over a walker used to make me mutter, "Put me out of my misery if I get like that." Now I mutter, just as fervently, "The bull looks different, the bull looks different." Now I realize how presumptuous it is to assume that

I know what's going through her head, let alone that she's worse off than I am. No one wants to be pitied, and it turns the object of pity into just that: an object instead of a person.

A friend's father was completely paralyzed along his left side by a stroke at seventy-six. The man spent the next seventeen years in a wheelchair, in a nursing home. After one routine visit, he told his daughter, "I just have to say this has been about a perfect day." Her last present to him was the Berlitz textbook he'd requested so he could learn to speak Spanish with one of his doctors. Before I started this project, I'd have assumed that life with severe disabilities had little to offer, and that my friend's father would have been better off dead. As the saying goes, "There are very few people who want to live to be one hundred—and most of them are in their late nineties."

Glossing over the very real challenges of late life does no one any favors, but neither does the assumption that even highly circumscribed lives are not worth living. Contact with olders and people with disabilities brings home the enormous variation in their circumstances, both physical and psychological, and in the ways in which they have adapted. Such encounters force us to recalibrate, to question assumptions, to swear to avoid or struggle to emulate. The lessons can be pragmatic or profound. As Dr. Marc Agronin put it rather grandiloquently: "Face-to-face encounters with older individuals force us to look momentarily into an eternal abyss and trigger unanswerable questions about life and death that can bring wonder as easily as fear and despair."[3]

It makes sense to operate on the basis of what we think we'd be feeling or thinking under the same circumstances. It's a projection, though, and different from empathy, which is the attempt to see the world from someone else's perspective. We often guess wrong. Repelled by physical decline, anchored in our own point in the life course, focused on loss, we tend to grossly underestimate the quality of life of the very old, especially if they're severely disabled and/or live in an "old-age home." We miss the beauties and intimacies of those last chapters, their pleasures local and all the more keenly experienced.

FEAR OF DEATH DIMINISHES WITH AGE

When I first encountered the fact that the very old don't worry about dying, I was skeptical. Then it turned out to be true of the people I interviewed, like eighty-two-year-old Boeing troubleshooter Anthony Mucci. "Oh, I'm glad you brought that up," he said, jumping up and returning to the breakfast nook in his tidy St. Louis ranch house with a Xeroxed photo. "That's his casket, and there's mine," his wife Rose explained. "We picked them out ten years ago." Were they afraid? "Not really," said Mucci. "There's only one thing on this earth that I want to do that I haven't, and that's see my grandson Adam graduate from medical school."

Over lunch on Manhattan's Upper East Side, I asked the eminent geriatrician Robert Butler what had surprised him about the aging process as he moved into his eighties. "The only thing, and I don't know if it's a surprise or not, is that I think you become less uneasy about death," he replied. "I'd say that in the middle years I became more conscious of it. In fact Schopenhauer said mid-life is that point in time of life when you begin to think backwards from death instead of forward from birth, which I thought was a pretty shrewd observation."

At ninety, *New Yorker* writer Roger Angell wondered "why I don't think about my approaching visitor, Death. He was often on my mind thirty or forty years ago, I believe, though more of a stranger. Death terrified me then, because I had so many engagements . . . though I'm in no hurry about the meeting, I feel I know him almost too well by now."[4]

I also heard it anecdotally from geriatricians: The very old don't want to die, and they especially don't want to die in pain, but they're not afraid. "We project our terror of death onto the aged . . . And yet in my fifteen years of working in nursing homes, I have never heard a patient tell me that he or she was afraid of death," said

Dr. Agronin, who works in one of the largest nursing homes in the United States, where the average age of his patients is about ninety. "Sometimes there is acceptance, other times anticipation, but most often there is no great concern. Life goes on in death's shadows."[5]

Over and over, participants in Karl Pillemer's Legacy Project said, "I wish I hadn't spent so much time worrying."[6] Life is short, they said. Say it now, travel more, worry less. What other advice did they have for younger people? "Don't worry so much about dying, because we don't." Eventually I encountered it in a scientific paper (so it *must* be true): "Younger adults consistently report higher fear of death than older adults."[7] The odds of ending up in that far bigger piece of the pie chart comforted me. But I didn't really believe it until I learned why.

THE GIFT OF THE BOUNDED FUTURE

It turns out that the awareness that time is short doesn't fill people with dread. It makes people spend their time more wisely. Laura Carstensen of the Stanford Longevity Center brought this point home at a seminar at the Columbia Journalism School in 2012. Her research shows that humans always set goals in a temporal context, and that those time lines change as a function of mortality. Those who perceive their time as short typically attach greater importance to finding emotional meaning and satisfaction in life, and invest fewer resources into gathering information and expanding horizons. For example, Carstensen quipped, "Young people will go to cocktail parties because they might meet somebody who will be useful to them in the future, even though nobody I know actually likes going to cocktail parties." Older people are more likely to give priority to existing relationships and to spend time going deeper into activities they know to be satisfying.

Younger people with terminal illnesses seem to view their social world as very old people do (prioritizing a small and intimate circle). Older people, when offered a miracle drug that would greatly extend their life spans, make choices that resemble those of healthy, younger ones, opting to take more social risks and undertake long-term challenges.[8] These findings have helped discredit disengagement theory, which posited that older people naturally withdraw from society in innate preparation for death. Instead, it turns out that they're deepening important relationships and focusing on activities they know will be rewarding. As Carstensen put it at the seminar, "A lot of what we thought was a unidirectional, experienced-based change associated with aging in some biological way turns out to be much more malleable."

Jonathan Weiner, author of the book *Long for this World: The Strange Science of Immortality,* interviewed Carstensen at the seminar and brought up a parakeet he'd had as a kid. Aware of the dimensions of its cage, the bird would scrunch down if lifted upward on a finger. "It seems to me that all of us of a certain age sense ourselves beginning to scrunch in some psychological way," he observed. "You're urging us to recognize that the cage, the space above us, has changed. That we don't have to scrunch the way we had been."

That's biology, Carstensen countered gently, pointing out that both birds and people behave differently when constraints are finite versus open-ended. She believes the "scrunching down" to be a positive behavioral adaptation to the constraints that all humans live with. "We need to prepare deeply and to focus [when time grows short]," she said. "That's when some people do their best work and have their best relationships. It would be bad for old people to be like young people, and vice versa." The "secret of a happy old age" lies in acknowledging that life's possibilities, though unpredictable right to the end, are finite. In other words, the awareness that death is growing close frees us from anxiety about that very fact. It's not a paradox. It only seems like one because it's so hard to get our heads around.

A companion and equally counterintuitive notion is that a long future can be oppressive. When we're young, we're constantly wondering about what lies ahead and whether we're doing our best to prepare for it. As time goes by and our paths reveal themselves, that anxiety diminishes. "In some ways—I think of this as the silver lining of growing older—we're relieved of the burden of the future the older we get," Carstensen said in an interview on NPR.[9] When she described how goals change over time, with youngers preparing for the long term while olders savor the moment, she said, "Almost every time, some young person will come up to me afterward and say, 'How do I get old faster? How can I live in that state?'" (I have a suggestion: become an Old Person in Training.)

Timelessness and agelessness are companion notions, seducing us with the promise of endless summers and boundless futures. They're also traps, as ancient myths about the curse of eternal youth remind us. Asked what he valued most about life, the great German writer Thomas Mann replied, "Transitoriness. But is not transitoriness—the perishableness of life—something very sad? No! It is the very soul of existence. It imparts value, dignity, interest to life. . . . Timelessness—in the sense of time never ending, never beginning—is a stagnant nothing. It is absolutely uninteresting."[10] As wise people across countries and cultures continue to remind us, there's no present if there's no ending.

Children live in the moment because they don't have the cognitive ability to do anything else. Olders do it because they know that time is running out. They don't want to waste their time. And living in the present is what makes people happy. As painter Marcia Muth put it, "As you age toward ninety you realize that somewhere along the line there's a stop. That's it. So every day is something you want to live really to the fullest." Hospital visits and funerals—potent reminders of mortality—crowd the calendars of the old, for whom denial is no longer an option. How excellent that this should buttress a sense of well-being. Life is short, and all the sweeter once we're able to inhabit that fact.

Children live in the moment because that's all they know. Olders do it because time is running out. And living in the present is what makes people happy.

WHAT IS LIFE WORTH, AND
WHICH LIVES ARE WORTH LIVING?

Life does not have to be lived large, in space or time, in order to be enjoyable and fulfilling. Painfully little of this awareness enters the cultural conversation about population aging and the end of life, where fear and ignorance prevail. Much of the rhetoric is outright hostile, focusing on old people—sick old people, yet!—who have the temerity to stick around. Older bodies benefit from medical treatment just as much as younger bodies, including serious interventions like organ transplants, chemotherapy, and dialysis. Much discussion centers on this "high-cost" group, although a 2015 study from the National Bureau of Economic Research determined that "medical expenses before death do not appear to be an important driver of the high and increasing medical spending found in the U.S."[11] Healthcare costs for Americans over sixty-five in their final year of life amounted to only 7 percent of total U.S. medical expenses.

Undertreatment typically goes unmentioned due to the fact that medical problems in older patients are often wrongly assumed to be untreatable, written off to age itself, or go undetected entirely. There's little discussion of the role that sexism plays in undertreatment: Women are more likely to be poorer, and to be coerced by the medical establishment into accepting substandard treatment. Or racism: These issues are all the more acute for people of color. Or ableism: We underestimate the quality of life of people with disabilities, and ensure ignorance by looking away. All, of course, are compounded by class.

Most people can agree that terminally ill patients who are mentally competent should be able to exert meaningful control over the circumstances of their deaths. This issue goes by many names, including euthanasia, assisted suicide, right-to-die, and mercy killing, and for a lot of good reasons the culture wars really heat up around it. Felicitously timed to coincide with the release of an upcoming novel, bad-boy British writer Martin Amis made headlines in 2010 for proposing "euthanasia booths" on street corners where old people could do themselves in with "a martini and a medal." Amis unconvincingly maintained that his comments were meant to be "satirical" rather than "glib," but there's something to offend just about everyone in his prediction that "a population of demented, very old people, like an invasion of terrible immigrants, [will be] stinking up the restaurants and cafes and shops."[12]

Sounds Orwellian, doesn't it? Yet it's become commonplace to hear even middle-aged people worry about becoming a burden and wondering whether the ethical alternative to living too long will be to commit suicide. This punitive "solution" to the costs of end-of-life is consistent with political reluctance to support the health and well-being of society's most vulnerable citizens. What "live too long" really means is "cost too much," despite the fact that according to the non-profit Alliance for Aging Research, only about 3 percent of the 4,800 Americans over sixty-five who die every day incur very high costs (and whose expenses therefore make up a disproportionate share of the 7 percent of total U.S. medical expenses that go to older Americans in their final year of life).[13] Only 3 percent, and it would be lower if American medicine weren't geared toward keeping some people alive at any cost and lousy at helping people die well—reasons to welcome the growing embrace of palliative care and hospice programs.

An ageist culture casts the problem in terms of increasing numbers of old people who inconveniently refuse to die, when the underlying issue is the changing nature of healthcare. Very sick people used to die fast. Modern drugs and procedures now prolong both the struggle with disease and its inevitable end. Before antibiotics, for example, pneumonia was called "the old man's friend" because patients often died peacefully in their sleep. Now the default is to treat it aggressively, because many high-tech interventions are profitable, and often legally mandated. The life expectancy of people with many different kinds of cancer has increased, and we're better at managing chronic conditions like heart disease and high blood pressure. These developments and interventions blur the line between the ill and the dying, and render decision-making all the more fraught.

Sometimes the patient's wishes are clear, as in the case of my partner's mother, Ruth, whose first move when she was hospitalized with pneumonia at ninety-two was to rescind her DNR. (A DNR, which stands for "do not resuscitate," is a legal instruction to the healthcare team not to give CPR if a person's heart and/or breathing stops.) It's more complicated when the patient becomes too ill to speak for herself, as was the case when my grandmother came down with pneumonia at almost ninety-one. Her children conferred with her GP of many years, who agreed to withhold antibiotics, and Granny did indeed die peacefully at home. So, for that matter, did Ruth two years later.

Things get even *more* complicated in the absence of ethical advocates, or consensus. Whose interests are in play besides those of the patient, and who is her advocate if she needs one? It's not a particularly radical leap to conceive of assisted suicide and euthanasia as a form of discrimination against the old, the ill, the disabled, and those who are no longer economically productive, cloaked in the rhetoric of compassion. After all, writes social worker Elizabeth Schneewind, "If it is rational to commit suicide when one has no hope of becoming more productive or useful and when society discounts one, why should this not equally apply to the severely physically ill or developmentally disabled or those with degenerative diseases?"[14] People who are suffering should have that right. But the flip side of that argument—you are useless and should go away—is unacceptable.

People who are suffering should have that right to end their lives. But the flip side of that argument— you are useless and should go away—is unacceptable.

Schneewind's question provoked people with disabilities to form the brilliantly named group Not Dead Yet. A grassroots organization, it demands legal protection "for the targets of so-called 'mercy killing,' whose lives are seen as worthless." In her memoir *My Body Politic*, Simi Linton describes some of the members at a 1997 protest in front of the Supreme Court:

> *The shouters were saying, in effect, my life is worth living. That incontinence, respirator dependency, twenty-four-hour attendant care, pain, paralysis, blindness, and other conditions often depicted as tragic and intolerable don't determine a wish to die. It is, more often, institutionalization, guilt about being a burden to others, fear of being alone and debilitated, poverty, inadequate medical coverage—all these things that lead to depression and a sense of hopelessness.*[15]

The same politicians who complain about the costs of universal healthcare draw heavily on their superb, taxpayer-funded coverage, including Senator Ted Kennedy, a lifelong advocate of healthcare reform, when diagnosed with brain cancer. But as economic risks are increasingly shifted from employers and the government onto individuals, the ill and disabled come under increasing pressure to "do the right thing." At any age and in any condition, a person has the right to *want to stay alive*. The thought of a society whose members have to defend that right is truly chilling.

Will that right become less self-evident? Will we allow the burden of proof to shift to the ill and vulnerable? Will the right to want to stay alive become an ever-taller order in a cutthroat capitalist culture grappling with its own decline? That is ageism and ableism at their most toxic. Consider poet Ed Meek's prognostication in the *Boston Globe* magazine that "Young people may get tired of paying for baby boomers who refuse to die."[16] "Should people be expected to refuse beneficial medical treatment just because they're not young anymore? What else can 'refuse to die' imply?" responded cultural critic Margaret Gullette sternly in a letter to the editor.[17] Warning of the slippery slope between prerogative and obligation, Gullette identified the key phrase: not "right to die" but "duty to die."[10] In a society repelled by physical decline, that line gets blurry alarmingly fast.

Why do we, as a country, find spending money on humans nearing the ends of their lives more ethically problematic than the millions we spend on teeny preemies at the beginning of it? Why is euthanasia routinely proposed as the "solution" to this imagined scarcity? This false dichotomy always crops up around healthcare rationing: Why spend money on old people who are going to die soon (even though no one says that last bit aloud) when we could spend it on kids? "Can you imagine a similar public debate based on race or sex?" asks Laura Carstensen in her book *A Long Bright Future*—that it would be acceptable to vaccinate girls but not boys, for example, or straight people but not gay ones? "Yet we have these discussions freely about age."[19]

IT'S COMPLICATED

My mother was a charter member of the Hemlock Society, the first national right-to-die organization. (It has since merged with Compassion & Choices, an organization that works to "expand choice at the end of life," to which I've belonged for decades.) Clinically depressed for decades, my mom was one of the very few members to actually commit suicide, and she made no secret of the prospect's appeal. On hearing of her death at seventy-four, the first question from most of her inner circle was, "Did she kill herself?" While I'll never fully come to terms with her decision, I respect it and am grateful for her clarity.

Fortunately for me, I don't suffer from depression, and I promised my children I wouldn't follow suit. Suicide is a wretched legacy. I, too, though, hope that luck and circumstances will converge to help me control the circumstances under which I die. I think we can count on my generation to diversify those circumstances and to make them more humane. The very old may not fear death, but they do fear a ghastly, painful precursor. No one wants a long and costly exit hooked up to machines, and opting out should be easier.

Making dying better, however, is no substitute for making *living* better in those last days, weeks, or months. On a personal level, that means resisting "duty to die" thinking. On a political level, it means effecting large-scale social change. In *Being Mortal*, Dr. Atul Gawande writes, "Our most cruel failure in how we treat the sick and the aged is the failure to recognize that they have priorities beyond merely being safe and living longer; that the chance to shape one's story is essential to sustaining meaning in life; that we have the opportunity to refashion our institutions, our culture, and our conversations in ways that transform the possibilities for the last chapters of everyone's lives."[20] Ideally, that means making space for an ongoing conversation about what matters most to us.

DISCUSS WHAT YOU THINK YOU'LL WANT AT THE END

My doctor has a copy of my living will and healthcare proxy. My kids know where to find the file and what I think I'll want. Next up: a tattoo of "put me in the bed by the window" across my collarbones; I'll need to see the sky, and a tree wouldn't hurt. I hope it won't come to that. I hope to die at home, where Team Ashton won't have to cede control to Team Hospital. My partner's mom wouldn't discuss any of this because she thought it meant we wished she were dead and because she remained in relentless denial of her own aging and mortality. Had she and her husband been hospitalized at the end, I think they would have wanted every possible intervention, and if it comes to that, I bet their son will too. His criterion is that he wants to hang in until he can no longer have a meaningful conversation. He's since broadened his definition of conversation to include communication of any sort: smile, tapping of hoof, twitching of snout.

Bob has chosen his son, Murphy, as his medical proxy because he thinks I'll pull the proverbial plug the minute he stops being entertaining. My proxy is my sister, because it'll be easier for her to pull it when the time comes, and I think that's what I'll want. But who knows? The bull looks different. I've learned that the way we die is highly unpredictable, and that my age and condition may have remarkably little bearing on what I end up wanting—and deserve.

One thing's for sure: It's essential to discuss our hopes, fears, and priorities with those we love, ideally well before they need to be acted upon. Don't wait. No one is thinking clearly when "something happens," as it inevitably does. The nonprofit Conversation Project offers smart and sensitive suggestions in their starter kit. As it points out, the place to start talking is the kitchen table, not the intensive care unit, so that fewer people die in ways they wouldn't have chosen and fewer care partners have to grapple with uncertainty and guilt. That conversation is critical, because if we're too squeamish to *talk* about our own end-of-life priorities, we can't expect more of the medical establishment.

The value of discussing end-of-life wishes is gaining visibility thanks to ethicists, activists, and physicians like Gawande, who is training doctors to make these five questions part of routine end-of-life care:

- What is your understanding of the situation and its potential outcomes?
- What are your fears and what are your hopes?
- Which goals and priorities are most important?
- What trade-offs are you willing to make, and what outcomes are unacceptable? And later on,
- What would a good day look like?[21]

IT'S STILL REALLY COMPLICATED

I've printed out my living will and medical power of attorney and stuck them in the same file, but I'm no longer smug about having my papers in order. Brooke Hopkins, a retired English professor, had recently updated a living will declining procedures that would "unnaturally postpone or prolong the dying process" in the event of a grievous illness or injury. The lines seemed clearly drawn to his wife, bioethicist Peggy Battin, an internationally respected champion of end-of-life choices, and author of seven books about how we die. Then, in 2008, Hopkins broke his neck in a bike accident, and by the time Battin reached the hospital Hopkins was entangled in life-support machinery and paralyzed from the shoulders down.

The bull looked different. Life remained worthwhile. Again and again, Hopkins opted for equipment and procedures that kept him alive in the face of constant pain, infections, and setbacks. At times Battin had to make decisions for him, at which point things got even more complicated. "Alongside her physically ravaged husband, she would watch lofty ideas be trumped by reality—and would discover just how messy, raw, and muddled the end of life can be," wrote Robin Henig in a moving profile in the *New York Times Magazine*.[22] Closer to home, a friend's eighty-three-year-old mother had been crystal clear about wanting no extreme measures if her heart failed. When it did, she felt differently. She was too weak for a triple bypass, so surgeons installed two stents during a highly risky seven-hour surgery—extreme measures by any definition. Two weeks later she fired the visiting nurses and went back to playing the violin in her string quartet. An active year and a half later, she died, having played with the quartet that afternoon.

A study conducted by Peggy Battin in 2007 was one of the first to look empirically at whether people in Oregon and the Netherlands, where assisted suicide is legal, were being coerced into choosing to end their lives. She and her colleagues were relieved to find that the people who used it tended to be better off and more educated than those considered more vulnerable. What she's become more aware of is "not the influence of a greedy relative or a cost-conscious state that wants you to die, but pressure from a much-loved spouse or partner who wants you to live. The very presence of these loved ones undercuts the notion of true autonomy." The "right" thing to do can be impossible for even the best-intentioned parties to agree on.

Four years after his accident, in December 2012 on a blog he and his wife maintained together,[23] Hopkins wrote, "I've tried to just let [my own catastrophe] be part of me, part of who I am becoming, and to always keep in mind how extraordinarily much I've gained, not just what I've lost." The couple concluded that "this story doesn't end, and it doesn't need to be a tragedy. It's still a story of love, even if it's love under trial." A year and a half later, Hopkins requested that all the medical equipment—ventilator, diaphragmatic pacer, external oxygen, cardiac pacemaker, feeding tube—be removed and that he be referred to hospice care. After enrolling him, the hospice staff asked what date he'd like the ventilator withdrawn. "Today," he replied. The professor died peacefully at home a few hours later.

With the help of a devoted team, Hopkins got what he wanted—control over the circumstances of his death. His advocates paid close attention to his wishes and fears and were able to discuss them in the largest possible context: what his death meant to him and the people he loved. Ignoring the dying older person's wishes, whether for more intervention or less, is a form of elder abuse. In a landmark victory for the rights of the terminally ill, the nonprofit organization Compassion & Choices won the first court judgment to that effect in 2001, when eighty-five-year-old William Bergman was dying agonizingly of mesothelioma and doctors declined to prescribe more effective pain medication. Their case on behalf of ninety-two-year-old Marjorie Mangiaruca, who received full cardio-pulmonary resuscitation from an EMT team in violation of her "do not resuscitate" order and died five days later in the hospital, is pending.

The profit-driven, often legally mandated interventionist default of the medical-industrial complex is powerful. That's why a colleague of mine made sure she or her sister was in the hospital room when their ninety-four-year-old mother was dying of Alzheimer's and related complications. "We were watching Mom's vital signs slow on the monitors. She was at the very end, and in walks an orderly with an X-ray machine! We nearly bit his head off, poor guy;

he was just following orders. So in comes the doctor, who says, 'We think something's obstructing your mother's breathing. Don't you want us to look into it?'"

Brooke Hopkins and my mother were outliers. Most of us never choose death, no matter how degraded our quality of life may appear. Most of us will enter the ranks of the disabled bit by bit, not, like Hopkins, with brutal suddenness. In the ultimate reckoning, it may matter less than we think. Television producer Ruth Friendly's first husband died in the middle of a sentence in their breakfast nook, her second slowly after a series of strokes. I asked her something I'd always wondered: Was a sudden death more devastating, or was it more bearable than the alternative? Friendly reflected, then replied, "They're both worse."

Whether or not the bull looks different is beside the point. At any age, the criteria for medical procedures, to quote bioethicist Felicia Ackerman, should be the "desire to stay alive, medical need, and a reasonable chance that the procedure will work."[24] That's it.

EXAMINE BIAS. EMBRACE UNCERTAINTY

Checking on a new arrival at the nursing home where he's the mental health director, Dr. Marc Agronin found the ninety-three-year-old woman silent in her wheelchair, silhouetted against her window by the fierce Florida sun. He introduced himself, asked why she'd moved in, and learned of the recent death of her husband of seventy-three years. Overwhelmed by the thought of her loss, the doctor leaned in, offered heartfelt condolences, and asked what widowhood felt like after so many years of marriage. Her answer came after a pause. "Heaven."[25] She'd endured decades with a gruff, verbally abusive man and was happy to be released. Chagrined, Agronin realized that he'd made the classic mistake of assuming that he knew what another person was experiencing. Throwing herself into activities and friendships, the new widow made the most of the five years that remained to her.

We see old age through the lens of loss. From the outside what people lose as they age is more obvious than what they gain. The losses are real and wrenching. But from the inside, the experience is different. Abandoning preconceptions takes open-mindedness as well as imagination. Perspectives shift. Look at Pete Townshend, who, as the twenty-year-old lead guitarist for The Who immortalized the lyric "Things they do look awful cold / Hope I die before I get old." Born in 1945, Townshend now has a blog that sings a very different song. An August 2012 post describes making music, producing shows, traveling, and playing the harmonica with his two-year-old grandson. "It was my first musical instrument. Pretty easy, all you have to do is breathe," Townshend wrote. "I hope I retain that facility for a few more years. Life is very good."[26]

We see old age through the lens of loss. The losses are real and wrenching. But from the inside, the experience is different.

BRING DEATH AND DYING OUT OF THE CLOSET

One reason that death is so little discussed is that few contemporary Americans have ever seen a dead person, once a routine part of family life. Bodies are whisked out of retirement homes at night, as though the dead just disappeared. This makes it easier to avoid confronting mortality, but it has consequences. "Segregating the old and the sick enables a fantasy, as baseless as the fantasy of capitalism's endless expansion, of youth and health as eternal, in which old age can seem to be an inexplicably bad lifestyle choice, like eating junk food or buying a minivan, that you can avoid if you're well-educated or hip enough," Tim Kreider wrote in a witty essay called "You Are Going to Die."[27]

The tide may be turning. "Death salons" and "death cafes," where people can convene for biological, psychological, and anthropological perspectives on the Grim Reaper, are cropping up across the country. These meet-ups are a reaction against the sanitization of death that occurred during the 1800s, when it started being outsourced to hospitals, and the attendant rituals relocated from parlor to funeral parlor. The movement is hip! Check out Caitlin Doughty's *Ask A Mortician* YouTube videos. ("You got death questions, we got death answers.") In 2015 Doughty opened a funeral home in Los Angeles that offers help with home funerals, enabling people to wash, dress, and sit with their dead, instead of leaving these intimate tasks to strangers. There's even a Tumblr blog called *Selfies At Funerals*, which is possibly an example of young people engaging with death and dying and possibly the worst idea ever.

Another development is the emergence of the death doula, also known as an end-of-life doula or death midwife. Greek for "woman who serves," the word "doula" is more commonly associated with childbirth, but growing numbers are being trained to help people transition out of this world as well as into it. Duties can range from regular bedside visits to helping with paperwork and communicating with doctors, to providing support for family and friends. As these doulas know well, death is a hugely meaningful experience, especially for those who make it part of life. A commenter on my blog recommended a short stint volunteering in a hospice. "That way we would all see what dying looks like, stop being afraid of dying people, develop compassion and awareness of the needs of other people *in this moment*, and recognize our own selves in the faces of other dying human beings," he wrote. "Then maybe as a society we would figure out how to treat dying as a natural transition." It would serve us better. People with intimate and prolonged exposure to death in settings where it's viewed as a normal part of life, like hospice staff and suicide prevention workers, are less anxious about it. Mexican culture celebrates the Day of the Dead, a ritual that dates back nearly forty centuries. Based on the cycle of life and celebrating rather than fearing death, this festival joyfully connects the living to those they love who have passed on.

Another important piece is to develop new end-of-life rituals and traditions that bind generations, and even nurture communities. Bob and I came back from Vietnam, where many homes have little shrines to ancestors, enthused by the idea of a family altar. Our kids haven't exactly jumped on the idea, but we haven't built one our-selves yet either. As I attend more memorial services, I'm making mental notes of bits I like best. (Memo to self: talk s_l_o_w_l_y. Al-low time for people to savor the slide show. Don't sanitize.) Longer lives give us time to think deeply about how to transfer what we know and value to those who come after. Stories give objects mean-ing: Have we told the tale of that portrait or Jell-O mold so the next generation knows why we held on to it, and why they might want to? Have we told our own stories? Which traces of ourselves would we like to persist, and perhaps to benefit others, once we're no longer around?

CHAPTER NINE

OCCUPY AGE! BEYOND AGEISM

A few years ago an e-mail landed in my inbox titled "The Ageing Party!" It read, "I am ageing! On April 29th I will celebrate thirty-four years of ageing. Please save the date. I would LOVE to see you, celebrate with you, hug you, and toast with you. If you are partial to ageing, come to the ageing party!" I asked the birthday girl if I could take some credit for having inspired the invite, and if so, whether I could post it, anonymously or not. "Of course you inspired!!!" she responded. "Of course post away with my name in **BOLD**!!" So, happy birthday, **Masha Feiguinova**, for joyfully occupying age.

Occupying age doesn't mean old age. It means acknowledging and embracing the actual process of change on which we embark the day we're born. Aging means living, and birthdays commemorate that happy fact.

Why does an aging party like Masha's seem like such a wild idea? Because conventional thinking holds that someone in her thirties is too young to be "aging" and too old—already!—to be happy about it. Why else do we celebrate birthdays up till twenty-eight or so, then treat them with increasing alarm up until, say, seventy-five, then dust off the balloons again? Because we're brainwashed by a culture that reduces older people to the grotesque caricatures that birthday cards routinely offer up. Institutionalized ageism is responsible for producing those cards, and internalized ageism for the fact that they sell.

Long before the term "It sucks" entered the vernacular, I promised myself I'd never forget how much it truly sucked to be thirteen. (New school, mean girls, acne, bad glasses, hair that refused to be straight, extreme dorkiness.) I've kept that promise, and things have mercifully continued to look up. What's next? All bets are off, except for the fact that the longer we live, the more different from each other we become—and the more likely it is that our lives will diverge from popular culture's cramped, oppressive script. Intuitively we know this. Lived experience brings the lesson home. The transitions we're conditioned to dread materialize differently, or not at all.

How to jimmy open that crack, that disconnect between script and reality, that twinge of cognitive dissonance? To turn that glimmer of awareness into conscious thought? To turn *that* awareness into a grasp of the social and economic institutions that attempt to shape our aging? To reject those meanings and develop our own? Last but not least, to take them out into the culture at large? To shift the entire conversation around longevity—from deficit to opportunity, from dependence to interdependence, from burden to gift—and transform our internal experience along with it.

The longer we live, the more likely that our lives will diverge from popular culture's cramped, oppressive script.

It won't happen until we replace ageist stereotypes and stories with more diverse and accurate ones.

That won't happen without a mass shift of consciousness on the part of people of all ages.

THE PERSONAL IS POLITICAL

My previous book, *Cutting Loose: Why Women Who End Their Marriages Do So Well*, is about why it's hard to have an egalitarian marriage in a society that treats men and women very differently. (Hint: patriarchy.) It involved years of immersion in the history of feminism and women's rights, not to mention unsnarling my own relation to the material, and it wasn't until a good year after publication that I realized sheepishly that writing the book had raised my consciousness.

That phrase "consciousness raising" originated with the women's movement, as did "the personal is political." Both phrases were attached to a seminal 1969 essay by feminist Carol Hanisch about the role of consciousness-raising in understanding the cause of collective problems. "Can you imagine what would happen if women [and] blacks . . . would stop blaming ourselves for our sad situations?" Hanisch asked. "That is what the black movement is doing in its own way. We shall do it in ours. We are only starting to stop blaming ourselves. We also feel like we are thinking for our- selves for the first time in our lives."[1]

Until feminism taught them new scripts, many women blamed themselves for their second-class status. It took a movement, itself catalyzed by countless consciousness-raising sessions around the world, to change that. The women's movement woke people up to the fact that the obstacles women faced weren't "all in our head" but the result of entrenched systems at work: patriarchy, sexism, capitalism. It took getting my consciousness raised for me to grasp that egalitarian marriages are elusive not because wives are wimpy or husbands bullies, but because a sexist society values men's and women's bodies and experiences differently. Those same en- trenched systems of discrimination oppress us all.

It wasn't until I started this project that I realized the degree to which my anxieties about growing old were, again, in large part a function of the society in which I live. (I did grasp it faster this time around.) It's not loving a man that makes life harder for gay guys; it's homophobia. It's not the color of their skin that makes life harder for people of color; it's racism. It's not having vaginas that makes life harder for women; it's sexism. And it's ageism, far more than the pas- sage of time, that makes growing older far harder than it has to be.

Women still face discrimination on many fronts, but powerful movements like #MeToo have raised awareness of the many faces of sexism and the need to confront them. When it comes to ageism, on the other hand, most people aren't sure what it looks or sounds like, or even what the word means. That's why I started a Q&A blog called *Yo, Is This Ageist?* (modeled on the superb *Yo, Is This Racist?*), and why people like Rhonda submit notes like this: "I am reading about so many of the things that have happened to me and upset me.

When I would talk to my family about it they acted like I was just overly sensitive about my age, when in actuality I was being subject to ageism." The task is to become aware of the political context of personal experience. *Yo* helped Rhonda realize that she should stop blaming herself, her insecurities, or her age for the discrimination she has encountered. Once our consciousness has been raised, we can stop faulting ourselves, take control of our stories, critique ageist thinking and doctrine, and work toward change. Change requires awareness. Think of it as a mind-set intervention.

EVERYONE IS AGEIST

"Bias is more automatic, ambiguous, and ambivalent than people typically assume," says Susan Fiske, a psychology professor at Princeton who studies stereotypes.[2] Almost everyone displays unconscious biases against marginalized groups, even when we've been socialized to know better. Attitudes aren't necessarily about distaste or dislike, either; they can be about shielding and protecting people from presumed incompetence or vulnerability. That, too, is bias.

Almost all of us are prejudiced against older people, and olders themselves are no exception. Ageism is woven into the fabric of life, reinforced by the media and popular culture at every turn, and seldom challenged. How could anyone be entirely free of it? "Why can't we stop ageism?" asks ethicist and gerontologist Harry R. Moody. "For some answers, start by looking in the mirror—and look around you." Considering Botox in your twenties or thirties for "wrinkle prevention"? (It's a thing.) Think about who profits from your anxiety. Flinching because the wrinkle ship has sailed? Think about who profits from your self-loathing.

It's harder to unlearn than to learn, especially when it comes to values. The critical starting point is to acknowledge our own prejudices.

Do unconscious associations reflect actual prejudice or merely the mindless absorption of cultural signals? It doesn't really matter; either way, they affect how we behave. The good news is that we can change, although the process requires genuine soul-searching and reflection. It's harder to unlearn than to learn, especially when it comes to values. The critical starting point is to acknowledge our own prejudices.

The next step is to work toward making our own behavior and beliefs less ageist. We're complicit if we lie about our age or sculpt our faces into rigid masks. We're complicit if we head for people our own age at a social gathering, on the assumption that we wouldn't have common interests across an age gap, or they wouldn't want to talk to us. We're complicit if we mutter under our breaths about the "little old lady" holding up the checkout line. No judgment—we're all ageist—but it's time.

The next step is harder: pointing out ageist behavior or attitudes in other people. Educating others, kindly and tactfully, sends that change outward like ripples across a pond. Silence sanctions, and it too has consequences. A 2013 study suggests that if you're confronted by prejudice and don't object to it, you'll actually become more prejudiced yourself. As a way to resolve the internal conflict, to make your behavior and your beliefs more consistent, your attitudes shift in a more prejudiced direction.[3]

Acknowledging bias is an uncomfortable task and an ongoing one, as I'm reminded on a regular basis. Make the effort and the rewards are real—and you can't get that genie back in the bottle. I hear regularly from people who've begun to reject age shame that they instantly feel relieved and empowered. As we travel this path—from accepting stigma to perceiving it as unjust and realizing that we can challenge it through collective action—we experience what sociologist Doug McAdam calls "cognitive liberation." It's a fantastic feeling, and it is the linchpin of movement-building.

The only person in my old office who was older than I am drank my Kool-Aid and is glad she did. Not long ago she told me she'd nearly bitten the head off a woman who was complaining about how hard it was to turn thirty. I gently pointed out that the forces that are flipping that twenty-nine-year-old out are the same ones that make her own upcoming seventieth so fraught. We're allies, not enemies. She got it. It'll take millions more conversations to build the coalitions that a movement requires, but it's happening. An intergenerational world is straight-up a better world. We're all in this together.

CONSCIOUSNESS-RAISING BEGINS AT HOME

My poor kids. My son Murphy, a computer scientist, was talking about mathematics research and the fact that a lot of important papers hadn't yet been posted to an online archive. "The problem is that a lot of them are by people who are really old now," he said. Uh oh. The issue, I chided, wasn't age but technological illiteracy. Older scientists were indeed less likely to race to post their work online, but it was wrong to assume so on the basis of age alone. Although he probably felt like kicking me, he got it, and he thinks of it differently now.

Here's a generous e-mail from my daughter's partner, Emily, a musician and yoga teacher:

Wednesday night my band had a gig and I got home super late. Operating on about 3 hrs. of sleep, I showed up at my early yoga class and had to give myself a major pep talk, like, "Okay! You can do this: just phone it in, it's only a one-hour class," etc. When I walked in the room, I noticed there was an older man in the class, and I instantly thought to myself, "Oh GREAT. This is all I need: an old guy who can't bend over, and whom I have to worry about busting a knee-cap or breaking a hip-ugh, FML" etc. [FML is short for Fuck My Life. I had to look it up]. *He was probably in his mid-to-late seventies; definitely the oldest person I've ever taught.*

As soon as we started the opening sun salutations, I felt so ashamed and realized what an ageist idiot I had been. Dude had seriously the most beautiful practice of anyone in the room, and was arguably one of the best students I've ever taught, not only for his strength, flexibility, timing, and beautiful breathing, but for his courage. When I tried to teach forearm stand (an inverted balance posture where you're just on your forearms) he was the ONLY one in the class who attempted it. He didn't make it all the way up, but he at least TRIED, which is more than I can say for the other five students in the class who just rested in child's pose after my demo, each of whom was a good forty years his junior. I just thought I'd share that with you because I felt like "A-HA! I just proved Ashton's whole point."

I came home the same week to these questions from my other son's fiancée, Agnieszka, a science teacher: "Does ageism exist in art? What would happen if we went to all those nursing homes with pens, paints, blank notebooks, tape recorders, film crews? . . . I feel like we often think that olders have done all their growth and are now just undergoing a steady decline. But aging could be seen as a necessary journey that leads to new experiences and develops our minds in novel ways. When I write this I keep thinking about older artists like Georgia O'Keeffe and Yayoi Kusama." She signed it (my favorite part) "your fellow older in training."

Some old people in training are born, not made, and Agnieszka is one of them. As a child she spent weekends and summers with her grandparents in two Polish mountain villages, and she's always gravitated toward much older people. She also has a keen sense of social justice and would have made her way to this awareness without any goosing on my part. Goosed without reprieve, the rest of my family and a ton of friends have joined her as old people in training. They may wish I'd give it a rest, but I think they're glad they're making the transition.

IF YOU SEE SOMETHING, SAY SOMETHING

There are ways to confront prejudice without being a jerk about it, although it's easier to go with the flow. A few summers ago I decided it was time for a new shirt for dancing, and headed into a favorite shop. When I explained my mission to the saleswoman, her response was, "With sleeves, of course?"

"No, I plan to work up a sweat," I replied, irritated and taken aback, and walked away. What should I have done instead? Asked "Why would you think that?" And not in an aggressive, how-do-you-know-I-don't-have-Michelle-Obama-arms-anymore kind of way. She'd have been flustered, I would have let her off the hook, and she would have learned something. But it was easier to let it go, and I missed the opportunity.

I knew I had to step up when a phrase in an e-mail from my college pal Lewis caught my attention. The offending phrase appeared in a note to a bunch of classmates who pass around photos of get-togethers and nostalgia-based music recommendations. The context was a boating foray during which fun was had and alcohol consumed, the latter "not like gin and juice at DKE but as fun as we 60+ers could manage."

"Re: 60+ers comment," I wrote Lewis, "keep in mind that you'd never make a gratuitous dig on the basis of someone's race or sex, and that age should be no exception. Now descending from soapbox—"

He pushed back: "I don't know anybody who doesn't note a difference and decline in physical and/or mental capabilities at our age. Adding humor lessens the sting of recognizing the truth. So 60+er comments/jokes/etc. such as mine are not at all in the same league as racist or sexist positions. They could be seen as such in the hands of people who are younger and using it to deny employment or even validity to anyone older."

Lewis was employing a classic defense mechanism: You've lost your sense of humor. People tell ageist jokes all the time, even in bastions of political correctness—listen for 'em on NPR. They can be funny as hell. They also draw on the stereotype of olders as asexual, physically weak, and mentally impaired. And while it's okay to make fun of people, it's not okay to discriminate against them. What makes comments like these discriminatory? The fact that we'd never mock the same deficits in a young person. I pushed back too: "Physical capacity does indeed decline, though so far my brain appears to be hanging in there. But your comment is rooted in internalized ageism: the assumption that 60+ers are actually less capable of fun than college kids, and in even more problematic stereotyping: the notion that all 60-year-olds are alike in this or any other regard."

Nor does the age of the offender matter. Ageism disempowers people at both ends of the age spectrum. And, oh yeah, all the people in the middle, which is why Masha's aging party seems preposterous to everyone for whom "aging" remains a dirty word. This year the e-mail arrived from her husband, who was planning a surprise party. "Masha is turning thirty-five years young," it began. Crap. I took a deep breath and wrote back, "You're gonna think I'm kidding, but last year Masha gave her birthday the extremely wonderful and radical name the Aging Party. I don't expect you to go that far. But she's not thirty-five years young, she's thirty-five years old, and she's good with it. So please don't use cutesy, denial-oriented ageist language to describe this wonderful event."

"Cutesy is my raison d'être. Nonetheless, point taken," Zor responded graciously. "Looking forward to dancing with you." Me too.

Lewis and I are still friends, and his point of view did shift a bit. A filmmaker who attended one of my talks put it this way: "The big takeaway is to see how much I have bought into the party line about what the future holds." A painter declared herself ready for the next step, after being "made uncomfortable by being forced to acknowledge my own ageist thoughts and self-denigration and ultimately fired up to fight it where I see it in myself and others." She's following the Quaker tradition of bearing witness: People who are present when an injustice occurs point out that it's wrong. Bear witness, and speak up. Things start small. No successful struggle began as a mass movement.

SOME PLACES TO START:

- Look for ways in which you *are* ageist instead of looking for evidence that you aren't. You can't challenge bias unless you're aware of it, and everyone's biased some of the time.
- If you're not sure whether something is ageist or not, think about whether the same language or image would be appropriate if the situation involved someone significantly older or younger. When does an amorously entwined couple get downgraded from "hot" to "adorable," for example? If your dentist spots a lot of cavities "for someone your age," on the other hand, it's probably all about the floss.
- Don't assume that older people aren't ageist. Plenty of them unthinkingly accept second-class status as "just the way things are."
- Don't compliment an older person by telling her she's "different"—fitter, stronger, more stylish—from other people her age. Saying "I can't believe you're seventy-five" implies that seventy-five-year-olds look a certain way. She can only accept the compliment at the expense of other women her age. And it implies that you'll stop admiring this attribute or capacity when it stops being exceptional. Instead, compliment her purse or her power lift.
- Watch out for sanitized or romanticized views of aging: depictions of sexless, placidly smiling olders enjoying their golden years on a porch swing, or doing splits in dance competitions, or playing the token wise elder. Whitewashing only masks anxiety. Idealized depictions of late life distract from the real challenges of aging and the need to confront them.
- Talk to people significantly older and younger than you, and listen carefully. If you don't know many of them, seek them out.
- Don't use "still" when describing a routine activity, because it suggests that the activity makes the person an outlier. Older people are not *still* driving, going to the gym and the office, traveling,

having sex, etc. They're just doing them, like countless others. It's a hard habit to break, but just leave it out.

- The next time the sight of someone with severe disabilities makes you think, "Put a pillow over my head if I get like that," remember: The bull looks different.
- The next time someone asks how old you are, tell them the truth. Then ask why they wanted to know, or what feels different now that they have a number, and why. If you're asking a child how old they are, tell them your age first.
- Instead of telling people they look great for their age, tell them they look great. If someone says, "You look great for your age," resist the impulse to thank them. Say, just as brightly, "You look great for your age too!"
- Don't use adjectives for older people that you wouldn't apply to younger ones, like "spry" and "feisty" and "kindly." Try "active," "opinionated," and "kind." Children are "little," "cute," and "childlike." Their grandparents are not. Colors and communities are vibrant; people are energetic or memorable.
- Avoid youth-centric language like "young at heart" or "youthful" or "young for your years." Instead, use specific descriptors like "playful" or "full of energy" or "charismatic" or "enthusiastic"— attributes that are age-independent.
- Have you ever heard anyone describe themselves as "elderly"? Avoid the word. Skip "*the* elderly," too; it implies infirmity and suggests that advanced age lumps people into some kind of uniform category, when nothing could be further from the case.
- Nix "grandmotherly" unless the topic is grandmotherhood. It reduces women to their reproductive status, leaves out the child-free, and is desexualizing.
- Look for beauty in older faces and bodies. It is there.
- Don't assume someone is too old—or too young—to weigh in on a topic or take on a responsibility.
- Assume capacity, not incapacity. Speak to an older person the

same way you would to a younger one. Offer help if it seems appropriate, but don't insist.

- Train yourself to notice when everyone in a group is the same age, and unless there's some legitimate reason, speak up about it.
- The next time you wonder whether an outfit, or an attitude, or an outing is age-appropriate, reconsider the question. For adults, there's no such thing.
- Start or join a consciousness-raising group around age bias. Consciousness-raising is a tool that uses the power of personal experiences to unpack unconscious prejudices and to call for social change. You can download a free booklet—*"Who Me, Ageist?" How To Start Your Own Consciousness-Raising Group*—at thischairrocks.com/resources. It includes a list of other anti-ageism resources.
- Don't assume this topic is only relevant for older people. Ageism affects everyone.

EXPECT PUSHBACK

Social change unsettles. We use defenses to avoid discomfort or conflict. Activist Kathy Sporre came up with this list of typical responses to being called out for ageist behavior:[4]

- Global thinking: it's okay because "everyone does it," as in, "Everyone buys 'over-the-hill' birthday cards." Maybe so, but it doesn't make the cards any less objectionable.
- Rationalizing: "I was just kidding. I didn't mean to hurt anyone's feelings." That may be true, but negative speech has an effect. Intent is irrelevant.
- Minimizing: "Ageism isn't as bad as racism/global warming/ lymphoma, so what's the big deal?" This just deflects the conversation.
- Blaming: "If you had to deal with them every day, you'd call them cranky old coots too!" This shifts responsibility for the ageist behavior onto others—often olders themselves.

These evasive maneuvers maintain the status quo. The goal when we challenge them isn't to "win" the point, since being confrontational typically makes the other person dig in, but to give them a new perspective to chew on. Speaking at an anti-ageism roundtable, I called out some problematic language I'd heard from others during the meeting, including "gray tsunami," which likens population aging to a terrifying natural disaster. Of course I didn't name names, but a woman came over afterward and declared, "I *like* that language, it's not derogatory, and I'm sticking with it." Okay, then! But perhaps she'll think twice the next time.

If people get defensive, odds are that the conversation is hitting close to home and touching on unexamined attitudes. It can be very difficult for someone to understand that their intentions are beside the point, to let those intentions fall away, and to focus on the message itself. Listen carefully and empathetically, and try to hear what it says about you as well as about the other person.

What if you're on the receiving end of an ageist comment? Comments can be not only inappropriate but downright bizarre— "I'm so glad you're still up and around," for example. It can be hard not to be snippy, as I was with the saleswoman in the clothing store, or tongue-tied, or to manage more than a disbelieving, "Huh?" Here's an all-purpose rejoinder: "What do you mean by that?" Or "Why would you say that?" Pose the question in a neutral way—not aggressively or sarcastically, because you wouldn't want to be labeled feisty or crotchety, now would you?—and then just listen.

If you're on the receiving end of an ageist comment, ask, "What do you mean?" Then just listen.

This way you don't have to explain why the comment was unacceptable; the other person has to figure it out. They have to think about why they're suddenly squirming (instead of you). Those moments stick with us. A friend approached an older woman with a cane at an intersection and asked loudly, "May I help you?" In return she received an angry earful, not for the offer of assistance but for the assumption that the older woman was hard of hearing. It was an embarrassing lesson she never forgot. Instead of bristling, suppose the older woman had gently asked, "Why are you speaking so loudly?" The younger woman would have learned the lesson less painfully, and her well-meaning offer might have been accepted. The point is not to embarrass, but to make someone reflect for a moment. It's more educational than any mini-lecture could ever be, and both parties, whatever their ages, benefit from an even-handed exchange.

TOWARD AN ALL-AGE-FRIENDLY WORLD

Ridding ourselves of internalized ageism and becoming Old People in Training are important tasks in their own right. Their value increases exponentially if it helps us see resistance to ageism as part of a broader cultural revolution.

There will be resistance. Fundamental paradigm shifts threaten the role, income, and identity of established professionals, whether the field is buggy-making or print publishing. When electric light came on the scene, the value of Procter & Gamble's brilliant chemists plummeted, because they were in the candle-making business, not lighting experts. Many in the field of aging will resist this shift because they're

Resisting ageism is part of a broader cultural revolution.

professionally and personally invested, consciously or not, in a decline-oriented model of aging. It's terrific that AARP has begun to confront ageism through their #DisruptAging initiative. Doing so in full means acknowledging octo- and nonagenarians as their constituents along with the young old, foregrounding disability rights, and embracing aging in all its forms—not just the "successful" version. Those are high-stakes moves in today's cultural climate, although change is underway.

What changes would we like to see? Strict divisions of any sort—whether between young, middle-aged, and old, or between home, school, and work, or between work and retirement—are not just artificial and increasingly obsolete. They are antithetical to the immense and necessary task of shaping and taking advantage of longer lives. In order to make the most of more healthy years, care for those who need it, and share these burdens and blessings across four living generations, we need to see these categories as commingled, messy, blended, and parallel, rather than as isolated silos, reflecting life itself in all its complexity. If careers started later and peaked in our late fifties and sixties, we'd have more time early on to study, to figure out what we're good at, and to be at home with kids while they're small. Transitioning gradually out of the workforce would enable us to pass on what we've learned and to plan for retirement, which we'd still have time to enjoy. Living, learning, and working together would facilitate intergenerational friendships and partnerships, and turn everyone into Old People in Training.

A social compact for longer lives would support contact and transfers of all kinds across generations; we needn't look any further than Social Security for an outstanding fiscal example. This stable and secure source of income has kept millions of Americans out of poverty, especially olders and people with disabilities, and in the process helped keep their families afloat. A social compact for longer lives would opt for integration over age apartheid, in the form of affordable, multi-generational housing, adequate and accessible public transportation, and universal compliance with the Americans with Disabilities Act. It would provide families—defined not by biology but by long-term mutual commitment—with subsidized caregiving at decent wages, and treat those workers with dignity. It would enforce the Elder Justice Act and the Age Discrimination in Employment Act.

How else could we move toward an all-age-friendly world?

- Increase opportunities for older people to contribute socially, civically, and economically—from libraries and schools and community centers and museums to farmers' markets and sporting events and community gardens—and support these new roles

237

as they evolve. Not just places to go but ways to get there, and not just bingo but activities that offer learning opportunities and trust and occasions to create and build.

- Help older people work longer by continuing to train them, offering flexible hours, increasing accessibility, and enabling transitions to part-time employment.
- Invest in research into the biology of aging. What triggers aging in our tissues and cells, why does it occur, and what genetic, physiological, and environmental factors underlie these changes? We have very few answers to these basic questions.
- Include older subjects in studies of physical, psychological, and social function, and in clinical trials of pharmaceuticals and new treatments unless there is a non-age-related reason for exclusion.
- Develop clinical guidelines for screening older patients (including questions about elder abuse, alcohol and drug use, sexual health, and care partner stress) and demand that evidence-based treatment be applied to olders with cardiac disease.
- Improve reimbursement for practicing geriatricians and encourage and fund physicians, nurse practitioners, and physician assistants who want to be trained and certified in geriatric medicine.
- Explicitly include olders in health-promotion campaigns, since both physical and mental health can improve at any age.
- Fund research into the social implications of longevity: how to integrate an active fourth generation into public and private life; how to enable olders to continue to contribute and care for them when they cannot; what roles technology could play; how attitudes toward marriage and family structures will be affected.
- Make education more friendly to older learners with accessible locations, flexible schedules, a full range of course offerings, scholarships, and integration into the school community.
- Introduce ageism into elementary-school curricula, so that children learn about it when they're taught about other forms of prejudice.
- Fund the Elder Justice Act, the federal government's most com-

prehensive response to the problem of elder abuse. Passed in 2010, it has received only one appropriation of $4 million.

- Support care partners in their stressful, exhausting, and important work. Over forty million Americans provide unpaid care, earn no Social Security credits, receive no paid leave, and have limited access to resources like training, family counseling, and time off. Nearly five million grandparents provide primary care to grandchildren, yet they receive only 10 percent of the funds from the National Family Caregiver Support Program, the only federal program of its kind.[5] People who leave the paid labor force to provide care for others (of any age) should continue to earn Social Security credits.
- Ensure income security for older Americans after they leave paid employment.
- Develop a comprehensive, public-private partnership to provide the long-term care that many olders will eventually require in some form. Most are in denial about it, which is one reason there's no real funding for long-term care.
- Adjust the healthcare system to improve geriatric treatment and provide public insurance for long-term care.
- Create new secular and spiritual rites of passage.
- Identify ageism as an overarching issue on any aging-related agenda, and prioritize anti-ageism initiatives.

Those are big asks. Yet experts quoted in *Gauging Aging*, a report issued in 2015 by the Leaders of Aging Organizations (AARP, the American Federation for Aging Research, the American Geriatrics Society, the American Society on Aging, the Gerontological Society of America, the National Council on Aging, and the National Hispanic Council on Aging) think these goals are achievable. They argue that although an aging society has the potential to strain public resources like Social Security and Medicare, "We are wealthy enough for an aging population."[6] The key is to make public spending more efficient, and to realign priorities.

The list could go on and on. Thousands of smart people—experts in medicine, health and workforce policy, urban planning, education, economics, law, design, and the humanities—are thinking hard about how to meet these challenges. Now is the perfect time for an active collaboration between all these fields, and more, to figure out ways to support those scenarios. Confronting ageism is fundamental to all of them, and ageism is a perfect target for compound advocacy. We cannot make the most of longer lives within a society that perpetuates and profits from age discrimination.

My call to action skews toward the first and foundational step of confronting internalized ageism, but that's only the first step. Although I'm leaving it to political economists to explain the function of ageism within the capitalist system, it's clear that upending discrimination on the basis of age will require fundamental changes in the way society is structured. We have to come up with fairer and broader ways to assess productivity, devise more ways for older people to continue to contribute, support them in these endeavors, and decouple the value of a human being from success along any of these metrics.

This social change demands that we join the struggle against racism, sexism, ableism, and homophobia as well. As the poet Audre Lorde said, "There is no such thing as a single-issue struggle because we don't live single-issue lives." Likewise, activists for other social justice causes would do well to consider how ageism hampers their efforts, and to raise awareness and work against it. When we come together at all ages for whatever cause matters most, whether a political campaign or a community garden, we make that effort more effective. Not only that: By having friends and comrades who are older and younger than ourselves, we dismantle ageism organically.

Like the ongoing movements that continue to challenge entrenched systems of racism and sexism, overcoming ageism is going to take a lot of determined people of all ages working to overturn "the way things are." That means a lot of uncomfortable reassessments, difficult conversations, and outright conflict, not just over healthcare and housing but about when we stop valuing people, and why—not because we grow old, but because we do so in an ageist world. That struggle is essential if we want to create a world in which people can find meaning and purpose at every stage of life.

Reshaping the landscape means challenging a system that values people in terms of conventional economic productivity instead of their full worth as human beings. The fundamental question is whether or not there is some age or stage at which people become disposable. Those who think not should ask that question, often and aloud, of the politicians I call virtuecrats, who equate personal goodness with material good fortune, consider poverty a moral failing, and make a repellent distinction between the "deserving" and "undeserving" poor. Why can't we have a society that values *all* of its members, educates a corps of geriatric specialists to help olders stay as healthy as possible, and supports collaboration between families, neighbors, and friends to keep everyone safe and connected to the world?

A revelatory encounter with a recording of Bessie Smith singing "Nobody in Town Can Bake a Sweet Jelly Roll Like Mine" introduced playwright August Wilson to the blues. He described it as "a birth, a baptism, a resurrection of my consciousness that I was a representative of a culture and a carrier of some very valuable antecedents."[7] Looking around, the twenty-year-old began looking at the olders in his community not as beaten-down and useless but as valuable sources of living history. He hung out in a Pittsburgh Hill District cigar store and pool hall and listened to them talk about baseball and city politics and their lives when they were young—a rich collective history of which, Wilson realized, he was a part. It "turned my ear, my heart, and whatever analytical tools I possessed to embrace this world."[8]

Everyone has access to worlds like Wilson's. Let's inhabit them. As Old People in Training of all ages and from all walks of life, let's take matters into our own hands and build an all-age-friendly society. It would be as hospitable to strollers as wheelchairs. Its members would acknowledge and respect differences in age, connect across them, and decline to leverage them against one another. Let's investigate the strategies that people put in place as they age, listen to what they need and want, and work toward a society in which preparing for late life is a collective as well as an individual endeavor. Imagine!

IT'LL BE WORTH IT

"Speak your mind, even if your voice shakes," said Gray Panthers founder Maggie Kuhn, who questioned the depiction of olders as sexless and incapacitated, called late life a time of "liberation and self-determination,"[9] and had no trouble envisioning critical roles for older members of society as watchdogs, advocates, educators, and futurists. Not to mention as backward-understanders; as Danish philosopher Søren Kierkegaard observed, "Life can only be understood backwards; but it must be lived forwards."

Age is different from race or gender because it is a universal condition. This sets ageism apart from racism or sexism or ableism, and paradoxically makes identification with the cause more elusive. Members of radical movements generally define themselves in opposition to the mainstream, but everyone ages. People of all ages, unite! We have nothing to lose but our prejudices.

When we swallow the notion that two-thirds of life is decline, the mind and body conform prematurely to expectations of frailty and debility. These perceptions inform our explicit and implicit attitudes toward age and aging. They also *People of all ages, unite!* profoundly influence how—and whether—people of different ages interact, and how youngers envision the future that awaits them. Every Old Person in Training has a part to play in transforming personal and cultural attitudes toward longevity. Some will take it further, exposing the prevailing view of population aging as a threat to powerful economic interests as well as to personal empowerment.

AGE PRIDE!

Unlike the "temporarily able-bodied" (as the rest of us are known to people with disabilities) who assiduously avoid canes, walkers, and anything else that might associate us with infirmity, disability rights activists howl, "I'm disabled, hear me roar." By claiming the status as integral to their identity, they destigmatize it. Over the past four decades, they've built a movement based on the premise that "There is no pity or tragedy in disability, and that it is society's myths, fears, and stereotypes that most make being disabled difficult."[10] You could swap "aging" and "old" for "disability" and "disabled" in that powerful statement, especially since long life is indisputably no loss but unequivocally a gift. Many millions of Americans now take growing pride in identifying as disabled, a stunning transition in a society that exalts intelligence and physical perfection.

Words like "asylum" and "retarded" and even "handicapped" have been demoted from the lexicon. Our fear of mental health issues, invisible and terrifying, runs even deeper. Yet a burgeoning "mad pride" movement has emerged to combat the stigma and celebrate the culture and identity of people the world has labeled "mentally ill." Only a few decades ago, being gay was a shameful secret; now closets are for clothes, and same-sex marriage is legal in America. Spurred by the foundational civil rights movement, each of these groups has nudged the U.S. closer to a society that values and respects all its members.

Isn't it time to put age equality, likewise a matter of civil and human rights, on the agenda? Discrimination on the basis of age is as unacceptable as discrimination on the basis of any other aspect of ourselves that we cannot change. Imagine the postwar generation, their children, and *their* children finding common cause in a fact- rather than fear-based view of growing older, and mobilizing against the discrimination that makes aging in America so much more difficult than it should be. This is about the world we want those children, who may well live to be one hundred, to inherit.

Naming and claiming and de-shaming are crucial components of all successful social movements. The Black Power movement had "Black is beautiful." Helen Reddy's song "I Am Woman" became the anthem of the women's movement. "Nothing about us without us," declare people with disabilities, insisting on visibility and participation. Gay rights activists chant, "We're here, we're queer, get used to it!" It's time for "We're old, we're bold, behold!" to join that playlist. It's time for a radical aging movement, and for age pride. Parents revel in their children's accomplishments; as youth recedes, why not take pride in having come this far and in our aspirations to make the most of whatever the future holds?

Age pride isn't just for dissed teenagers or dismissed olders. Age pride is for Maggie Kuhn, who said, "We must be proud of our age," and who, if she'd lived long enough, would have beaten me to "Occupy age!" Age pride is for everyone who refuses to regret waking up a day older, who acknowledges long life as the privilege it is, and who is prepared to challenge the power structures that underlie all discrimination. We are all aging. Each of us benefits when we make common cause against oppression. Age pride is for everyone.

NOTES

INTRODUCTION

1   "A Profile of Older Americans: 2016," Administration for Community Living, U.S. Department of Health and Human Services, 7, https://www .acl.gov/sites/default/files/Aging%20and%20Disability%20in%20America /2016-Profile.pdf.

2   "A Profile of Older Americans: 2017," Administration for Community Living, U.S. Department of Health and Human Services, 15, https://www.acl.gov/ sites/default/Aging%20and %20Disability%20in%20America/2017Older AmericansProfile.pdf.

3   Kenneth M. Langa, Eric B. Larsen, Eileen M. Crimmins, "A Comparison of the Prevalence of Dementia in the United States in 2000 and 2012," *Journal of the American Medical Association-Internal Medicine*, January 2017. 2017;177(1):51–58. doi:10.1001/jamainternmed.2016.6807

4   Greg O'Neill, Director, National Academy on an Aging Society, "Discussion of Social, Economic, Policy and Scientific Drivers of Change Affecting Healthy Aging, Productive Engagement and Ageism—'What this means to Mrs. Jones'" (presentation at the 2010 Age Boom Academy, sponsored by The Atlantic Philanthropies, New York, June 7, 2010).

5   Laura L. Carstensen, *A Long Bright Future* (New York: Broadway Books, 2009), 26.

6   David G. Blanchflower and Andrew J. Oswald, "Is well-being U-shaped over the life cycle?" *Social Science & Medicine*, Elsevier, vol. 66(8); 1733–1749, April 2008, http://www.nber.org/papers/w12935; Jonathan Rauch, "The Real Roots of Midlife Crisis," *The Atlantic*, December 2014, http://www .theatlantic.com/magazine/archive/2014/12/the-real-roots-of-midlife-crisis /382235/; Yang, Yang. 2008. "Social Inequalities in Happiness in the U.S. 1972–2004: An Age-Period-Cohort Analysis." *American Sociological Review*, 73: 204–226, http://news.uchicago.edu/article/2008/04/16/age-comes -happiness-university-chicago-study-shows.

CHAPTER ONE

WHERE AGEISM COMES FROM AND WHAT IT DOES

1   David Hackett Fischer, *Growing Old in America* (New York: Oxford University Press, 1978), 134.

2   Becca Levy and Mahzarin R. Banaji, "Implicit Ageism," in *Ageism: Stereotyping and Prejudice Against Older Persons*, ed. Todd D. Nelson (Cambridge: MIT Press, 2004), 67.

3   Robert N. Butler, *Why Survive? Being Old in America* (New York: Harper & Row, 1975), 47.

4   National Center on Elder Abuse, Administration on Aging, Department of Health and Human Services, "Elder Abuse: The Size of the Problem," citing, among other sources, Acierno, R., Hernandez, M. A., Amstadter, A. B., Resnick, H. S., Steve, K., Muzzy, W., et al. (2010). Prevalence and correlates of emotional, physical, sexual, and financial abuse and potential neglect in the United States: The national elder mistreatment study. *American Journal of Public Health*, 100(2), 292–297, http://www.ncea.aoa.gov/Library/Data /index.aspx.

5   Cari Romm, "Battling Ageism With Subliminal Messages," *The Atlantic*, October 22, 2014, http://www.theatlantic.com/health/archive/2014/10 /battling-ageism-with-subliminal-messages/381762/.

6   Todd D. Nelson, "Ageism: Prejudice Against Our Feared Future Self," *Journal of Social Issues,* 61 (2005); 207–222, referencing the work of Giles et al., 1994; Giles, Fox, & Smith, 1993.

7   Sarit A. Golub, Allan Filipowicz, and Ellen J. Langer, "Acting Your Age," in *Ageism: Stereotyping and Prejudice Against Older Persons*, ed. Todd D. Nelson (Cambridge: MIT Press, 2004), 292.

8   Zoe Williams, "We Should Celebrate Enhanced Longevity," *The Age*, July 25, 2009, http://www.theage.com.au/federal-politics/we-should -celebrate-enhanced-longevity-20090724-dw3g.html.

9   Anthony Webb, "Do Health and Longevity Create Wealth?" Institute for

Ethics and Emerging Technologies, Alliance for Health & the Future at the International Longevity Centre Policy Report, 2006, http://ieet.org/course /Webb-Health&Wealth.pdf.

10 Philip Longman, "Think Again: Global Aging," *Foreign Policy*, October 12, 2010, http://www.foreignpolicy.com/articles/2010/10/11/think_again _global_aging.

11 Andrea Charise, "Rising Tide, Grey Tsunami: Charting the History of a Dangerous Metaphor," Canadian Geriatrics Society Podcast Series, Episode 3, 2012. Now posted at: http://canadiangeriatrics.ca/wp-content/uploads/2017/10 /Rising-Tide-Grey-Tsunami-Charting-the-History-of-a-Dangerous-Metaphor .mp3 (via http://canadiangeriatrics.ca/resources/humanities/). And permanently archived at: http://www.utsc.utoronto.ca/people/acharise/talks/

12 Ted C. Fishman, "As Populations Age, a Chance for Younger Nations," *New York Times Magazine*, October 14, 2010, http://www.nytimes.com/2010/10 /17/magazine/17Aging-t.html.

13 Thomas Edsall, "Who is Poor?" *New York Times*, March 13, 2013, http://opinionator.blogs.nytimes.com/2013/03/13/who-is-poor/.

14 Fishman, op. cit.

15 Frank Furedi, preface to *The Imaginary Time Bomb* by Phil Mullan (London: I.B. Tauris & Co., 2002), xii.

16 Phil Mullan, *The Imaginary Time Bomb* (London: I.B. Tauris & Co., 2002), p. 94.

17 Longman, op. cit.

18 Martha Albertson Fineman and Stu Marvel, "The right's latest Obamacare lie: Scapegoating America's seniors," *Slate.com*, November 7, 2013, http:// www.salon.com/2013/11/07/the_rights_latest_obamacare_lie_scapegoating _americas_seniors/.

19 A. Palangkaraya and J. Yong, "Population ageing and its implications on aggregate health care demand: empirical evidence from 22 OECD countries," *International Journal of Heath Care Finance Econ* (2009), 391–402. doi: 10.1007/s10754-009-9057-3. http://www.ncbi.nlm.nih.gov/pubmed/19301123.

20 D.E. Kingsley, "Aging and health care costs: narrative versus reality,"

Poverty Public Policy. 2015;7(1):3–21. doi: http://dx.doi.org/10.1002/pop4.89. http://apps.who.int/iris/bitstream/10665/186468/1/WHO_FWC_ALC_15 .01_eng.pdf?ua=1.

21   Matthew C. Klein, "How Americans Die," *Bloomberg View*, April 17, 2014, http://www.bloomberg.com/dataview/2014-04-17/how-americans-die.html.

22   John W. Rowe and Robert L. Kahn, *Successful Aging* (New York: Dell Publishing, 1998), 186.

23   "The Longevity Economy: Generating economic growth and new opportunities for business," by Oxford Economics for AARP, September 2016, p. 14, http://www.aarp.org/content/dam/aarp/home-and-family/personal -technology/2016/09/2016-Longevity-Economy-AARP.pdf.

24   "The Longevity Economy: Generating economic growth and new opportunities for business," by Oxford Economics for AARP, 2013, p. 4, http://www .aarp.org/content/dam/aarp/home-and-family/personal-technology/2013-10 /Longevity-Economy-Generating-New-Growth-AARP.pdf.

25   Joseph F. Coughlin, *The Longevity Economy: Unlocking the World's Fastest- Growing, Most Misunderstood Market* (NY: Public Affairs, 2017), 8.

26   Whitney Johnson, "Entrepreneurs Get Better With Age," *Harvard Business Review*, June 27, 2013, https://hbr.org/2013/06/entrepreneurs-get-better-with.

27   "Value of Senior Volunteers to U.S. Economy Estimated at $75 Billion," Corporation for National and Community Service, May 20, 2015, https:// www.nationalservice.gov/newsroom/press-releases/2015/value-senior -volunteers-us-economy-estimated-75-billion.

28   David Costanza, "Can We Please Stop Talking About Generations as if They Are a Thing?," *Slate* magazine, April 13, 2018, https://slate.com /technology/2018/04/the-evidence-behind-generations-is-lacking.html.

29   Phil Mullan, *The Imaginary Time Bomb*, op. cit., xix.

30   Lincoln Caplan, "The Boomer Fallacy: Why Greedy Geezers *Aren't* Destroying Our Financial Future," *The American Scholar*, Summer 2014, 20.

31   Christopher Farrell, "Disproving Beliefs About the Economy and Aging," *New York Times*, May 13, 2016, https://www.nytimes.com/2016/05/14/your -money/disproving-beliefs-about-the-economy-and-aging.html.

32   Anne Karpf, *How to Age* (London: Macmillan, 2014), 31.

33   Gretchen Livingston, "At Grandmother's House We Stay," Pew Research Center report, September 4, 2013, http://www.pewsocialtrends.org/2013/09 /04/at-grandmothers-house-we-stay/.

34   MacArthur Foundation Network on an Aging Society, "Facts & Fictions About an Aging America," *Contexts*, vol. 8, no. 4, November, 2009, http://www.macfound.org/press/publications/facts-fictions-about-aging -america/.

35   Pew Charitable Trusts Economic Mobility Project, "When Baby Boomers Delay Retirement, Do Younger Workers Suffer?" September 13, 2012, http://www.pewtrusts.org/en/research-and-analysis/issue-briefs/2012/09 /13/when-baby-boomers-delay-retirement-do-younger-workers-suffer.

36   Altman, Ros CBE. *A New Vision for Older Workers: Retain, Retrain, Recruit.* Report to Government. March 2015, https://www.gov.uk/government /publications/a-new-vision-for-older-workers-retain-retrain-recruit.

37   Fischer, *Growing Old in America*, 199.

38   Lincoln Caplan, "The Boomer Fallacy: Why Greedy Geezers *Aren't* Destroying Our Financial Future," *American Scholar*, Summer, 2014, 26.

39   Canadian Institute for Health Information, "Health Care in Canada, 2011–A Focus on Seniors and Aging," ix, https://secure.cihi.ca/free_products /HCIC_2011_seniors_report_en.pdf,

40   E. Lindland, M. Fond, A. Haydon, and N. Kendall-Taylor (2015). "Gauging aging: Mapping the gaps between expert and public understandings of aging in America." Washington, DC: FrameWorks Institute, http://www .frameworksinstitute.org/pubs/mtg/gaugingaging/page7.html.

41   Kevin M. Murphy and Robert H.Topel, "The Value of Health and Longev-ity" (June 2005). National Bureau of Economic Research Working Paper No. w11405. Available through Social Science Research Network: http:// papers.ssrn.com/sol3/papers.cfm?abstract_id=742364.

42   "Aging and the Macroeconomy: Long-Term Implications of an Older Population," September 2012, National Research Council, http://www.rci .rutgers.edu/~khartman/libguides/agingandmacroeconomybriefreport.pdf.

43   Susan Jacoby. *Never Say Die: The Myth and Marketing of the New Old Age* (New York: Pantheon, 2011), p. 37.

44   Jill Lepore, "The Force: How much military is enough?" *New Yorker,* January 28, 2013.

45   Central Intelligence Agency, *The World Factbook*, "Country Comparison: Life Expectancy at Birth," https://www.cia.gov/library/publications/the -world-factbook/rankorder/2102rank.html.

46   Barry Bosworth, Gary Burtless, and Kan Zhang, "Later Retirement, Inequality in Old Age, and the Growing Gap in Longevity Between Rich and Poor," The Brookings Institution, January 2016, https://www .brookings.edu/wp-content/uploads/2016/02/BosworthBurtlessZhang _retirementinequalitylongevity_012815.pdf.

47   *NPR, Talk of the Nation,* "In 'Shoot My Man,' Mosley Tells Tale of Atone- ment," by NPR Staff, January 26, 2012, http://www.npr.org/2012/01/26 /145913466/in-shoot-my-man-mosley-tells-tale-of-atonement.

CHAPTER TWO

OUR AGES, OURSELVES: IDENTITY

1   Anne Karpf, "'Ageing is a mixture of gains and losses': why we shouldn't fear getting old," *The Guardian,* January 3, 2014, http://www.theguardian .com/society/2014/jan/04/ageing-mixture-gains-losses.

2   Laura Shapiro, "What It Means to Be Middle Aged," *New York Times Book Review,* January 13, 2012, http://www.nytimes.com/2012/01/15/books /review/in-our-prime-the-invention-of-middle-age-by-patricia-cohen-book -review.html.

3   Butler, *Why Survive?*, 14.

4   Paul Taylor et al., "Growing Old in America: Expectations vs. Reality," *Pew Research Center's Social and Demographic Trends Report,* June 29, 2009, 3.

5   Sarit A. Golub, Allan Filipowicz, and Ellen J. Langer, "Acting Your Age" in *Ageism: Stereotyping and Prejudice Against Older Persons,* ed. Todd D. Nelson (Cambridge: MIT Press, 2004), 278.

6   Susan Krauss Whitbourne and Joel R. Sneed, "The Paradox of Well-Being, Identity Processes, and Stereotype Threat: Ageism and Its Potential Relationships to the Self in Later Life," in *Ageism: Stereotyping and Prejudice Against Older Persons,* ed. Todd D. Nelson (Cambridge: MIT Press, 2004), 287.

7   Sarit A. Golub, Allan Filipowicz, and Ellen J. Langer, "Acting Your Age" in *Ageism: Stereotyping and Prejudice Against Older Persons,* ed. Todd D. Nelson (Cambridge: MIT Press, 2004), 288.

8   Golub, Filipowicz, and Langer, "Acting Your Age," 282.

9   Judith Warner, "I Feel It Coming Together," *New York Times,* October 15, 2009, http://opinionator.blogs.nytimes.com/2009/10/15/i-feel-it-coming-together.

10 Sasha Frere-Jones, "Brit Pop," *New Yorker,* December 16, 2013, www.newyorker.com/magazine/2013/12/16/brit-pop.

11 University of Warwick, "Middle-Aged Misery Spans the Globe," *ScienceDaily,* January 30, 2008, http://www.sciencedaily.com/releases/2008/01/080129080710.htm.

12 Lynne Segal, *Out of Time: The Pleasures and the Perils of Aging* (London: Verso Books, 2013), Kindle edition.

13 Wendy Lustbader, *Life Gets Better: The Unexpected Pleasures of Growing Older* (New York: Jeremy P. Tarcher/Penguin, 2011), 125.

14 "Gerotranscendence: A Possible Path Toward Wisdom in Old Age," pamphlet, Uppsala University, Sweden, http://www.soc.uu.se/digitalAssets/149/149866_folder.pdf.

15 Molly Andrews, "The Seductiveness of Agelessness," *Aging and Society,* vol. 19, no. 3 (1999), 301–318.

16 Alex Morris, "The Prettiest Boy in the World," *New York,* August 14, 2011, http://nymag.com/fashion/11/fall/andrej-pejic/.

17 *NYU Local* blog, April 21, 2014, http://nyulocal.com/on-campus/2014/04/21/local-stops-internet-teenagers-jesus-flume-and-america/.

18 Elaine Showalter, introduction to *Out of Time: The Pleasures and the Perils of Aging,* by Lynne Segal (London: Verso Books, 2013), Kindle edition.

19 Personal e-mail to author, via Paula Span, May 8, 2013.

20 Naomi Wolf, "Madonna: The Director's Cut," *Harper's Bazaar*, Nov 9, 2011, http://www.harpersbazaar.com/celebrity/news/madonna-interview-1211.

21 "Alabama Mayor, 91, Admits Stealing $201K from Town," AP, October 12, 2012, http://www.cbsnews.com/8301-201_162-57531139/alabama-mayor-91 -admits-stealing-$201k-from-town/.

22 Harry R. Moody, *Human Values in Aging* newsletter, August 1, 2009.

23 Anne Karpf, *How to Age* (London: Macmillan, 2014), 65.

24 Ina Jaffe and NPR Staff, "'Silver Tsunami,' And Other Terms That Can Irk the Over-65 Set," National Public Radio, May 19, 2014, http://www.npr.org /2014/05/19/313133555/silver-tsunami-and-other-terms-that-can-irk-the -over-65-set.

25 Margaret Cruikshank, *Learning to Be Old: Gender, Culture and Aging* (Lanham, MD: Rowman & Littlefield, 2013), 3.

26 Paula Span, "Aging's Misunderstood Virtues," *New York Times*, August 30, 2010, http://newoldage.blogs.nytimes.com/2010/08/30/appreciating-the -peculiar-virtues-of-old-age/.

27 Laura Carstensen, *A Long Bright Future*, 228.

CHAPTER THREE

FORGET MEMORY: THE OLDER BRAIN

1 Rowe and Kahn, *Successful Aging*, 44.

2 Margaret Morganroth Gullette, "Our Irrational Fear of Forgetting," *New York Times*, May 21, 2011, http://www.nytimes.com/2011/05/22/opinion /22gullette.html.

3 Laura Carstensen, professor of psychology, Stanford University, and director, Stanford Center on Longevity, "The Science of Aging," (presentation at the 2012 Age Boom Academy, sponsored by the Atlantic Philanthropies, AARP and the *New York Times*, New York, NY), March 24, 2012.

4 Gina Kolata, "U.S. Dementia Rates Are Dropping Even as Population

Ages," *New York Times*, November. 21, 2016, https://www.nytimes.com /2016/11/21/health/dementia-rates-united-states.html.

5   Margaret Morganroth Gullette, "Our Irrational Fear of Forgetting."

6   "11/14: Alzheimer's Most Feared Disease," by Marist Poll, November 15, 2012, http://maristpoll.marist.edu/1114-alzheimers-most-feared-disease/.

7   Robert McCann and Howard Giles, "Ageism in the Workplace: A Communication Perspective," in *Ageism: Stereotyping and Prejudice Against Older Persons*, ed. Todd D. Nelson (Cambridge: The MIT Press, 2004), 171.

8   Erving Goffman, *Stigma: Notes on the Management of Spoiled Identity* (New York: Simon and Schuster, 2009), 3.

9   Peter J. Whitehouse and Daniel George, *The Myth of Alzheimer's: What You Aren't Being Told About Today's Most Dreaded Diagnosis* (New York: St. Martin's Press, 2008), Kindle edition.

10 Andy Coghlan, "New Alzheimer's drugs: What do they do and could they be a cure?" *New Scientist*, July 22, 2015, https://www.newscientist.com/article /dn27941-new-alzheimers-drugs-what-do-they-do-and-could-they-be-a-cure/.

11 Toby Williamson, "My Name Is Not Dementia: People with Dementia Discuss Quality of Life Indicators," published by the Alzheimer's Society (UK), 2010.

12 Sousan Hammad, "Islands of Amnesia," *Guernica*, February 26, 2014, http://www.guernicamag.com/daily/sousan-hammad-islands-of-amnesia/

13 Margaret Morganroth Gullette, "Keeping the Conversation Going." *Jewish Daily Forward*, September 30, 2012, http://forward.com/articles/163585 /keeping-the-conversation-going/?p=all#ixzz2jJRYbpKg.

14 Anne Basting, "Coping With Alzheimer's," Letter to the Editor, *New York Times*, June 4, 2011, http://www.nytimes.com/2011/06/05/opinion /l05alzheimers.html.

15 Nina Strohminger and Shaun Nichols, "Your Brain, Your Disease, Your Self," *New York Times*, August 21, 2015, http://www.nytimes.com/2015/08 /23/opinion/your-brain-your-disease-your-self.html.

16 Whitehouse and George, *The Myth of Alzheimer's*, Kindle edition.

17   Tara Bahrampour, "Proposed budget for Alzheimer's research may rise by over 50 percent," *Washington Post*, December 16, 2015, http:www.washington post.com/local/social-issues/proposed-budget-for-alzheimers-research-may-rise-by-over-50-percent/2015/12/16.

18   Bureau of Labor Statistics, Occupational Employment and Wages, May 2017, 39-9021 Personal Care Aides. https://www.bls.gov/ocs/current/ocs399021.html.

19   Molly Wagster, Branch Chief, Neuropsychology of Aging, National Institute on Aging, "The Aging Body," presentation at "Longevity: America Ages Seminar," sponsored by the Knight Foundation for Specialized Journalism, University of Maryland, Towson, MD, April 9, 2008.

20   Patricia A. Coyle et al., "Effect of Purpose in Life on the Relation Between Alzheimer Disease Pathologic Changes on Cognitive Function in Advanced Age," *Arch Gen Psychiatry*, 2012 May; 69(5): 499–505. doi: 10.1001/archgenpsychiatry.2011.1487, http://www.ncbi.nlm.nih.gov/pmc/articles/PMC3389510/.

21   Benedict Carey, "At the Bridge Table, Clues to a Lucid Old Age," *New York Times*, May 21, 2009, http://www.nytimes.com/2009/05/22/health/research/22brain.html.

22   Joe Verghese, Richard B. Lipton, Mindy J. Katz, Charles B. Hall, Carol A. Derby, Gail Kuslansky, Anne F. Ambrose, Martin Sliwinski, and Herman Buschke, "Leisure Activities and the Risk of Dementia in the Elderly," *New England Journal of Medicine* (June 19, 2003); 348:2508–2516. DOI: 10.1056/NEJMoa022252, http://www.nejm.org/doi/full/10.1056/NEJMoa022252.

23   John W. Rowe, MD, and Robert L. Kahn, PhD, *Successful Aging* (New York: Dell Publishing, 1998), 20.

24   Gene Cohen, MD, director, Center on Aging, Health and Humanities, George Washington University, "The New Senior Moment: Positive Changes Because of Aging," presentation at "Longevity: America Ages Seminar" sponsored by the Knight Foundation for Specialized Journalism, University of Maryland, Towson, MD, April 7, 2008.

25   Roberto Cabeza, Nicole D. Anderson, Jill K. Locantore, and Anthony R.

McIntosh, "Aging Gracefully: Compensatory Brain Activity in High-Performing Older Adults," (2002), doi:10.1006/nimg.2002.1280. http://cabezalab.org/wp-content/uploads/2011/11/Cabeza02_AgingGracefully_Neuroimage.pdf

26   Benedict Carey, "Older Really Can Mean Wiser," *New York Times*, March 16, 2015, http://www.nytimes.com/2015/03/17/health/older-really-can-mean-wiser.html.

27   Joshua K. Hartshorne and Laura T. Germaine, "When Does Cognitive Functioning Peak? The Asynchronous Rise and Fall of Different Cognitive Abilities Across the Life Span," *Psychological Science* (2015), doi:10.1177/0956797614567339.

28   Michael Ramscar, Peter Hendrix, Cyrus Shaoul, Petar Milin, and Harald Baayen, "The Myth of Cognitive Decline: Non-Linear Dynamics of Lifelong Learning," *Topics in Cognitive Science* (2014), 5–42, DOI: 10.1111/tops.12078.

29   cbreaux.blogspot.com.

30   E-mail correspondence with author, August 13, 2015.

31   Kathleen Woodward, "Against Wisdom: The Social Politics of Anger and Aging," *Cultural Critique*, 51 (Spring 2002): 186–218.

32   Vaillant, *Aging Well*, 5.

33   Nicholas Bakalar, "Happiness May Come With Age, Study Says," *New York Times*, May 31, 2010, http://www.nytimes.com/2010/06/01/health/research/01happy.html.

34   Laura Carstensen, "Why Should We Look Forward To Getting Older?" interview with NPR/TED Staff • June 22, 2015, Part 4 of the TED Radio Hour episode "Shifting Time," http://krcu.org/post/why-should-we-look-forward-getting-older.

35   Nicholas Bakalar, "Happiness May Come With Age, Study Says," *New York Times*, May 31, 2010, http://www.nytimes.com/2010/06/01/health/research/01happy.html.

36   Jonathan Rauch, "The Real Roots of Midlife Crisis," *The Atlantic*, December, 2014, p. 90.

37 "The U-bend of Life," *Economist*, December 16, 2010, http://www
.economist.com/node/17722567.

38 Karl Pillemer, "Why Family and Social Relationships Matter," presentation
at the 2012 Age Boom Academy, sponsored by the Atlantic Philanthropies,
AARP and the *New York Times*, New York, NY, March 24, 2012.

39 Wendy Lustbader, "Who Speaks for Older Adults," presentation at Age
Boom Academy, New York, NY, sponsored by the Atlantic Philanthropies,
September 9, 2013.

40 Lustbader, *Life Gets Better*, 124.

41 Jane Fonda, "Life's Third Act," TEDWomen, December, 2011, http://www
.ted.com/talks/jane_fonda_life_s_third_act.html#.TwizbBCoYnd.e-mail.

42 Muriel Gillick, *The Denial of Aging: Perpetual Youth, Eternal Life, and Other
Dangerous Fantasies* (Cambridge: Harvard University Press, 2006), 266.

43 Hannah Seligson, "An Age-Old Dilemma for Women: To Lie or Not to Lie,"
New York Times, June 27, 2015, http://www.nytimes.com/2015/06/28/style
/an-age-old-dilemma-for-women.html.

44 Sarah Ditum, "How old age became a fashion trend," *The Guardian*,
October 19, 2012, http://www.theguardian.com/commentisfree/2012/oct/19
/fashion-old-women.

45 Paul Taylor, et al., "Growing Old in America: Expectations vs. Reality," *Pew
Research Report* (June 29, 2009), 59.

46 Louis Begley, "Age and Its Awful Discontents," *New York Times*, March 17,
2012, http://www.nytimes.com/2012/03/18/opinion/sunday/age-and-its
-discontents.html.

CHAPTER FOUR

HEALTH, NOT YOUTH: THE OLDER BODY

1 Anti-Ageism Taskforce at The International Longevity Center, "Ageism in
America," 2005, 25, http://www.mailman.columbia.edu/sites/default/files
/Ageism_in_America.pdf.

2   Gillick, *The Denial of Aging*, op. cit., p. 36.

3   Jay Olshansky, "The Demographic Perspective on Longevity," presentation at the 2009 Age Boom Academy, sponsored by the *New York Times* with support from the Glenn and MetLife Foundations, New York, NY, May 31, 2009.

4   *Brian Lehrer Show*, "The World Envies Our Wrinkles," March 27, 2015, http://www.wnyc.org/story/how-think-about-aging/.

5   "Good Survival Rates Found in Heart Surgery for Aged," *Associated Press*, November 10, 2008, http://www.nytimes.com/2008/11/11/health/research/11heart.html.

6   Maureen Mackey, "Ageism in Medicine: How It Appears, Why It Can Hurt You," *AARP Bulletin*, November 18, 2010, http://www.aarp.org/entertainment/books/info-11-2010/author_speaks_ageism_in_medicine.html.

7   "Access all ages: assessing the impact of age on access to surgical treatment," Age UK & The Royal College of Surgeons of England, RCSENG—Communications, 2012, https://www.rcseng.ac.uk/publications/docs/access-all-ages.

8   "Access all ages 2: Exploring variations in access to surgery among older people," Age UK & The Royal College of Surgeons of England, 2014, http://www.rcseng.ac.uk/news/docs/access-all-ages-2.

9   Monisha Pasupathi and Corinna E. Lockenhoff, "Ageist Behavior," in *Ageism: Stereotyping and Prejudice Against Older Persons*, ed. Todd D. Nelson (Cambridge: The MIT Press, 2004), 208.

10 Pasupathi and Lockenhoff, "Ageist Behavior," 206.

11 Pasupathi and Lockenhoff, "Ageist Behavior," 209.

12 J. Lazarou et al., "Why Learn about Adverse Drug Reactions (ADR)?" Institute of Medicine, National Academy Press, 2000; *JAMA* 1998;279(15):1200–1205; Gurwitz J. H. et al. *Am J Med* 2000;109(2):87–94, http://www.fda.gov/Drugs/GuidanceComplianceRegulatoryInformation/Surveillance/AdverseDrugEffects/ucm070461.htm.

    Website of the U.S Food and Drug Administration: http://www.fda.gov

/Drugs/DevelopmentApprovalProcess/DevelopmentResources
/DrugInteractionsLabeling/ucm114848.htm.

13   Richard W. Pretorius, Gordana Gataric, Steven K. Swedlund, and John R. Miller, "Reducing the Risk of Adverse Drug Events," *Am Fam Physician*, 2013 Mar 1;87(5), 331–336.

14   Paula Span, "The Clinical Trial Is Open. The Elderly Need Not Apply," *New York Times*, April 13, 2018, https://www.nytimes.com/2018/04/13/health /elderly-clinical-trials.html.

15   "Ageism in America," International Longevity Center, p. 35.

16   Joan C. Chrisler, Angela Barney and Brigida Palatino, "Ageism can be Hazardous to Women's Health: Ageism, Sexism, and Stereotypes of Older Women in the Healthcare System," *Journal of Social Issues*, vol. 72, no. 1, 2016, pp. 86–104 doi: 10.1111/josi.12157.

17   Laura Carstensen, "The Science of Aging," presentation at the 2012 Age Boom Academy, sponsored by the Atlantic Philanthropies, AARP and the *New York Times*, New York, NY, March 24, 2012.

18   Paula Span, "Even Fewer Geriatricians in Training," *New York Times*, January 9, 2013, http://newoldage.blogs.nytimes.com/2013/01/09/even -fewer-geriatricians-in-training/.

19   Kristen Gerencher, "Poor prognosis for care of elderly," CBS. *MarketWatch .com*, June 12, 2003, http://www.marketwatch.com/story/fighting-a-dearth -of-geriatric-medicine-professionals.

20   Anne Kingston, "Why it's time to face up to old age," *Maclean's*, October 13, 2014, http://www.macleans.ca/society/health/an-age-old -problem/.

21   Atul Gawande, *Being Mortal* (New York: Metropolitan Books, 2014), Kindle edition.

22   Albert L. Siu and John C. Beck, "Physician Satisfaction with Career Choices in Geriatrics," *The Gerontologist*, vol. 30, no. 4, 529–534, http:// gerontologist.oxfordjournals.org/content/30/4.toc.

23   J. Paul Leigh, Daniel J. Tancredi, and Richard L. Kravitz, "Physician career

satisfaction within specialties," *BMC Health Services Research* (2009), 9:166, http://www.biomedcentral.com/1472-6963/9/166.

24 Monisha Pasupathi and Corinna E. Lockenhoff, "Ageist Behavior," in *Ageism: Stereotyping and Prejudice Against Older Persons*, ed. Todd D. Nelson (Cambridge: The MIT Press, 2004), 202.

25 Ibid., 202.

26 National Institute of Health, "Disability in Older Adults," updated on June 30, 2018, http://report.nih.gov/nihfactsheets/ViewFactSheet.aspx?csid=37.

27 Harvard University, "Longer life, disability free: Increases in life expectancy accompanied by increase in disability-free life expectancy, study shows," *ScienceDaily*, 6 June 2016, www.sciencedaily.com/releases/2016/06/160606120039.htm.

28 Nicholas Bakalar, "Gentlemen, 5 Easy Steps to Living Long and Well," *New York Times*, February 19, 2008, http://www.nytimes.com/2008/02/19/health/19agin.html.

29 "Quick Statistics Compiled by the National Institute on Deafness and Other Communication Disorders (NIDCD)," https://www.nidcd.nih.gov/health/statistics/quick-statistics-hearing, page updated December 15, 2016.

30 Frank R. Lin, E. Jeffrey Metter, Richard J. O'Brien, Susan M. Resnick, Alan B. Zonderman, and Luigi Ferrucci, "Hearing Loss and Incident Dementia," *JAMA Neurology*, vol. 68, no. 2, February 14, 2011 *Arch Neurol.* 2011;68(2):214–220. doi:10.1001/archneurol.2010.362, http://archneur.jamanetwork.com/article.aspx?articleid=802291.

31 Gregg Easterbrook, "What Happens When We All Live to Be 100?," *The Atlantic*, October, 2014.

32 Rowe and Kahn, *Successful Aging*, 30.

33 Jane E. Brody, "100 Candles on Her Next Cake, and Three R's to Get Her There," *New York Times*, October 18, 2010, http://www.nytimes.com/2010/10/19/health/19brody.html.

34 John Leland, *Happiness Is A Choice You Make: Lessons from a Year Among*

the Oldest Old (New York: Sarah Crichton Books, Farrar, Straus & Giroux, 2018), 13.

35   Jane Gross, "How Many of You Expect to Die?" *New York Times*, July 8, 2008, http://newoldage.blogs.nytimes.com/2008/07/08/how-many-of-you -expect-to-die/?hp.

36   Becca R. Levy, Martin D. Slade, Robert Pietrzak, Luigi Ferruci, "Positive age beliefs protect against dementia even among elders with high-risk gene," *PLOS One*, February 7, 2018, https://doi.org/10.1371/journal.pone.0191004.

37   Gretchen Reynolds, "Exercise to Age Well, Whatever Your Age," *New York Times*, January 29, 2014, http://well.blogs.nytimes.com/2014/01/29 /exercise-to-age-well-regardless-of-age/.

38   "Dr. Mark Lachs—'Treat Me Not My Age,'" *Annuity News Now*, uploaded to YouTube November 15, 2010, http://www.youtube.com/watch?v=vz_lgvBsBpE.

39   "Living to 120 and Beyond: Americans' Views on Aging, Medical Advances and Radical Life Extension," Pew Research Religion & Public Life Project, August 6, 2013, http://www.pewforum.org/2013/08/06/living-to-120-and -beyond-americans-views-on-aging-medical-advances-and-radical-life -extension/.

40   "Aging Through The Eyes of A Doctor," *The Today Show*, Feb 17, 2011, http://www.today.com/id/41610799/ns/today-today_health/#.UmE_C5TF1As.

41   Cruikshank, *Learning to Be Old*, 37.

42   Ibid., p. 42.

43   Paula Span, "A Workout for the Mind," *New York Times*, October 20, 2014, http://newoldage.blogs.nytimes.com/2014/10/30/a-workout-for-the-mind/.

44   Karin A. Ouchida and Mark S. Lachs, "Not for Doctors Only: Ageism in Healthcare," *Generations*, vol. 39(3), Fall 2015, 47.

45   Becca R. Levy, Corey Pilver, Pil H. Chung, and Martin D. Slade, "Subliminal Strengthening Improving Older Individuals' Physical Function Over Time With an Implicit-Age-Stereotype Intervention," *Psychological Science*, October 17, 2014 0956797614551970, http://pss.sagepub.com/content/early /2014/10/17/0956797614551970.abstract.

46   Becca R. Levy, Martin D. Slade, Terrence E. Murphy, and Thomas M. Gill, "Association Between Positive Age Stereotypes and Recovery From Disability in Older Persons," *JAMA*. 2012;308(19):1972–1973. doi:10.1001/jama.2012.14541.

47   Becca R. Levy, Martin D. Slade, Suzanne R. Kunkel, Stanislav V. Kasl, "Longevity increased by positive self-perceptions of aging." *Journal of Personality and Social Psychology*, vol. 83(2), Aug. 2002, 261–270, http://psycnet.apa.org/journals/psp/83/2/261/.

CHAPTER FIVE

NO EXPIRATION DATE: SEX AND INTIMACY

1   Simi Linton, *My Body Politic: A Memoir* (Ann Arbor: University of Michigan Press, 2010), 85.

2   Cynthia Rich, "Ageism and the Politics of Beauty," in *Look Me in the Eye: Old Women, Aging and Ageism*, by Barbara Macdonald with Cynthia Rich (San Francisco: Spinsters Book Company, 1991), 143.

3   Anti-Ageism Taskforce of the International Longevity Center, "Ageism in America," 52, http://www.mailman.columbia.edu/sites/default/files/Ageism_in_America.pdf.

4   Stacy L. Smith, Marc Choueiti, Elizabeth Scofield, and Dr. Katherine Pieper, "Gender Inequality in 500 Popular Films: Examining On-Screen Portrayals and Behind-the-Scenes Employment Patterns in Motion Pictures Released between 2007–2012," Annenberg School for Communication & Journalism, University of Southern California, 2013.

5   "Over Sixty, Underestimated: A Look at Aging on the 'Silver' Screen in Best Picture Nominated Films," by Stacy L. Smith, PhD, Marc Choueiti, & Katherine Pieper, PhD, USC Annenberg School for Communication and Journalism, February, 2017, http://annenberg.usc.edu/sites/default/files/Over_Sixty_Underestimated_Report_2_14_17_Final.pdf.

6   Andrea Peyser, "Sleazy Geezer Society Meeting Now in Session," *New York*

Post, June 1, 2011, http://nypost.com/2011/06/01/sleazy-geezer-society -meeting-now-in-session/.

7   Arianna Rebolini, "These Confessions from Women in Their Eighties Will Challenge Your Views on Sexuality," *BuzzFeed*, February 6, 2014, http:// www.buzzfeed.com/ariannarebolini/these-confessions-from-women-in -their-eighties-will-challeng.

8   Lindy West, "Women in Their 70s Say They're Having Way Hotter Sex than You," *Jezebel*, February 6, 2014, http://jezebel.com/women-in-their -70s-say-theyre-having-way-hotter-sex-th-1516813341.

9   Cynthia Rich, "The Women in the Tower," in *Look Me in the Eye: Old Women, Aging and Ageism*, 78.

10   Susan Sontag, "The Double Standard of Aging," *Saturday Review*, September 23, 1972, 28–38.

11   Carina Chocano, "Girls Love Math. We Never Stop Doing It," *New York Times*, November 16, 2012, http://www.nytimes.com/2012/11/18/magazine /girls-love-math-we-never-stop-doing-it.html.

12   Miranda Prynne, "Beautiful actresses suffer more from ageism, says Angela Lansbury," *London Telegraph*, January 23, 2014, http://www.telegraph .co.uk/culture/theatre/10591490/Beautiful-actresses-suffer-more-from -ageism-says-Angela-Lansbury.html.

13   Frank Greve, "As seniors live longer they find 'love expectancy' also grows," *McClatchy Newspapers*, July 16, 2008, http://www.mcclatchydc.com/news /politics-government/article24491419.html.

14   "HIV Among People Aged 50 and Over," Division of HIV/AIDS Prevention, National Center for HIV/AIDS, Viral Hepatitis, Sexual Transmitted Diseases and Tuberculosis Prevention, Centers for Disease Control and Prevention, February 12, 2018, http://www.cdc.gov/hiv/group/age/olderamericans /index.html.

15   Stacy Tessler Lindau. MD, et al., "A Study of Sexuality and Health among Older Adults in the United States," *New England Journal of Medicine* (2007); 357:762–774, August 23, 2007, DOI: 10.1056/NEJMoa067423; http://www.nejm.org/doi/full/10.1056/NEJMoa067423.

16 Christian Rudder, *Dataclysm* (New York: Crown Publishers, 2014), 91.

17 Jon Pareles, "As Ever, the Wisdom Of a Lovin' Heart," *New York Times*, April 29, 2002, http://www.nytimes.com/2002/04/29/arts/pop-review-as -ever-the-wisdom-of-a-lovin-heart.html.

18 Gullette, *Agewise*, 130.

19 June Arnold, *Sister Gin* (Plainfield, VT: Daughters Inc., 1975), 129.

20 Louis Begley, "Old Love," *New York Times*, August 8, 2012, http://www .nytimes.com/2012/08/12/opinion/sunday/old-love.html.

21 Grace Paley, excerpt from "Here" from *Begin Again: Collected Poems* (New York: Farrar, Straus, and Giroux, 2000), 177.

22 Jan Hoffmann, "Married Sex Gets Better in the Golden Years," *New York Times,* February 23, 2015, http://well.blogs.nytimes.com/2015/02/23 /married-sex-gets-better-in-the-golden-years/.

23 *Still Doing It: The Intimate Lives of Women Over 60*, website for book and movie by Deirdre Fishel and Diana Holtzberg, http://www.stilldoingit.com/.

24 Lynne Segal, *Out of Time*, Kindle edition.

25 Mireille Silcoff, "Why Your Grandpa Is Cooler Than You," *New York Times Magazine,* April 26, 2013, http://www.nytimes.com/2013/04/28/magazine /why-your-grandpa-is-cooler-than-you.html.

26 *Fabulous Fashionistas*, directed by Sue Bourne, television documentary, first broadcast on Channel 4 (U.K.) September 14, 2013, http://www .channel4.com/programmes/fabulous-fashionistas.

27 Sarah Ditum, "How old age became a fashion trend," *The Guardian*, October 19, 2012, http://www.theguardian.com/commentisfree/2012/oct/19 /fashion-old-women.

28 "Antiaging Products and Services: The Global Market," *MarketWatch*, Aug. 19, 2013, http://www.marketwatch.com/story/antiaging-products-and-services -the-global-market-2013-08-19

29 Abby Ellin, "Raise Your Hand for an Engagement Selfie," *New York Times*, May 25, 2014.

30 Amia Srinivasan, "Does anyone have the right to sex?" *London Review of*

Books, vol. 40, no. 6, March 22, 2018, pp. 5–10, https://www.lrb.co.uk/v40/no6/amia-srinivasan/does-anyone-have-the-right-to-sex

31   *This American Life*, Episode 589: "Tell Me I'm Fat," June 17, 2016, https://www.thisamericanlife.org/589/transcript

32   "Frances McDormand on Aging," interview with Katie Couric posted on Yahoo News on Nov 6, 2014, https://www.youtube.com/watch?v=NZLQojPcuwQ.

33   Dominique Browning, "The Case for Laugh Lines," *New York Times*, May 26, 2011, http://www.nytimes.com/2011/05/29/fashion/dominique-brownings-argument-for-natural-aging.html.

34   Chuck Nyren, "Going Nutty Over Older Women's Bodies," *Huffington Post* blog, May 29, 2014, https://www.huffingtonpost.com/chuck-nyren/aging-bodies_b_5360313.html.

35   Brown, S. L., Lin, I.-F., & Payne, K. K. (2012). "Age Variation in the Divorce Rate, 1990–2010 (FP-12-05). National Center for Family & Marriage Research," http://www.bgsu.edu/content/ dam/BGSU/college-of-arts-and-sciences/NCFMR/ documents/FP/FP-12-05.pdf; https://contemporaryfamilies.org/growing-risk-brief-report/

36   Mike Albo, "Love Has No Bounds," *AARP* magazine, January 18, 2018, https://www.aarp.org/disrupt-aging/stories/solutions/info-2018/how-online-dating-shatters-ageism.html.

CHAPTER SIX

NOT DONE YET: THE WORKPLACE

1   Catherine Rampell, "In Hard Economy for All Ages, Older Isn't Better . . . It's Brutal," *New York Times*, February 2, 2013, http://www.nytimes.com/2013/02/03/business/americans-closest-to-retirement-were-hardest-hit-by-recession.html.

2   Michael Winerip, "Pushed Out of a Job Early," *New York Times*, December 6, 2013, http://mobile.nytimes.com/2013/12/07/booming/pushed-out-of-a-job-early.html.

3   Tara Siegel Bernard, "'Too Little Too Late': Bankruptcy Booms Among Older Americans," *New York Times*, August 5, 2018, https://nytimes .com/2018/08/05/business/bankruptcy-older-americans.html

4   Matthew S. Rutledge, Steven A. Sass, and Jorge D. Ramos-Mercado, "How Job Options Narrow for Older Workers by Socioeconomic Status," Center for Retirement Research at Boston College, IB#16-13, August, 2016, http://crr .bc.edu/briefs/how-job-options-narrow-for-older-workers-by-socioeconomic -status/.

5   Robert McCann and Howard Giles, "Ageism in the Workplace: A Communication Perspective," in *Ageism: Stereotyping and Prejudice Against Older Persons*, ed. Todd D. Nelson (Cambridge: The MIT Press, 2004), 170.

6   Shankar Vedantam, "Older Americans May Be Happier Than Younger Ones," *Washington Post*, July 14, 2008, http://www.washingtonpost.com /wp-dyn/content/article/2008/07/13/AR2008071301641_pf.html.

7   Nathaniel Reade, "The Surprising Truth About Older Workers," *AARP* magazine, August/September 2013, http://www.aarp.org/work/job-hunting /info-07-2013/older-workers-more-valuable.html.

8   David Hackett Fischer, *Growing Old in America* (New York: Oxford University Press, 1978), 211.

9   Pew Charitable Trusts, "A Look at Access to Employer-Based Retirement Plans and Participation in the States," January 13, 2016, www.pewtrusts .org/en/research-and-analysis/reports/2016/01/a-look-at-access-to-employer -based-retirement-plans-and-participation-in-the-states

10   Tricia Neuman, Vice President, Henry J. Kaiser Family Foundation, "Present Economics of Older America," presentation at the 2013 Age Boom Academy, sponsored by the Atlantic Philanthropies, New York, NY, September 9, 2013.

11   Liana Fox and José Pacas, "Deconstructing Poverty Rates among the 65 and Older Population: Why Has Poverty Increased Since 2015?," April 26, 2018, Working Paper Number: SEHSD-WP2018-13, https://www.census.gov /library/working-papers/2018/demo/SEHSD-WP2018-13.html

12   National Council on Aging, "Economic Security for Seniors Facts Sheet,"

2016, http://www.ncoa.org/press-room/fact-sheets/economic-security-for
.html.

13 Social Security Administration Fact Sheet, 2017, https://www.ssa.gov/news
/press/factsheets/basicfact-alt.pdf.

14 Carmen DeNavas-Walt, Bernadette D. Proctor, Jessica C. Smith, "Income,
Poverty, and Health Insurance in the United States: 2012," U.S. Census
Bureau. Issued September 2013, 21, http://www.census.gov/prod/2013pubs
/p60-245.pdf.

15 National Women's Law Center, "Facts About the Wage Gap," September 13,
2016, https://nwlc.org/resources/faq-about-the-wage-gap/.

16 Joan Entmacher, Katherine Gallagher Robbins, Julie Vogtman, and Lauren
Frohlich, The National Women's Law Center, "Insecure & Unequal:
Poverty and Income among Women and Families 2000–2012," 2013.

17 Robert McCann and Howard Giles, "Ageism in the Workplace: A Communication Perspective," in *Ageism: Stereotyping and Prejudice Against Older
Persons*, ed. Todd D. Nelson (Cambridge: The MIT Press, 2004), 170.

18 Abigail Van Buren, "Dear Abby: Single mom rips older workers for staying
on the job too long," *Mercury News*, September 6, 2013, http://www
.pottsmerc.com/article/20130905/LIFE01/130909807/dear-abby-single
-mom-rips-older-workers-for-staying-on-the-job-too-long.

19 "Working Longer: The Disappearing Divide Between Work Life and
Retirement," The AP-NORC Center's Working Longer Study, May, 2016, p. 4,
http://www.apnorc.org/projects/Pages/HTML%20Reports/working-longer
-the-disappearing-divide-between-work-life-and-retirement-issue-brief.aspx.

20 Kathleen Geier, "Deserving vs. undeserving poor—for the love of God,
here we go again," *Washington Monthly*, December 21, 2013, http://www
.washingtonmonthly.com/political-animal-a/2013_12/deserving_vs
_undeserving_poor048302.php.

21 "When Baby Boomers Delay Retirement, Do Younger Workers Suffer?" Pew
Charitable Trusts Economic Mobility Project report, p. 4, http://www
.pewstates.org/uploadedFiles/PCS_Assets/2012/EMP_retirement_delay.pdf.

22   Dora L. Costa, *The Evolution of Retirement—An American Economic History 1880–1990* (Chicago: University of Chicago Press, 1998), 12.

23   David C. Wilson, "When Equal Opportunity Knocks," *Gallup Business Journal*, April 13, 2006, http://businessjournal.gallup.com/content/22378 /When-Equal-Opportunity-Knocks.aspx#1.

24   Kimberly Palmer, "10 Things You Should Know About Age Discrimination" *AARP*, 2017, https://www.aarp.org/work/on-the-job/info-2017/age -discrimination-facts.html.

25   Noam Scheiber, "The Brutal Ageism of Tech," *New Republic,* March 23, 2014, http://www.newrepublic.com/article/117088/silicons-valleys-brutal-ageism.

26   "Age Discrimination," *New York Times* editorial, July 6, 2009, http://www .nytimes.com/2009/07/07/opinion/07tue2.html.

27   Adam Cohen, "After 40 Years, Age Discrimination Still Gets Second-Class Treatment," *New York Times*, November 6, 2009, http://www.nytimes.com /2009/11/07/opinion/07sat4.html.

28   Fischer, op. cit., 214.

29   William E. Gibson, "A New Bill to Stop Ageism," *AARP*, March 1, 2017, http://www.aarp.org/politics-society/advocacy/info-2017/congress-bill-stop -age-discrimination-fd.html.

30   Peter Gosselin, "Federal Court May Decide If Employers Can Reject Older Job Seekers to Protect 'Image,'" *ProPublica,* Jan. 31, 2017, https://www .pressreader.com/usa/san-francisco-chronicle/20170228/281496456064058.

31   "10 Thing You May Not Know about Boomers Today," fact sheet accompanying the 2007 PBS Series *The Boomer Century*, http://www.pbs.org /boomercentury/tenthings.html.

32   Marc Freedman, "The Big Shift," interview with Mike Cuthbert, *AARP Prime Time Radio*, April 26, 2011, http://www.aarp.org/health/longevity /info-04-2011/the-big-shift.html.

33   Ursula Staudinger, Director, Columbia Aging Center, "Demographic Change: Opportunities and Challenges for Corporations," presentation at

the 2013 Age Boom Academy, sponsored by the Atlantic Philanthropies, New York, NY, September 10, 2013.

34 "When Retirement Goes Wrong," Michael Martin, host, *NPR Special Series: Money Coach*, March 13, 2013, http://www.npr.org/2013/03/13/174198166 /when-retirement-goes-wrong.

35 Rowe and Kahn, *Successful Aging*, 33.

36 Cruikshank, *Learning to Be Old*, 48.

37 Joyce Carol Oates, *More* magazine, June 2009.

38 Nardine Saad, "Anne Hathaway, 32, is losing roles to younger stars: 'I was that 24-year-old once,'" *Los Angeles Times*, September 4, 2015, http://www .latimes.com/entertainment/gossip/la-et-mg-anne-hathaway-ageism -hollywood-losing-roles-glamour-uk-20150904-story.html.

39 Ellis Cose, "Why It Makes No Sense to Fire Older Workers," *Newsweek*, October 28, 2009, http://www.newsweek.com/why-it-makes-no-sense-fire -older-workers-cose-81355.

CHAPTER SEVEN

LONG LIFE IS A TEAM SPORT: THE INDEPENDENCE TRAP

1 "Across the States: Profiles of Long-Services and Supports," AARP Public Policy Institute, 2012, 7, http://www.aarp.org/content/dam/aarp/research /public_policy_institute/ltc/2012/across-the-states-2012-executive-summary -AARP-ppi-ltc.pdf.

2 "A Profile of Older Americans: 2012. Administration on Aging," U.S. Department of Health and Human Services, 5, http://www.aoa.gov/Aging _Statistics/Profile/2012/docs/2012profile.pdf.

3 Renee Stepler, "Smaller Share of Women Ages 65 and Older Are Living Alone," Pew Research Center, February 2016, http://www.pewsocialtrends .org/2016/02/18/smaller-share-of-women-ages-65-and-older-are-living-alone/.

4 Shaoni Bhattacharya, "European heatwave caused 35,000 deaths," *New Scientist*, October 10, 2003, http://www.newscientist.com/article/dn4259 -european-heatwave-caused-35000-deaths.html#.U8PTgo1dXqo.

5   "Dying Alone," interview with Eric Klinenberg, University of Chicago Press, http://www.press.uchicago.edu/Misc/Chicago/443213in.html.

6   Anne C. Roark, "With Friends Aplenty, Many Widows Choose Singlehood," *New York Times*, July 13, 2009, http://newoldage.blogs.nytimes.com/2009 /07/13/with-friends-aplenty-many-widows-choose-singlehood/.

7   A Profile of Older Americans 2016, Administration on Aging, Administration for Community Living, U.S. Dept. of Health and Human Services, p. 7, https://www.acl.gov/sites/default/files/Aging%20and%20Disabil ity%20in%20America/2016-Profile.pdf.

8   Alice Fisher, "Aging-in-Place: It Can Be Detrimental to Your Health," *Radical Age Movement* blog, Jun 15, 2014, http://theradicalagemovement .com/2014/09/27/ageing-in-place-it-can-be-detrimental-to-your-health/.

9   *US News & World Report*, "Best Nursing Homes for 2017–18" report, https://health.usnews.com/best-nursing-homes/area/ny/hebrew-home-for -the-aged-at-riverdale-335020

10   "The Eden Alternative," PBS interview with Dr. Bill Thomas, undated, http://www.pbs.org/thoushalthonor/eden/.

11   Peter Uhlenberg and Jenny de Jong Gierveld, "Age-Segregation in Later Life: An Examination of Personal Networks," *Ageing & Society* 24 (2004): 5–28.

12   Linda Carroll, "Alzheimer's extracts a high price on caregivers, too," *NBC News*, September 5, 2013 at 10:02 AM ET, http://www.nbcnews.com/health /alzheimers-extracts-high-price-caregivers-too-8C11070658.

13   Gullette, *Agewise*, 29.

14   Ibid.

15   John Leland, *Happiness Is a Choice You Make: Lessons from a Year Among the Oldest Old* (New York: Sarah Crichton Books, 2018), p. 114.

16   Elana D. Buch, "Beyond Independence: Older Chicagoans Living Valued Lives," in *Successful Aging as a Contemporary Obsession: Global Perspectives*, ed. Sarah Lamb (Rutgers University Press, 2017), 87.

17   Patricia Cohen, "Why Women Quit Working: It's Not for the Reasons Men

Do," *New York Times*, January 24, 2017, https://www.nytimes.com/2017/01 /24/business/economy/women-labor-force.html.

18 Debora MacKenzie, "Women live longer than men but suffer more years of poor health," *NewScientist*, March 17, 2016, https://www.newscientist.com /article/2081497-women-live-longer-than-men-but-suffer-more-years-of -poor-health/.

19 Pew Research Center, "Internet/Broadband Fact Sheet," February 5, 2017, http://www.pewinternet.org/fact-sheet/internet-broadband/.

20 Rachel Levy, *Grandma Got STEM* blog, http://ggstem.wordpress.com/.

21 Peter Uhlenberg and Jenny de Jong Gierveld, "Age-Segregation in Later Life: An Examination of Personal Networks," *Ageing & Society* 24 (2004): 5–28.

22 Vaillant, *Aging Well*, 163.

23 Lustbader, *Life Gets Better*, 159.

24 Ibid., 168.

25 Atul Gawande, *Being Mortal* (New York: Metropolitan Books), 146.

26 Jan Baars, "Aging, Autonomy and Justice. Beyond Independence." Lecture at receipt of the GSA Social Gerontology Theory Award, November 22, 2013, New Orleans (unpublished manuscript).

27 Meika Loe, "Asking for Help As We Age Actually Fosters Autonomy," *Aging Today*, June 19, 2013, http://www.asaging.org/blog/asking-help-we -age-actually-fosters-autonomy?goback=.gde_3876337_member _257938510.

28 Lustbader, *Life Gets Better*, 72.

29 Robert McG. Thomas, Jr., "Maggie Kuhn, 89, the Founder Of the Gray Panthers, Is Dead," *New York Times*, April 23, 1995, http://www.nytimes .com/1995/04/23/obituaries/maggie-kuhn-89-the-founder-of-the-gray -panthers-is-dead.html.

CHAPTER EIGHT

THE BULL LOOKS DIFFERENT: THE END OF LIFE

1   Joel Tsevat, Neal V. Dawson, Albert W. Wu, et al., "Health Values of
    Hospitalized Patients 80 Years or Older," *Journal of the American Medical
    Association*, 279, no. 5 (February 4, 1998): 371–375, https://jhu.pure.elsevier
    .com/en/publications/health-values-of-hospitalized-patients-80-years-or
    -older-4.

2   Kenneth E. Covinsky, Albert W. Wu, C. Set Landefeld; Alfred F. Connors,
    Russell S. Phillips, . . . [+], "Health status versus quality of life in older
    patients: does the distinction matter?" *The American Journal of Medicine*,
    Volume 106 (4), Apr 1, 1999, http://www.amjmed.com/article/S0002
    -9343(99)00052-2/fulltext

3   Marc E. Agronin, *How We Age: A Doctor's Journey into the Heart of Growing
    Old* (New York, Da Capo Press, 2011), 9.

4   Roger Angell, "This Old Man: Life in the Nineties," *New Yorker*, February 17 &
    24, 2014, 63.

5   Marc E. Agronin, "Old Age, From Youth's Narrow Prism," *New York Times*,
    March 1, 2010, http://www.nytimes.com/2010/03/02/health/02case.html.

6   Karl Pillemer, *30 Lessons for Living: Tried and True Advice from the Wisest
    Americans* (New York: Hudson Street Press, 2011), 217.

7   J. A. Thorson and F. C. Powell, (2000), "Death anxiety in younger and
    older adults." In A. Tomer (Ed.), *Death attitudes and the older adult:
    Theories, concepts, and applications* (pp. 123–136). Philadelphia: Taylor &
    Francis. Also Pillemer, 141.

8   Laura L. Carstensen, "The Influence of a Sense of Time on Human
    Development," *Science* magazine, Vol. 312, 30 June 2006, Vol. 312 no. 5782
    pp. 1913–1915 DOI: 10.1126/science.1127488

9   Interview on KRCU Radio with Laura Carstensen by NPR/TED staff, "Why
    Should We Look Forward To Getting Older?," aired June 22, 2015, http://
    krcu.org/post/why-should-we-look-forward-getting-older.

10   Thomas Mann, "Life Grows in the Soil of Time," in *This I Believe: The Personal Philosophies of Remarkable Men and Women*, Jay Allison and Dan Gediman, eds., Henry Holt & Company, 2007, 151.

11   Mariacristina De Nardi, Eric French, John Bailey Jones, Jeremy McCauley, "Medical Spending of the U.S. Elderly," National Bureau of Economic Research, NBER Working Paper No. 21270, June 2015 (DOI): 10.3386/w21270, http://www.advisory.com/daily-briefing/2015/06/22/new-data -could-change-how-you-think-about-end-of-life-care-costs.

12   Caroline Davies, "Martin Amis in new row over 'euthanasia booths,'" *The Guardian*, January 24, 2010, http://www.theguardian.com/books/2010/jan /24/martin-amis-euthanasia-booths-alzheimers.

13   James H. Schulz & Robert H. Binstock, *Aging Nation: The Economics and Politics of Growing Older in America*, Baltimore, 2008, 190.

14   Elizabeth Hughes Schneewind, "Of Ageism, Suicide and Limiting Life," *Journal of Gerontological Social Work*, Vol. 23(1/2) 1994, [p. 146].

15   Linton, *My Body Politic*, 226.

16   Ed Meek, "The millennial-boomer alliance," *Boston Globe* magazine, September 15, 2013, http://www.bostonglobe.com/magazine/2013/09/14 /why-millennials-bond-with-their-boomer-parents/yO932V5sUVj205pEXTyQSJ /story.html.

17   Margaret Gullette, Letter to the editor, *Boston Globe*, September 28, 2013, http://www.bostonglobe.com/magazine/2013/09/28/readers-respond-articles -baby-boomers-day-care-costs/ctTZKV6BuUAp8fgHiSPUPJ/story.html.

18   Gullette, *Agewise*, 43.

19   Carstensen, *A Long Bright Future*, 36.

20   Gawande, Atul, *Being Mortal* (New York: Metropolitan, 2014). Kindle edition.

21   Ibid.

22   Robin Marantz Henig, "A Life-or-Death Situation," *New York Times Magazine*, July 17, 2013, http://www.nytimes.com/2013/07/21/magazine/a -life-or-death-situation.html.

23   http://brookeandpeggy.blogspot.com/.

24 Ackerman, August 2009, private communication with Margaret Morgan-roth Gullette, op. cit., 52.

25 Marc E. Agronin, "Old Age, From Youth's Narrow Prism," *New York Times*, March 1, 2010, http://www.nytimes.com/2010/03/02/health/02case .html.

26 Pete Townshend, *Pete Townshend Summer Blog*, http://thewho.com/blog /story/summer-blog/#qgVSm9y9jTPjE4dY.99.

27 Tim Kreider, "You are going to die," *New York Times*, January 30, 2013, http://opinionator.blogs.nytimes.com/2013/01/20/you-are-going-to-die/.

CHAPTER NINE

OCCUPY AGE! BEYOND AGEISM

1 Carol Hanisch, "The Personal Is the Political," originally published in *Notes from the Second Year: Women's Liberation*, 1970, http://www.carolhanisch.org /CHwritings/PIP.html.

2 Nicholas Kristof, "She Gets No Respect: Sexism Persists, Even Among the Enlightened," *New York Times*, June 11, 2014, http://www.nytimes.com /2014/06/12/opinion/nicholas-kristof-she-gets-no-respect.html.

3 Heather M Rasinski et al., "I Guess What He Said Wasn't That Bad," doi:10 .1177/0146167213484769Pers *Soc Psychol Bull*, July 2013 vol. 39 no. 7 856-869856-869, http://psp.sagepub.com/content/39/7/856.

4 Kathy Sporre, "Ageism Hides in Plain Sight," *Journal on Active Aging*, November/December 2011, Vol. 10 Issue 6, p74 www.icaa.cc.

5 Robert R. Blancato and Meredeith Ponder "The Public Policies We Need to Address Ageism," *Generations*, Fall, 2015, Vol, 39, No 3, p. 92.

6 "Gauging Aging: Mapping the Gaps between Expert and Public Under-standing of Aging in America." A FrameWorks Research Report by Eric Lindland, Marissa Fond, Abigail Haydon and Nathaniel Kendall-Taylor. FrameWorks Institute, Washington, DC, 2015, http://www .frameworksinstitute.org/pubs/mtg/gaugingaging/page7.html.

7 McCarter Theatre Center, "There is a black person talking: How blues

and Bearden inspired Wilson's own profound articulation of the black tradition," http://www.mccarter.org/fences/3-explore/thereisablackperson talking.html.

8   Mark William Rocha, "August Wilson and the Four B's Influences," in *August Wilson: A Casebook*, edited by Marilyn Elkins (New York, 1994), 565.

9   "Remembering Maggie Kuhn: Gray Panthers Founder On The 5 Myths Of Aging," 1978 interview with Ken Dychtwald, *Huffington Post*, 05/31/2012, http://www.huffingtonpost.com/ken-dychtwald/the-myths-of-aging_b _1556481.html.

10   Shapiro, Joseph, *No Pity*, 5.

INDEX

275

NPR, 57, 92, 118, 209, 230

nursing homes, 4–5, 14, 19, 36, 66, 94, 124, 162, 171, 173, 195, 206–7, 229

Nyad, Diana, 52

Nyren, Chuck, 138

O

Oates, Joyce Carol, 162

Occupy Sandy, 153

OKCupid, 124, 127

O'Keeffe, Georgia, 229

"old age dependency ratio," 30–31, 142

"olders," 10

"old person in training," 58–61

Olshansky, S. Jay, 91

Omar, Mahmoud Abdel-Salam, 119

optimism, 84, 108, 175, 176

Orange County, California, 73

"organ recital," 109

orgasm, 116, 130, 132

O'Shaughnessy, Jacky, 134

osteoarthritis, 90

Oswald, Andrew J., 81

OurTime.com, 124

outercourse, 132

Out of Time: The Pleasures and the Perils of Aging (Lynne Segal), 47

Oxford English Dictionary, 13

P

Paley, Grace, 129

Parkinson's disease, 179

patriarchy, 121, 140, 224, 225

Pejić, Andrej, 50

Pemberton Park (Kansas City), 175

penis, 131, 132

Pew Charitable Trust, 151

Pew Research Center, 31, 32, 40, 47, 86, 111

physician-assisted suicide, 20, 178, 210, 212, 217

Pillemer, Karl, 81–82, 187, 189, 207

Playboy, 116

polyamory, 140

Poo, Ai-jen

   The Age of Dignity: Preparing for the Elder Boom in a Changing America, 68

population aging, 5, 22, 23, 25–28, 32–33, 51, 62, 96, 98, 113, 152, 210, 235, 239, 242

postwar generation, 27–29, 45, 86, 124, 146, 172, 173, 243

poverty, 24, 25, 33, 57, 107, 146–47, 151, 166, 213, 237, 241

   line, 147

"premature cognitive commitments," 41–42

Price, Joan, 126

   Naked at Our Age, 126

Princeton University, 226

productivity, 21, 23, 31, 36, 37, 56–57, 60, 152, 161–65, 212, 240, 241

The Program for All-Inclusive Care for the Elderly (PACE), 68

prophecies, self-fulfilling, 41–43

psychiatric care, 94